HARDPRESS.NET
HOME OF HARD-TO-FIND BOOKS

Works
by John Hollingshead

Address:
HardPress
8345 NW 66TH ST #2561
MIAMI FL 33166-2626
USA
Email: info@hardpress.net

P. O. angl. 169 $\frac{b}{}$

(6)

Hollingshead

TO-DAY.

TO-DAY

ESSAYS AND MISCELLANIES

BY

JOHN HOLLINGSHEAD

AUTHOR OF "UNDERGROUND LONDON," "ODD JOURNEYS," "UNDER BOW BELLS,"
"RAGGED LONDON," ETC., ETC.

VOL. I.—DAY THOUGHTS

LONDON

GROOMBRIDGE AND SONS

PATERNOSTER ROW

MDCCCLXV.

ARKILD, PROCTER, LONDON.

PREFACE.

———◆———

THESE two volumes of Essays and Miscellanies, dealing almost exclusively with the present as distinguished from the past, are reprinted, by the kind permission of the various editors and proprietors, from " Good Words," " All the Year Round," " Once a Week," the " Daily News," and many other London Magazines and Journals. The only pride I feel in collecting these papers at the wish of my publishers, is in finding that while writing for a living in many periodicals of very opposite views, I have always consistently maintained my own Benthamite principles.

JOHN HOLLINGSHEAD.

LONDON, *October*, 1864.

CONTENTS.

———◆———

TO-DAY.

SHOP.

THOSE who are very familiar with the old town of Green-wich, particularly with that most ancient portion which lies off the High Street towards the river, may probably have noticed a little barber's shop, distinguished by the usual outward signs of the barber's trade, and the inscription, "Hackblock: established 1750." The top part of this house is built of wood—of black tarred planks which would be like the side of a ship, if they were not as frail-looking as an egg-chest. The shop part is very low, and is entered by a sunken narrow doorway at the bottom of two well-worn stone steps. The outside of this house might be considered rather repulsive by people who are fond of new brick-work and stucco, but the inside leaves nothing to be desired in neatness and cleanliness. The roof, of course, is low, the floor has a down-hill tendency towards the fire-place; the looking-glass over the mantel-shelf is of that quality which makes the human face look as muddy as a bad photograph; but the floor is always well sanded, the towels are spotless, and those

1

who keep the shop are evidently devoted to their business. They are a father and son; and though the bulk of the work falls on the younger of the two, the elder does all he can to help, and they evidently live very comfortably together. The father is a little, thin man, nearly eighty years of age, always dressed in drab knee-breeches, with very white stockings, and wearing an apron, and a waistcoat with black sleeves. His hair is very scanty and white, but it is made the most of by judicious brushing and combing; and the son, though a young man about thirty-eight, and careful about his appearance, hardly looks as thoroughly healthy and fresh as his father. Both are what are popularly called well-spoken persons, that is, persons who have had some little education in their youth, which has clung to them in after life; and they are consequently free from the flippancy which is so general amongst common barbers.

Anybody who entered the shaving-shop of the Hackblocks, father and son, for the first time, might suppose that the calm life within had gone on for years without any break or hindrance; that the son was a young man without impulse or ambition, who had always been tied to his father's apron-strings, and was content with an apparently stagnant existence. To those who are drunk with the romance of self-help, who believe that to wander is to thrive, that every boy can become at will a Lord Mayor, or a Lord Chancellor, this contentment of young Hackblock, must appear very mean and degrading. Young Hackblock, however, would not be fairly judged by such observers, though his youthful ambition, fed by a restless uncle, an old Greenwich pensioner, was not much to be proud of, if estimated by results.

Commonplace as this old barber's shop and their

keepers look, still they have their story, to tell which—
and we think it is worth telling—we must go back nearly
ten years.

Early in the year 1853, on a cold spring morning, old
Hackblock entered his shop—the same shop we have just
been describing—rather dejected in appearance. He was
then ten years younger than he is now, but he looked quite
as old, and more careworn. His niece, Fanny Hackblock,
was in the shop when he entered, dusting the scanty furniture, and arranging the old-fashioned shaving-chair with
its crutch-like back, for the day's business. Fanny's father,
old Hackblock's brother, was a Greenwich pensioner, and
Fanny, though she attended to her uncle as much as
possible, got her living in the town as a bonnet-maker.
She was a young woman about eight-and-twenty, not what
is called pretty, and very plainly dressed.

" Good morning, uncle," said Fanny, as old Hackblock
entered.

" Ah, Fanny," said old Hackblock, with a slight air of
abstraction, " making the old place tidy as usual ? No
one's been in to be shaved ?"

" No, uncle," returned Fanny, " or I should have called
you."

" They never do come on a Wednesday," said old Hackblock. " I might as well shut the shop up on that day, if
it wasn't for cutting children's hair in the afternoon,
because it's half-holiday at the schools."

" And that's a job, uncle, I _know_ you wouldn't lose."

" I like to pat their heads and finger their little curls,"
said old Hackblock, half musingly ; " although," he added
sadly, " they often remind me of my poor lost boy."

" I see father was here yesterday," continued Fanny,
trying to change the conversation, " by the mess the

stove was in with tobacco-ashes. I wish you wouldn't let him smoke so much; I'm sure it isn't good for him."

"He does as he chooses, Fanny; just as he chooses. Though I'm his elder brother, I don't like to stint him in his pipe, because they're rather strict up at Greenwich Hospital yonder; but I'll never forgive him for causing my poor boy to run away, by his wild yarns about glory, adventures, and foreign countries."

"Let bygones be bygones, uncle," said Fanny, persuasively.

"That's the way with relations," continued old Hackblock, partly to himself; "they always interfere with your family affairs, always know better what to do with your children than you do yourself."

"Father thought he was doing all for the best."

"It was cruel, very cruel; just as the boy was nearly ready to take my place, and handled his razor so cleverly."

"Cousin Harry was quite as much to blame for going as father was for persuading him to go, when he knew you were almost alone in the world."

"There's the pinch, Fanny, there's the pinch," continued old Hackblock, this time addressing his remarks to his niece. "Perhaps I ought to be glad that he had the spirit to go, but I'm not. When *she* dropped off, the mother of them all, and they all followed her except him, I certainly hoped to keep him near me. It may have been a weak, womanish feeling, but I couldn't help it."

"Of course not," replied Fanny, sympathizing with her uncle's evident emotion.

"And then the business, too," continued the old man; "it requires a young, steady hand to keep it together. I sometimes think that it's going, slipping through my old fingers."

"Oh, no, uncle," returned Fanny; "that's impossible. You've been established too long to lose your customers. People don't forget those who've served them for fifty years."

"Fifty years?" exclaimed old Hackblock, in a tone of petulant pride. "More than that, Fanny; more than that. A hundred years at least, if you count the time my father had it before me."

"Of course; I'd forgotten that, which makes it all the better."

"I wish I could think so," continued old Hackblock, in a desponding manner, as he fetched a razor from a side-table, and stropped it slowly on a strop; "I wish I could think so; but my hand is sometimes very shaky, and people are so nervous about razors."

"Oh, no, they're not, uncle," said Fanny, trying to reassure him. "I heard old Mr. Jones, the baker, say, the other day, that he'd rather be shaved by you in the dark, than by all the chattering shopmen at the new hair-cutting 'saloon,' as they call it, in the High Street, by broad daylight."

"Ah, that's because I know all his pimples."

"Oh, no, uncle! I've heard others say the same who've got no pimples."

"Have you, Fanny?" said old Hackblock, brightening up a little. "Well, well, I know my business thoroughly, and that goes a long way. Half your barbers now-a-days who call themselves *professors* ought no more to be trusted with a chin or a head of hair than with a rowing-boat on the Thames. I don't care what a man's trade may be, but I do like him to learn it thoroughly and to take a pride in it."

Old Hackblock, at this point of the conversation, sat

down in the shaving-chair, continuing his task of stropping the razor, and at the same moment his brother, Boatswain Hackblock, the old Greenwich pensioner, entered the shop. Boatswain Hackblock was about five years younger than the barber, much stouter and stronger, with a red face, bushy eyebrows, and a very obstinate expression. His dress was the ordinary Greenwich pensioner's dress, he had a wooden leg of the old clumsy make to supply the place of a lost right limb; and to compensate him for this disfigurement, two medals, hanging by ribbons, glittered on his breast.

"Halloo, my hearties," roared out the boatswain, as he stumped heavily into the little shop, making the fire-irons tremble in the fender; "what cheer?"

"For goodness' sake, father," said Fanny, going up to him, "don't be quite so boisterous; you alarm the neighbourhood, and uncle's got his living to get!"

"Ay, ay," returned the old pensioner, a little softened; "give us a pipe of tobacco, and I'll bring myself to an anchor."

Fanny looked towards her uncle when she heard this request. Old Hackblock nodded his head, and then Fanny went to a jar in the window, from which she took what her father asked for.

"Don't make the stove in such a mess as you did yesterday," said Fanny, as she gave the tobacco to her father; "it took me half an hour to clean it this morning, and I shall have to fetch the time up at my bonnet-work."

"Oh, shiver the work," returned the old pensioner; "I believe, if the Hackblocks had their rights, they'd be riding in their carriages like admirals."

"Well, father," said Fanny, putting on her bonnet and

shawl, "when you've got a fortune to give me, I'll be a fine lady; but till that time comes I must grub on in the old hard-working way."

When Fanny had delivered this speech, she ran off to her work at the bonnet-maker's in the town, leaving her father and uncle together. The old pensioner prepared to enjoy himself with his pipe, while old Hackblock seemed to have sunk back into his former melancholy.

"Do you know what day this is?" said old Hackblock, addressing his brother, and stropping the razor slowly.

"I never keep any log, now," returned the old pensioner, through puffs of smoke, "and only remember the days when my pension becomes due, and the big-wigs come down to inspect us at the Hospital."

"Ah, it must be very pleasant to have such a bad memory, Jack," continued the old barber.

"What tack are you on now, Harry?" asked the old pensioner.

"This is the day on which *he* went away, exactly fourteen years ago: stole off in the night like a thief, without thinking of anybody but himself."

"Don't drag up that story; the boy thought it was all for the best."

"Of course *you* say so. If you hadn't filled his head with dreams about prize-money, glory, and Trafalgar, he might now have been a well-to-do barber."

"Of course he might," retorted the old pensioner, getting excited; "or a well-to-do tailor, or a bonnet-builder, like my girl—or—or—or any other landlubber."

The delivery of this speech, far from calming the old pensioner, seemed to excite him still more, and he stamped about the room with his wooden leg in a way that endangered the rather tender flooring.

"Now do be careful, Jack," exclaimed the old barber,
anxiously, " with that wooden leg of yours; you're not
dibbling a potato-field.   I can't afford to pay another
pound this quarter to mend the holes which you make in
the floor."

"Ay, ay," returned the old pensioner, becoming a little
quieter; "you're all very well, Harry, but you've got no
pride."

"What good's my boy done by his pride, or rather your
pride, which you put into him? He ran away from steady,
honest work, became a private soldier, was ordered about
for years from station to station like a dog, wrote home
just when he wanted a little money, and now Heaven only
knows whether he's alive or dead."

"That's because he went into the wrong service.   I
didn't want him to become a soldier, did I? If he'd not
been cross-grained, and had listened to me, he'd have been
a chief mate by this time, perhaps a captain."

"Not he; it's not in the family."

"Oh, isn't it?" returned the old pensioner, with great
self-importance, displaying the two medals on his breast
rather ostentatiously.

"Ah," said the old barber, rather sadly, "it's not the
first time, by a good many, that I've seen those medals, and
heard of them, too.   It's my belief the sight of their glitter
helped to make the boy discontented."

"If you can't understand what glory is, Harry, that's
not my fault; I can."

"Especially when your wooden leg goes through my
floor, and you bawl to me to pull you out."

"You wouldn't have me wear these medals for
nothing, would you?—walking about like a beadle who's
never earned his ribbons? You know you're as proud

of the bits of metal as I am, and, if not, you ought to be."

"Perhaps I am, Jack," replied the old barber, a little softened. "Perhaps I am."

"They're no disgrace, are they?"

"No, no," said the old barber, pettishly; "but one hero's quite enough in the family."

"Yes," retorted the old pensioner, "and so's one barber—more than enough."

"I take it very unkindly of you, Jack," said old Hackblock, "coming here and taunting me about my business. I've never disgraced the family in it, have I? It's what our father got his living at before us."

"I can't stomach it, Harry; it isn't manly. I can't bear to see a brother of mine compelled to take every scrubby fellow by the nose who pays him a penny to do so. Why, when I was in active service——"

"There," interposed old Hackblock, stopping his brother's words, "I don't want to hear any slaughter-house yarns. You'd have done your duty."

"Of course I should."

"And I'm doing mine. I only want to be left alone to do it. You've driven one member of the family out of the business—perhaps to die amongst strangers—be content with that."

"Well, come, Harry," said the old pensioner, after a slight pause, and in a softened manner, "don't let you and I be at sixes and sevens. There's plenty of people to quarrel with without two brothers going at it tooth and nail. Give us a bit more tobacco."

"You know where to find it," returned the old barber; adding, to himself, "you smoke all my little profit away on that article."

Boatswain Hackblock went to the window, helped himself out of the jar, and refilled his pipe. After this he came towards his brother.

"Harry," he said, "it wants six weeks to quarter-day."

"I'm glad to hear it, Jack," returned the old barber.

"That's because you've got to pay instead of to receive, Harry; I think I must get you to let me have another half-crown to keep me afloat till then."

"Afloat in grog, you mean."

"No, no," returned the old pensioner, apologetically.

Old Hackblock gave his brother the money, after a pause, but with a remark about barber's work not being quite as profitable as it used to be.

"You'd better make it a crown," said the old pensioner, "and then I shan't have to ask you again."

This second request was complied with, though not with a very good grace. Old Hackblock had not the firmness to say no, and yet he always felt irritated after he had given the money—for it was generally a gift in the name of a loan. To avoid more bickering on this occasion, he put on his hat to go out to shave a customer, asking his brother to mind the shop.

"I'll do my best, Harry," said the old pensioner, in answer to his request, "though it's not exactly in my way."

When old Hackblock had gone out, the old boatswain settled down over the fire with his pipe and a newspaper. It was the period when the Crimean war was at its height, to the great delight of the old pensioner. He had waited so long for a good war, as he called it, since the great French war in which he was engaged, that he began to think the art of fighting was lost for ever. The fact that the English were fighting side by side with the French, instead of against them, seemed to puzzle him a little, but

he solved the difficulty by supposing that it was all for the
best. Of course he retained his old prejudices, and called
the French "Mounseers;" but in this he was not far
behind many better-educated persons who now called them
"Mossoos." Like all obstinate, self-willed people, he never
liked to admit, even to himself, that he had made a mistake, and, therefore, he persisted in believing that his
nephew, young Harry Hackblock, was alive, well, and pros-
perous, though the runaway had not been heard of for
several years. The last that had been heard of him was
from the Cape of Good Hope, where he had been sent with
his regiment from the West Indies to quell a disturbance
among the Kaffirs. From the Cape his regiment had been
sent to the Crimea, at the outbreak of the war; and though
there was no evidence to show that he went with it, old
Boatswain Hackblock was determined to regard him as
alive and in the thick of the battle.

"He *must* be alive," said the old pensioner, as he pored
over the warlike news in the paper, "and *must* be doing
great things, for he's got more of my spirit in him than his
father's. *He* was never cut for a barber; oh, no; and
he'll turn up some day to prove that I was right, as I
always knew I was from the first."

Judgments formed on much surer grounds than those
which seemed to satisfy the old pensioner have been proved
to be false before now in the most striking manner, and we
can, therefore, hardly feel surprised that at that moment
the person old Boatswain Hackblock was talking and thinking about appeared in the low doorway. His dress looked
rather shabby and travel-stained, with nothing like military stiffness about it, and in stepping suddenly into the
shop he made an old hat look even worse by crushing it
against the door-sill. He was fourteen years of age when

he left home, and twenty-eight when he returned, and had forgotten, for the moment, that he had grown two feet higher in his wanderings.

"Everything seems very small," he said to himself, looking round; "the streets seem narrow, the distances short, the houses low. Most things have changed very much; I wonder whether father has changed with them."

Young Harry Hackblock, like all persons returning home after an absence of many years, seemed to have acquired a sudden delicacy of feeling. He felt that his father, whom he knew to be alive, from inquiries he had made in the town, must be getting old and feeble, and that it would hardly be kind to show himself too suddenly. Trusting to the disguise of a dense brown beard, which he had suffered to grow during his travels, and also to the change in his growth and appearance, he resolved to play the part of an ordinary customer for half-an-hour. He was curious to hear what his father really thought of his conduct in running away, and he was candid enough to admit to himself that he deserved very little tenderness.

He had no sooner entered the little shop in the manner we have described than he observed old Boatswain Hackblock reading the newspaper.

"I do believe that old Greenwich pensioner is my uncle," he said to himself, "and he's sitting, as usual, by father's fire. I don't think he's altogether a humbug, but he deceived me nicely with his yarns about glory."

Knowing his uncle's chief weakness, young Hackblock shouted out "shop," very loudly.

"Sir!" said the old boatswain, leaping in his seat, and turning round suddenly.

"Shop!" repeated young Hackblock, with marked emphasis.

" What d'ye come in without knocking for?" asked the old pensioner, indignantly.

" We never knock at *shops*," returned young Hackblock.

" I don't know anything about shops; what d'ye want?"

" A barber, of course."

" You'd better call another time. My brother (hem), Mr. Hackblock, is out."

" No, I shan't; I shall wait."

" Very well, sir, wait."

When Boatswain Hackblock had finished his part in this dialogue, he turned round rather sulkily to read his paper, sitting more closely than before over the fire, and leaving young Hackblock to do as he liked.

" A good guard to leave in charge of a shop," said the disguised nephew, to himself, " if you want to drive all the customers away. Ah," he continued, looking round the shop, " I suppose that's the old block on which I used to dress wigs, and that's the old strap on which I used to sharpen razors. I might have learned a worse trade than that, though I didn't think so at one time."

The mumblings of the young man appeared to disturb the old pensioner, and it is possible that another altercation would have ensued, if Fanny Hackblock had not entered at that moment. She had a large bonnet-box in her hand, which she placed on a side-table near the fireplace; and as young Hackblock was seated in the old, deep shaving-chair, she did not notice him for a minute or two.

" There," said she, audibly, taking off her bonnet and shawl, " I've brought as much work as I shall be able to get through this afternoon; and then, as it's a slack day with uncle, I can mind the shop while he takes a walk— I'm sure he wants it."

By this time she had observed young Hackblock, though without recognizing him, and she apologized for her uncle's absence, saying that he would be back in a few minutes.

"That must be my cousin Fanny, then," said young Hackblock to himself; " I'm sure I shouldn't have known her if I had met her in the street. She's more improved than her father has. His wooden leg's the only thing about him that's not altered for the worse ; but that, perhaps, is a new one."

Young Hackblock's reflections were here interrupted by the entrance of his father, who looked as if something had just occurred to annoy him.

"Fanny," said the old man, rather sadly, beckoning his niece towards him, and not seeming to notice anyone else, " you told me something this morning about old Mr. Jones, the baker."

" Yes, uncle," replied Fanny, " about his confidence in you."

"Was it true ?" asked the old man, with a slight look of suspicion.

"Uncle !" returned Fanny, hurt and astonished, "you don't think I'd deceive you ?"

" No—no."

"What's the matter ?"

"He's gone over to the rival shop—the ' *saloon*,' as they call it."

"Oh, he'll soon get tired of that," said Fanny, in a reassuring tone, though she inwardly hoped that some harm from careless shaving would happen to Mr. Jones's pimples.

"I suppose there's a good reason for it," said old Hackblock, resignedly ; " I'm not so quick and certain as I was,—I can't be,—I can't be."

" Rubbish," replied Fanny, rather coarsely, but with a good intention; " I know the reason. They take more loaves at the ' *saloon*' than we do. He's been bought over by that."

" Very likely, Fanny," continued the old man, " we can't eat more bread than we do unless another mouth was present. We eat as much now as we can pay for."

Young Hackblock overheard his conversation, and it had a strong effect upon him. He was just about to rise from the chair, and declare who he was, when he was checked by Fanny recalling the old barber to his business.

" You're forgetting a new customer, uncle," said Fanny, pointing to young Hackblock.

" I beg your pardon, sir," said the old man, addressing his son without knowing him, " but I've been rather put about. I'm not one who likes to neglect his business."

" I know that, I know that," replied young Hackblock.

Fanny went to the side-table and began her work, leaving the old barber to do his.

" Hair cut, or shaved, sir ?" said the old man, in a familiar, tradesmanlike tone.

" Well," returned young Hackblock, who had suddenly hit upon a plan for gradually making known who he was, " it may seem strange to you, but I want to get rid of this beard."

" Oh, no," returned old Hackblock; " not at all strange —not at all. It seems stranger to me that anybody should wear such a load of hair."

" What !" shouted Boatswain Hackblock, rousing himself, and looking round when he heard this,—" Wants his beard shaved off !—a full-grown beard shaved off ? He'll want his head shaved next !"

Young Hackblock merely smiled at this petulant outburst; but old Hackblock, thinking his customer would be offended, felt very nervous, and Fanny, sharing in the same feeling, tried to quiet her father. The old barber fetched his razor and strop, and prepared his lather, and the old boatswain turned once more to his newspaper.

"No one seems to know me," said young Hackblock to himself, as if he felt rather disappointed; "surely my father will recollect me when my beard is shaved off? I can't have grown entirely out of remembrance?"

"Are you a stranger in Greenwich, sir?" asked old Hackblock, as he made his preparations.

"Oh, no!" returned young Hackblock; "I know it very well, though I've been away from it for a long time. It seems a good deal changed."

"Still it's a nice place; I don't know a nicer place," said old Hackblock, admiringly.

"Of course not, and why?" again interrupted Boatswain Hackblock. "Because you've lived here, like a mushroom, all your life."

"I don't think that's any disgrace, father," said Fanny, defending her uncle.

"Nor I either," said young Hackblock.

"I've not done as well as I might," replied the old barber meekly; "but that's not altogether my fault. I know many rolling stones that haven't done much better."

"Ah, you may well say that," responded young Hackblock, with earnestness.

"Have you travelled much, sir?" inquired the old barber, as he stropped his razor.

"A good deal too much," was the answer.

"No one but a born landlubber *can* travel too much," exclaimed Boatswain Hackblock, again aroused.

"I *am* a born landlubber," returned young Hackblock.

"I'm sorry to hear it."

Fanny and old Hackblock again got very nervous, and the old barber even offered to check his brother; but young Hackblock motioned him to take no notice of the interruption, and he returned to his task.

"Your hair's very grey, sir, for a young man, and rather thin, too," said the old barber, speaking the truth, though he was uttering the common jargon of his trade.

"I wouldn't advise you to say much about that," replied young Hackblock.

"Why not?"

"Because I had it of you."

The old boatswain joined in here again with a loud, mocking laugh.

"If it's one of my wigs," returned the old barber, with some pride, "I don't wonder that it deceived me. They were always thought to be more natural than the real hair."

"I know they were," replied young Hackblock, beginning to be sorry for his joke: "but my hair is not a wig. When I said it was yours, I meant that it grew up under your guidance. You used to dress it and cut it," he added, feelingly, "and take a pride in it as if it was your own."

"Yes," roared out Boatswain Hackblock, "and soak it, as he does the whole of his customers, with dripping pomatum. Ha, ha! I don't wonder that it turned grey. You were caught there, brother Harry, completely caught."

"You always know everybody's business, Jack, better than your own," exclaimed the old barber, this time with some spirit. "I'm not responsible for a head of hair after it leaves my shop, am I? My memory's not so good as it was ; but I am sure this gentleman "—alluding to his un-recognized son—" has not been here for some years."

"Twelve or fourteen years, at least," replied young Hackblock.

"Ah," said the old barber, sadly, "about the time my foolish boy, Harry, ran away from his bread."

"Your name's Hackblock, isn't it?" asked the young man, with suppressed emotion.

"It is."

"Wasn't your son once in the army—a private in the 42nd Foot, which was moved from Jamaica, some years ago, to the Cape of Good Hope?"

"He was," replied the old barber, leaving off shaving his customer, while Fanny leaned forward to listen.

"Yes, yes, he was," exclaimed Boatswain Hackblock, this time chiming in anxiously, though pettishly.

"Then I'm sure I knew him," returned the young man, watching keenly the effect of his words on his father.

The old barber dropped his razor, and put up his hands towards his ears.

"Is—he—alive?" he asked, pausing between his words, and dreading to hear the reply.

Fanny and the old boatswain came forward.

"He is," replied the young man, quickly.

"Thank Heaven," said Fanny ; but old Hackblock could not speak. He wiped his face with a towel which he held in his hand, and trembled violently. Boatswain Hackblock took the good news less quietly.

"Of course he is ; I knew he was," he shouted, stamp-ing his wooden leg violently on the floor, "and doing well, too ? Eh, young man ?"

"What would you call well?" asked the young man, as

.the old barber tried to compose himself once more for his task of shaving.

"What should I call well?" asked Boatswain Hackblock, almost derisively; "why, promotion—rewards—reputation. Has he been in action? Did he wound many people, eh?"

"Yes, several," returned young Hackblock.

"Good, good!" was the response.

"How can you be so bloodthirsty, father," said Fanny, "when you've retired from business?"

"Don't talk to me," returned Boatswain Hackblock, impetuously; "an old salt never retires from business. What did he wound them with, eh, young man? the gun or the bayonet?"

"Neither."

"Neither?" asked the old barber, anxiously.

"What with, then?" inquired Boatswain Hackblock, with growing impatience. "A sword?"

"No," replied young Hackblock, still playing with his uncle's curiosity.

"What with, then? what with, then?" asked the old boatswain, now growing very red in the face, and stamping his wooden leg upon the ground.

"Well, if you must have it," replied young Hackblock, while his eyes twinkled, "it was a razor."

"A razor!" exclaimed the old pensioner, his brother, and Fanny, in chorus.

"Yes, a razor; there's nothing extraordinary in that; people are very easily wounded with razors."

"Don't beat about the bush, sir," said the old boatswain testily. "Is he promoted?"

"Yes," replied young Hackblock. "He became the barber of his regiment."

This announcement had the effect of making old Hack-block smile with satisfaction, while Fanny laughed out-right. Boatswain Hackblock, after the first explosion of rage, recovered himself sufficiently to speak, but not before he had stamped half round the shop in his usual style.

"Barber to his regiment!" he said, bitterly, "barber to his regiment! Why, hang me, he'd better have stopped at home—much better."

"I always said so, Jack, I always said so," returned the old barber, rather triumphantly. "What's bred in the bone, you know—it's my turn to laugh now."

"There's one comfort," retorted the old boatswain, clinging to his last chance of escape from defeat; "he'll have to fight in the Crimea—barber or no barber."

"He's not in the Crimea," said young Hackblock.

"Not in the Crimea?—not at the seat of war?" shouted the old boatswain, with renewed excitement.

"No; he bought out of his regiment some years ago, and started a small easy-shaving shop—much smaller than this—at Cape Town."

"Easy-shaving shop!" shouted Boatswain Hackblock, with riotous contempt, while the old barber's delight in-creased. "Easy cats'-meat shop! He's a disgrace to the family."

"No, Jack," said the old barber, interposing with much natural dignity and feeling; "I'm the best judge of that. I don't approve of his clumsiness with the razor, which this gentleman has mentioned—I can hardly believe in it when I know what a careful education I gave him, and how he used to shave the customers here. I don't approve of his not writing home for so many years—but—but I've heard nothing that tells me he's disgraced his family. He's not disgraced *me*!"

Young Hackblock could hardly suppress the emotion naturally aroused by this speech, but, by a great effort, he prevented himself rising to declare himself at once.

"You may well say what's bred in the bone," grumbled Boatswain Hackblock, as he retired to the fire-place to smoke, followed by Fanny—"none of you've got any proper pride except me."

The old barber, after this, resumed his task of shaving his customer, with a very shaking hand, and with many anxious inquiries about his supposed absent son.

"Tell me more, sir, about him," he said, "tell me more. Why didn't he write? He ought to have written."

"He ought," returned the young man, "but he has an excuse. He grew ashamed of drawing money from home after having run away, and made up his mind not to write until he could say that he was better off."

The old barber had now nearly half finished his task, and nearly one side of young Hackblock's beard had been shaved off. The old man seemed to be struggling with some thought or recollection, for he walked a few steps away from the shaving-chair, and looked curiously at his customer.

"He started in the business he had been bred up to," continued young Hackblock, appearing not to notice his father's change of manner, "hoping to get on, but several years soon passed without any luck."

"Strange!" murmured old Hackblock to himself, leaving his task again, and looking at his customer keenly from another point of view; "I can hardly hold the razor! I cannot be dreaming?"

"As he couldn't make a fortune," still continued young Hackblock, though with decreased command over himself, "he scraped together his passage money."

The old barber, by this time, had finished his task, and his son's face stood before him free from all its unfamiliar covering. The old man hesitated once more for a moment, but only for a moment, and before Fanny and the old boat-swain could get round the old shaving-chair, the father and son were re-united and the truth was revealed.

After the first burst of joy and astonishment was over, the old boatswain could not refrain from amusing himself at the expense of his brother.

"Harry," he said to the old barber, who was now sit-ting down half exhausted in the shaving-chair, "you're caught again. It's a wise father who doesn't know his own son, isn't it?"

"I *must* have known him all along, Jack," returned the old man, almost crying, "for I'm sure I never shaved any-body so badly in my life."

"Ah, tell that to the marines," replied the old boatswain, incredulously.

"Let us settle all family differences now," said the old barber, kindly, "and start afresh. We can't all be big-drummers, that we know; but we can all try with heart and soul to be good little ones."*

* The right of dramatising this story has been reserved and exer-cised by the author.

AN APRIL FOOL.

I HAPPENED to be at a well-known coast town in South Wales last April, at the time when the census had to be taken, and knowing the Chief Registrar of the district, I offered to become a volunteer enumerator. I had been so long idling, lounging, and making tours without having any particular object in view, that the chance of any useful occupation presented itself to me as an agreeable change. My friend very kindly gave me a choice of ground to go over, and I selected a small island—called Swamp Island—lying out in the Channel, about twenty miles from the coast, which had figured in the census tables of 1851 as possessing a population of three. As a wilderness it was only then beaten by Little Papa, one of the Shetland Islands, which held only one person—an old woman; and by Inchcolm, one of the Fife Islands, which sheltered only one man—a farm labourer. It was a pity, perhaps, that these two solitudes with their two inhabitants could not have been joined together in holy matrimony, forming one decent family on one tolerable island.

Very early on the morning appointed for my journey, I started in a large fishing-smack, the owner of which, for a small consideration, undertook to land me at my destination, and call for me again before night. I was full of curiosity as to what people, and how many, I should find on Swamp Island, but my boatmen could give me no information on this head. As there was no good fishing within several miles of the scrubby patch of sea-land to which I was bound, they had never taken the trouble even to inquire whether it was inhabited.

I landed with some difficulty, in a not very shallow creek, and should have been soaked through above my knees if I had not been protected by a thick waterproof dress. The weather had been rather rough during our few hours' voyage from the mainland—much rougher than I expected—and as I am no better sailor than nine-tenths of the human race, I felt a little qualmy. My companions immediately put off again to fish, and I was soon left to make friends with a few seagulls.

Having comforted myself with a little brandy and biscuit that I carried with me, I struggled up through the reeds, stones, and long grass, and prepared to begin my work. I got upon a hillock, and took a survey of the island through a telescope. The prospect was not encouraging. As far as I could see, there was nothing but a dead level of swampy earth and grass, broken here and there with small hillocks, like the one on which I stood. The island was stated by geographical authorities to be about ten miles long, and twelve broad, but the inequalities of the ground would not allow my telescope to range over a third of this space. As there was no house or hut in sight, nor any sign of a human being, I was compelled to walk on in the discharge of my duty. I strode along in the direction of the rising ground in front, now plunging into a hole, now stumbling over grass-covered blocks of stone, and blessing the practical genius who invented roads. One mile of walking on Swamp Island was equal to four miles on the mainland.

In about two hours I reached the distant ridge, and still found no traces of inhabitants. I was rather disappointed at this, though not surprised, for I could see nothing to tempt any one to settle on such a spot. The earth was chalky, and the vegetation scanty, to say nothing of the want of society. If the .three inhabitants who had figured in a former census had deserted the place, I felt that I could scarcely blame them.

I altered my course at this point, and followed the line of a shallow valley. I had not proceeded far, when I came to traces of mud, and a little farther on to a narrow channel of water. Keeping along the side of this inland stream, which I soon found to be a long tidal creek running down to the sea, I came suddenly on a large flat-bottomed boat, something between a fishing-punt and a barge, moored close to a bank on which stood a low hut, built chiefly with turf and stones. I lost no time in pushing open the half-closed door of this hut, and was met by a dense cloud of smoke which nearly choked and blinded me. It came from a fire of damp wood. When the fumes had partly blown off, I peeped through the door again, and saw an old man kneeling on the turf-floor, blowing the embers with his mouth. His dress was ragged; almost theatrical in its tatters, and his long dirty beard dragged through the ashes.

" Stand out of the draught," he said, angrily, without turning round, " and don't thwart me, pampered menial !"

I thought the style and tone of his address somewhat peculiar, and I soon explained who I was, and on what errand I came.

" Census ?" he said, standing up, and looking at me ; " why am I hunted about in this way ? I come miles beyond the land's-end for quiet, solitude, air. I can't breathe in cities—no man can breathe in cities; I fly to nature, and want to be left alone."

"We shall not trouble you again for ten years," I returned, amiably; "perhaps not then."

"Ten years!" he said, contemptuously, "what's ten years—what's twenty years—to one who has lived for centuries?"

"Eh?" I answered, pricking up my ears at this, "lived for centuries?"

"Yes," he said, "I have just completed my one hundred and seventy-sixth year."

"This sounds very remarkable," I replied, "and it is almost as strange to find you living in such a desert as this."

"You may think so," he said, shortly, "I don't."

"What name will you put down in this paper?" I asked, producing the official form, "and what profession?"

"Profession?" he inquired, vacantly.

"Occupation," I replied, "calling—in fact. What are you?"

"Ha, ha!"

"That's no answer," I said, in a dignified manner.

"What am I?" he continued; "what am I not? Do you think my history can be crammed into a line, or into a thousand lines? You've asked for it, and you shall have it. Sit down, and hear it."

I squatted on the turf floor in obedience to this request, which sounded like a command, and my wild-man-of-the-woods-looking host soon squatted opposite me.

"I am prepared," he began, "for any amount of doubt when I say that I never knew who my parents were; but I despise doubt, and those who feel it. I was found in a wood in a neighbourhood that it is idle to name, because it

was destroyed by an earthquake more than a hundred years
ago. I was discovered walking on my hands and feet,
climbing trees like a squirrel, and feeding on grass and
moss. The early habits thus implanted in me have never
altogether left me, and this is why you find me now living
contented on what you contemptuously term 'a desert.'
Many ignorant people were frightened at my singular
appearance, for my colour, at that time, was nearly
black——"

"I beg your pardon," I said, "but what do you call
your colour now?"

"No matter," he replied, "I hate to be interrupted."

"A huge dog," he continued, "was set at me, but I
awaited his attack without stirring from the place, and
gave him such a blow over the head with a club which I
held in my hand, that the animal fell dead, and his master
became respectful. After this feat I climbed a tree and
took a little repose on a branch, but was allured down by
some raw meat (I am still partial to raw meat), a bucket
of water, and a rabbit. I stripped off the skin of the rabbit,
and devoured the flesh ravenously. I was taken in charge
by a shepherd, who washed me, and found that the black
colour of my skin was not natural. I was considered fair,
and, on the whole, tolerably well formed, although very
short; and my fingers and thumbs were uncommonly
strong, which was ascribed to my practice of climbing
trees. On account of my wildness I was known as the
'shepherd's beast,' and it cost a deal of trouble to render
me a little tame. I was very dexterous in making holes in
the walls or roofs—too dexterous, no doubt, for the comfort
of my shepherd—and one day I crept through a space not
larger than a rat-hole, fled once more to the woods, and
became a gipsy.

" I was soon initiated into the arts and mysteries of the
wandering tribe I had joined, and was foremost in all ex-
ploits for which gipsies are famous. Being wonderfully
short for my age, which was considered then to be about
twenty or twenty-five years, I was exhibited as a famous
dwarf. My height was not more than two feet and a half,
and my weight fifty-six pounds. I was remarkably agile,
and could spring with ease from the ground to a table or
a mantel-shelf. I remember being told by a friend, who
died about a century and a half ago, that I was rather of a
morose temper, and extremely vain of myself, but this I
can hardly believe. I was once brought into a room, to
amuse the company, enclosed in an ordinary pie. I was
often teased by many of the visitors, and once, I admit,
I so far lost my temper as to challenge my enemy. He
came to the place of meeting armed only with a squirt, and
this so increased my anger that a real duel ensued, and, as
I was mounted on a chair to put me on a level with my
antagonist, I fired, and shot him dead.

" After this unfortunate adventure I fled from the town
and my gipsy friends, and sought my fortunes in another direction. I disguised myself as a female, and went on board
a large merchant vessel as a cook's attendant. I was looked
upon as a mere child, a girl of all work, and so escaped
much attention. I discharged my duties to the satisfaction
of my employers, and passed a very pleasant though hard-
working time until we came to an anchor at a port in the
Mediterranean. Here one of the sailors, a second mate,
became too idle to mend his own shirts, and he handed
them over to me, along with a lot of stockings requiring
footing, because I was the only female on board. Of course
I knew nothing of needlework, and yet was afraid to con-
fess my ignorance, for fear the deception I had practised

upon the captain and owners of the ship should be discovered. I saw no way out of the difficulty except flight;
so, throwing the unmended rags down the hold, I watched
my opportunity, rowed on shore in a boat, and mixed with
the natives of Genoa in my own proper character.

"I lived for several years very comfortably in a number of southern cities, doing little work, because living was
cheap, and the climate made it easy to sustain nature on a
very small quantity of food. Whether the warmth of this
part of the world acted on my system like the atmosphere
of a hothouse upon plants I never clearly understood, but
I grew so rapidly in height and strength, during the five
or six years of my travelling, that I soon began to excite
attention as a giant.

"I was not one of those common giants, who rely upon
creating wonder by their unwieldy size. I possessed many
accomplishments, both intellectual and physical. As a
posturer I was without a rival, and could exhibit, in the
most natural manner, almost every species of deformity
and dislocation. I amused myself with the tailors, by
sending for them to take my measure, and contriving so as
to have an immoderate rising in one of my shoulders.
When the clothes were brought home to be tried on, I had
shifted this hump to the other shoulder, and the tailors
took back the garments, apologizing for their mistake. I
played such tricks with the vertebræ of my back, that a
celebrated surgeon, before whom I appeared as a patient,
was so shocked at the sight he would not even attempt my
cure.

"I was now nearly nine feet high, and I made a trium-
phal tour from town to town. I had gone through the
whole circle of the sciences, could speak and write in ten
different languages, was an accomplished rider, dancer, and

singer, and a skilful performer on several musical instruments."

"Did you ever hear of a person called the 'Admirable Crichton?'" I asked, breaking into my host's narrative at this point.

"Crichton, Crichton," he answered, as if reflecting. "Was he a celebrated miser?"

"Not at all," I said; "he was a half-fabulous wonder of cleverness."

"Never heard of him in all my life," returned my host, pettishly, "and I don't see what the question has to do with my story.

"I will not weary you," he continued, "with a detailed account of my success in disputing with learned doctors, fighting with rampant gladiators, and performing many characters in an Italian play of my own writing. The narrative might possibly annoy you, by exciting envy. It is sufficient for me to tell you that I did all these things before I had reached the age of thirty. I distinguished myself in a much lower sphere by several displays of extraordinary strength, in which I pulled against two horses, lifted three hogsheads of water weighing nearly two thousand pounds, rolled up a very large pewter dish with my fingers, and raised a table six feet long, with half a hundred-weight fastened to it, in my teeth. I tied a kitchen poker round my neck like a cravat, and broke a rope about two inches thick.

"About this period I began to decrease in height, and to increase very much in breadth. Some of the doctors attributed the change to the fact that I had compressed myself in carrying an enormous weight upon my head during one of my exhibitions. Whatever was the immediate cause, I gradually grew stouter for ten years, until I weighed nearly fifty stone. My size was nearly three yards round the body; my legs measured a yard round the thigh; and a common suit of clothes cost me twenty pounds."

"Have you ever heard of Daniel Lambert?" I asked, again interrupting my host.

"Of course I have," he answered; "he was a running footman."

The coolness of this reply effectually silenced me, and I allowed the story to proceed without any further interruption.

"My excessive and increasing corpulence," he continued, "filled me with alarm, and I at last placed myself under strict rules of diet. This required a vast deal of sustained resolution, for almost from the beginning of my change in size I had been afflicted with a voracious appetite. I thought little of devouring at one meal as much as sixteen pounds of meat and bread, and there were times when my appetite was even more ravenous. My drinking was also in proportion to my eating, although I was never intoxicated. All this had to be changed, and I therefore copied the plan of Louis Cornaro, of whom *you* may have heard. It was a hard struggle, but I persevered. As I thought it prudent not to make a total alteration in my diet suddenly, I confined myself to a pint of ale a day, and used animal food sparingly. This method I soon found to answer to my satisfaction, for I felt easier and lighter, and my spirits became less oppressed. During the next two months I struck off half my drink, and more than half my animal food. I next gave up malt liquor, and confined myself entirely to water for about a year, at the end of which period I was able to do without any fluid except what I took in the way of medicine. I next avoided cheese, then butter, and at last was able to turn my back upon animal food, and to sustain myself entirely upon pudding made of sea-biscuit. I allowed myself very little sleep, generally going to bed at eight o'clock in the evening, sometimes even earlier, and rising about one o'clock in the morning. My voice, which I had entirely lost for several years, came back to me clear and strong; my flesh became firm, my complexion a good colour; and I reduced my weight at least forty stone."

"Did you ever weigh yourself, to test the truth of these figures?" I asked.

"Never. Prejudiced by a commonly prevailing superstition, which, of course, I see the folly of now, I never suffered myself to be put in the scales, either during the state of my extreme corpulence, or after my reduction."

"Why did you subject yourself to such very strict rules of diet?" I inquired; "stricter even than those which governed your teacher, Cornaro?"

"Because I was ten years older than Cornaro was when he began his regimen, and I therefore thought, on that account, a more severe and abstemious course was necessary. I was greatly influenced by Dr. Cheyne's opinion, that Cornaro would probably have lived longer had his regimen been more strict. Dr. Cheyne was right, as I have tested by experiment, and I have been right in following the advice of Dr. Cheyne. For more than a hundred years I have been fed upon a pudding, the composition of which you may be curious to learn, especially as you show a tendency to become stout, and are evidently not in very sound health. Take three pints of skimmed milk, boil them and pour them on one pound of the best sea-biscuit, broken into pieces: do this overnight, and then leave the ingredients to stand together until the following morning, when

you may add two eggs. This compound, being boiled in a
cloth about the space of an hour, will become a pudding of
sufficient consistency to be cut with a knife. No matter
what may have been the season—what festivities were
going on—what temptations there were to a little self
indulgence—I allowed myself only a pound and a half of
this pudding at four or five o'clock in the morning, as my
breakfast, and the same quantity at noon, as my dinner.
What is the result? At the age of a hundred and
ninety——"

"I beg your pardon," I said, "you told me you were
only one hundred and seventy-six."

"Did I?" he answered; "well, say one hundred and
seventy-six, then—we'll not quarrel about fourteen years—
at this age I am able to live cheerfully without company in
what, as I before remarked, you contemptuously style a
desert. I am active and vigorous, and in full possession of
more than my proper faculties. I am able, at times, to
pick out colours with my eyes closed, and to read a book
with my fingers' ends. Sometimes I can walk in my sleep
with even more security and speed than when I am awake;
which I look upon as a proof that my system of diet is
correct."

My host's story might probably have continued for
several hours longer, as I really had not sufficient determination to stop it, if we had not been interrupted at this
point by the appearance of a third person at the door of
the hut. The new comer was a man, about forty, and, if
dress were any sign of quality, I might have thought that
I had been entertained by the servant in the absence of the
master. I was not, however, left long in suspense as to the
relation in which the two islanders stood to each other, for

my ragged host immediately addressed the new comer in a loud, authoritative tone :—

"Pampered menial! Take off that dandy coat, and blow the fire."

The new comer obeyed this rude command rather slowly and sullenly, muttering something about not being so fond of rags as some people were.

"Silence!" again shouted my ragged host. "If Crusoe and Friday quarrel in private, let them preserve a certain decency before strangers."

I fancied preparations might be made to feed me with the sea-biscuit pudding I had heard described, and had not felt any particular wish to taste ; so, as my time on the island was drawing to a close, I rose to go. My host insisted on the "pampered menial" seeing me to the coast, and my proposed guide assured me that no one else was to be found upon the island.

"Worse luck," he said, as we left the hut together, "for he does try the best of tempers."

"You mean our eccentric friend yonder ?" I remarked, inquiringly, pointing back to the hut.

"Yes," he said. "If his friends didn't pay me very well, I should pitch him over, like a shot."

"Isn't there something the matter with his head ?" I asked, trying to put the question very delicately.

"Sometimes I think there is ; sometimes I don't. He took to this place because he was fond of fishing, though we never catch much worth speaking of. Even what the smacks catch is sent up to London, and we have to get it down again by signals."

"Fish ?" I said ; "I thought he lived upon nothing but pudding."

"Oh, he's been pitching that yarn into you, has he ?

He eats a precious sight more than I do, and thinks a good deal more about his dinner."

" I suppose," I said, " you have heard the extraordinary story of his life ?"

" Heard it ?" he returned, " I should think I have ! He goes over it about three times a week, or one hundred and fifty times a year. It all comes of reading of one book—the only book he's got with him—called ' Wilson's Wonderful Characters.' He muddles them all up together, and then goes and swears he's been through all the adventures, because his name happens to be Peter Wilson !"

" That looks like madness," I said. " Perhaps, however, it's as reliable as the book," I thought.

" So his friends think who live on the mainland opposite," returned my guide, " but I think the madness shows itself most in living here. They'll find that out some day, when I leave them, and they have to advertise for another ' companion ' to my gentleman."

When we arrived at the coast, we found my boatmen within hail. Before embarking, I inquired my guide's name, and, as he answered me, he seemed to have something on his mind.

" Can I do anything for you on the opposite shore ?" I asked, willing to make myself useful to the lonely islander.

" Well," he said, " there's one thing I want to ask you. Is that census return, as you call it, going to be put into print ?"

" Undoubtedly," I replied.

" What have you got him down as—the party up at the hut ?"

" Peter Wilson : no profession : age, one hundred and seventy-six."

" You can let that stand, if you like, but don't go and

call the island a private madhouse, and put me down as a keeper."

" How shall I describe you ?" I asked, willing to humour him.

" Call me a shepherd," he said. "Because I've got some friends on the opposite shore—especially a female friend—and I don't want to be laughed at."

I complied with his request in filling up the official form ; and he stands in his country's account-books as Giles Storks : profession, shepherd : age, forty-two.

THE SHOP-SIDE OF ART.

I.

THE earth is full of couples who are made for each other, not only of couples whose destiny it is to love, but of those whose destiny it is to hate. For every spider there is created a fly; for every cat a mouse; for every bird a worm; for every innocent bill-holder a more innocent bill-acceptor; and for every picture-dealer a picture-buyer. It is doubtful if that favourite target of small divines—the world—could be kept suspended in mid-air without such a provision of nature, and, therefore, if we record the habits and manners of antagonistic races, let us do it with so little party-feeling, and so much philosophical calmness, that something like the truth may be arrived at.

II.

Though Mr. Huggin was born some twenty years before Mr. Eizak Sleman came into existence, yet the latter gentleman was evidently destined to exert a peculiar influence over the former. The start that Mr. Huggin got in life over Mr. Sleman, seemed only to have been used in preparing for that gentleman's appearance. If money was accumulated by Mr. Huggin—and it *was* accumulated —in a business so unpictorial as the tallow-trade, it was allowed to grow in all its rank luxuriance, until Mr. Sleman presented himself to pluck it.

III.

In tracing the rise and progress of Mr. Eizak Sleman, we are struck by the many changes which a single name may undergo. The father of Mr. Sleman thought proper to sign himself Salamans, while another son gently changed his title to Slayman; a second to Sloman; and a third to Sleighman. The vowels are very accommodating. Another branch of the same family—an uncle of the subject of our sketch—went even further, and by adding "Van" to one end of his name, and the letter "n" to the other, he came out as Mr. Van Slemann. Without going into the question of how far individual taste may have had an influence in these changes, there is no doubt that they were found remarkably useful in all matters of business.

Young Eizak Sleman (or Solomons) was born in a mingled atmosphere of horses and art. If he had come into the world only ten years earlier, he might have found himself cradled in a low gaming-house; and ten years before that—about the time that Mr. Huggin was born— he might have wondered what took his father away for exactly seven years and a half—neither more nor less. As it was, however, he first saw the light in an obscure bye-street, and in a low brown shop, where betting-books had scarcely been driven out, and Holy Families (painted in oil) had hardly been gathered in. As he grew a little older, and able to use his eyes, he found that his father's permanent stock-in-trade was a large treacly portrait, much cracked, of a woman in a ruff, a couple of bronze candlesticks, a few pieces of dusty old china, some empty picture frames, and a parchment-coloured statuette of a figure that had no head, only half an arm, and one leg that wanted a foot. These things were always displayed in a coal-hole kind of gloom, and were never disturbed, either by buyer or seller.

As Eizak Sleman grew older still, and able to use his mind as well as his eyes, he was gradually taught some of the secrets of his father's business. He had the pleasure of seeing that business increase, and of learning the main principles upon which it was conducted. A thing of beauty is a joy for ever, was old Salaman's maxim, but only if you know how to deal with it.

The first step was to get the thing of beauty—the Holy Family, or the Head of the Madonna, as the case might be —and then to carefully. prepare it as bait for the trap. This picture was never one of those manufactured masses of paint and varnish that are popularly supposed to be produced, in any quantity, in certain garrets, and to be baked and smoked in any quantity, in certain ovens and kitchen chimneys. The class of buyers that old Salamans angled for were persons of some intelligence, some taste, much wealth, more vanity and cupidity, and a little judgment. These hucksters—for hucksters they were—could not be deceived by copies a week old, even if copyists of sufficient talent were to be drawn from more profitable work upon tenth-rate original pictures, or the reproduction of the modern masters. The common instinct of trade was against. this form of fraud. If the well-known worm-eaten wood, or the peculiar canvas of the old masters could be successfully imitated; what inducement would there be to exert this extra ingenuity, when a hundred safer and cheaper contemporary copies are to be found in the market ?

The chief works, then, that Eizak Sleman's father was always endeavouring to secure were pictures painted by

those few earnest pupils who had sat at the living feet of
the old masters. Sometimes the eyes of the masters had
rested approvingly upon these works, sometimes their
hands had kindly given them a touch of grace, beyond the
reach of the humble student of art. It may be that amongst
these nameless students were many who strove hard to
create something that the world should cherish, and who
sank to rest with a faint hope that they had accomplished
their task. The power of piercing into the distant future,
was kindly withheld from them, and they were spared the
pain of seeing their images of beauty mellowed with age,
encrusted with a thousand falsehoods, and patronized by
greasy touters in low sale-rooms. If the bitter destiny of
their lofty labour could have been unfolded to them, they
would surely have destroyed their handiwork, and the great
Sleman family would have been fed only upon those coarse
contemporary imitations that were openly painted and
sold in the lifetime of the masters by hucksters who knew
no guile.

The elder Salamans, however, did not confine his dealings to the stray pictures of antiquity, but he became a
patron of living art. He found out many British artists
whose necessities were slightly in advance of their income,
and while he played the Samaritan, he made many presentable additions to his pictorial stock. With these productions, and the pupil-pictures before described, which
required very little manipulation to transform them into
safe, current specimens of the genuine masters; a mass of
framed and unframed rubbish was freshened up, and a
catalogue prepared of a high-class periodical sale. This
sale was always largely supported by contributions from
the great Salaman's family; by pictures from " Slayman
and Co." (the eldest son) of Polyglot Square ; by bronzes

and articles of *vertù* from Humphrey " Sloman" (the second son) of Cameo Court, Oxford Street ; and by more " charming" pictorial productions from "Sleighman and Sleighman" (the third son) of Sligo Buildings, City. The sale always took place at the auction-rooms of Mr. Van Slemann (the brother of the elder Salamans), which were situated in a prominent part of Mudgate Hill, the chief thoroughfare of London. These rooms were very gay and enticing in front, very small and dark in the interior, and very crowded with a " choice collection of ancient and modern paintings." The safest flowers of this collection were placed in accessible positions, and in curious lights, while the sign-board and tea-board productions, a rather large majority of the stock, were turned, as if in shame, with their faces to the wall. They wanted nothing to set them off that a certain electro-plated taste could give them in the shape of frames, and if swelling lumps of gilding, rosewood cases, and faultless plate-glass would make great paintings, then these must have been very great, indeed.

On the morning of the sale, or the attempted sale, about half an hour before the official arrival of the auctioneer, a little crowd was always collected on Mudgate Hill, turning over the fluttering leaves of the catalogues that were nailed upon green-baize boards at the doorway, or looking at the great picture with which the trap was baited on that particular occasion, and which was displayed so as to catch the eye of passers-by at the single window in front. The greatest part of this crowd consisted of dummy-bidders, a number of middle-aged men, who were made up to play a part in such a manner, that they ought not to have deceived a child. A ragged-edged yellow collar on a starch-caked yellow shirt; a high black stock, worn just a little threadbare at the sides ; a well-brushed, thin black dress-coat, and rather shiny black trousers, that would bear no violent exercise; a well-cleaned pair of mended blucher boots; and a pair of ragged cotton gloves, are not the costume usually worn by wealthy collectors of art. Yet these were the men to the number of nearly a dozen, who were supposed to be regardless of money when a Rubens or a Correggio came in their way; and who, if not investing for themselves, were the confidential agents of Lord Mumble-peg, a devoted buyer of pictures, who was prevented by paralysis from attending personally at the sales. Poor wretches; they looked, with their clean-shaven, melancholy faces, as if the slightest whispered invitation to a substantial dinner at a snug, warm city tavern would have thrown them off their balance, and have caused them to fly, like a cloud of swallows, from the barren feast of paint.

Inside the auction-trap were the other members of the gang, the sprinkling of eager, confederate dealers; the four or five porters, who were probably "junior partners," and who looked like prize-fighters, and the usual number of "picture agents." As soon as a promising stranger entered the room, it was the business of one of these latter men to fasten on him, and explain the beauties and defects of the collection under sale. It must always be delightful to a man of refinement, to have such agreeable guides at his elbow, and to overlook their flavour of onions, tobacco, and stale clothes in admiration of their intense appreciation of art. There can, of course, be nothing to jar the most sensitive nerves in hearing a thick, hoarse, sponging-house voice enlarging upon the minute rendering of the crown of thorns, or in seeing a thick, black, grubby finger, half hooped with brassy rings, employed in pointing out the hidden touches of the agony in the garden. These picture-dealers certainly assume a very low standard of intellect in their patrons when they take no more trouble than this in selecting their confederates.

The sales at Mr. Van Slemann's were not entirely supported by family contributions, but were swollen by many "noble works," and "religious subjects," that were sent by other traders of a similar stamp. A fine of two shillings and sixpence upon every lot was found sufficient to cover the expenses upon these consignments, and pay the auctioneer a trifle for his trouble. When the sale of a high-priced picture to an ignorant but greedy purchaser did really occur, as it sometimes did, the transaction was saddled with, and able to bear, a commission of a very princely character. No man ever entered those rooms, or even peeped in at the window, who was not followed, and whose position in society was not thoroughly learnt, if he looked like, or promised to bud into, an innocent picture buyer. He may have been astonished to find that the pictorial treasures of his mansion were known to numbers of unsightly men, like sheriff's officers. He may have been astonished to find that after he had inquired about a landscape or a tavern scene, at the shop of "Slayman and Co.," his hall table was loaded the next morning with Claudes and Teniers from "Sleighman and Sleighman's" that had been left for his examination and approval by a strange man, a strange woman, or even a strange boy. He may have been astonished to find that his steps had been dogged from a print shop; and that when he wanted a little advice about a picture to guide his not very reliable judgment, the owner of the property seemed to know where he had applied for that advice, if not the exact words of the advice that had been given. He would have been more astonished, if he had not "bled freely," to find himself the purchaser of a fine, old, crusted collection of Italian saints, and half-a-dozen sturdy witnesses springing out of the ground, who had each and all a distinct recollection that he had promised to pay two thousand guineas for them. If he gave any indications that, with proper care and management, he was likely to become that sallow-faced, wild-eyed spectre, the collector who would "bleed to death," a net was woven round him from which there was little chance of escape ; he was fed with nothing but what was likely to encourage his one idea ; and he was never deserted until he was reduced to madness, or to a mere fruitless husk.

This is the great victim that every art huckster is always searching for, and who he knows is existing for him in some hidden corner of the world. His shops—his family organization—his " knock out" combinations—his delusive sales—are nothing but ingenious devices to employ his time, compared with the great mission of his life, the necessity for finding this victim in the crowd.

These were the experiences and the teachings that were constantly before young Eizak Sleman as he grew to be a man ; and when he attained that period of life, of course he became a picture-dealer.

IV.

And what had Mr. Huggin been doing for the last five-and-twenty years to prepare himself for the slaughter ? Beyond the fact already recorded that he had made money, and a good deal of money, in the tallow trade, he seemed to have reached the age of five-and-forty without being much the wiser for it.

His business was not sufficient to occupy his mind, and he wished to be known as something more than a successful merchant. There are many men who have a similar ambitious weakness.

He lived, from trading necessity, in a northern town, whose society had much of the Scottish pride of birth, and very little professed respect for riches. If Mr. Huggin had been single, this aristocratic haughtiness might doubtless have been softened, but as he was married, and had no children, there was little inducement to make it less hard than pride of ancestry ought, of course, to be. In vain did Mr. Huggin avail himself of the new philological lights, and trace his unpretending surname up to a Scandinavian god. His dinners were eaten, but eaten with silent contempt.

It was while suffering under this galling treatment, that, being unable to write a book or shake the senate, he formed the melancholy idea of setting up as a person of taste. He proceeded very gently, almost imperceptibly at first, as a man with his trading instincts and the knowledge of the value of money would naturally do, but by degrees he gained courage, or found that timidity was worse than useless in the art-collecting world. He deserted his prints and etchings, his Antonios and Bolswerts, for paintings of various qualities and many schools. He employed a provincial picture-dealer pretty constantly in commissions, a rude practitioner, like a country barber, with no more honesty than the great Salaman's family, but with hardly a fraction of their keenness and experience. This man was so clumsy in his operations, and so greedy of present profit, that he would have nipped the most promising innocent purchaser in the bud. Before, however, he could succeed in disgusting the mind and opening the eyes of Mr. Huggin, that gentleman was carried out of his reach for a time by important business in town.

V.

It was about this period that the death of Sir Saffron Hill, the great collector and connoisseur, was announced. Sir Saffron Hill had excited the envy and admiration of his tribe for more than half a century. The envy was bestowed upon his collection; the admiration upon his judgment. He was supposed to possess everything that was unique and valuable; he was supposed to know the imposition from the genuine thing at a single glance. If he declared a picture to be by the divine Raffaele, it was considered warranted; if he refused to say that a group of plump beauties were by the earthy Rubens, their reputation was considered to be hopelessly blasted. He had been heard to utter some contemptuous remarks about Guido, and Holy Venuses fell at once to a discount in the market. His opinion was sought even beyond the realms of high art, and he was sometimes asked to place his hand on the brown back of a violin, and to tell its trembling owner if it was really a Straduarius.

Sir Saffron Hill lived a lonely life in one of the old squares, with nothing but his beloved collection and a few vulgar, unsympathetic servants round him. If the latter had not been vulgar and unsympathetic, he would not have considered his smaller treasures so secure in their keeping. He was very unwilling to show his collection, and was a miser, in every sense of the word, although it has been the fashion never to associate this character with anything but money.

One evening, after dinner, Sir Saffron Hill was discovered dead in his easy chair, with his latest purchase, a small piece of palissy ware on the hearth-rug before him. There was abundance of dusty Utrecht velvet, tortoiseshell buhl, lapis-lazuli, ebony, Sevrès porcelain, oil-colour gems, and water-colour jewels, at his side and at his back, while a bust of one of the Cæsars, nearly over his head, seemed to be making faces at another Cæsar opposite, as if nothing had happened.

The death was rather welcomed by the art world than otherwise, as it promised to disperse a very large and valuable collection. The late unrivalled connoisseur had died without a will, and the two discarded children, a boy and girl, who came forward to claim the property, were not disposed either by education or by circumstances to retain it in its art form. A dozen hammers were trembling with eagerness, but the choice fell upon Messrs. Crystal and Ransom, the eminent auctioneers, and they received the usual instructions.

VI.

For days you could hardly get near the celebrated auction rooms in Plush Street, St. Coutts's, to view this magnificent released collection. The crowd was so great, and so mixed, that many persons of authority said it was like going to court. The Countess of Dura was seen struggling between Mr. Barrington from Whitechapel (*alias* "Duffing Jemmy") and a leading member of the great Salaman's family. The Duke of Majolica had his hat knocked over his patrician eyes. The street was full of carriages, cabs, and go-carts, and the spotless auctioneers were accused of favouring certain visitors by letting them in through a back skylight.

The second day's sale served to tone down this enthusiasm a little, and on the third day Mr. Huggin was passing by chance and found his way into the centre of the auction-room.

"Lot ninety-five," continued the auctioneer, rapidly, "An Interior—Van Pothaus—two figures at window—beautiful effect of pipe-light—credit alike to artist and collector—shall we say one hundred pounds?"

Two—three—five—ten hundred pounds were quickly offered from various parts of the crowd.

"Thousan' guinis," cried the eldest of the Salaman's family, Mr. Slayman, "and Co."

"One thousand and eighty pounds," exclaimed a feeble little gentleman in spectacles.

"One thousand and eighty pounds," repeated the auctioneer.

"Let Slayman 'av' it," shouted the venerable father of the Salaman's family.

"Mr. Salamans," said the auctioneer, sternly, "I must beg that you will abstain from interrupting the sale."

The sale went on, and a tall, severe-looking, middle-aged gentleman, in a white neck-tie, secured the picture with a solemn inclination of his head, and a commanding wave of his hand, for fifteen hundred pounds.

"Lord Eikey Drummond, I think?" said the auctioneer's clerk, as he recorded the purchaser's name.

The solemn inclination of the head was slowly repeated, and the Salaman's family looked as if they had made the acquaintance of a new picture buyer, before unknown to them.

Mr. Huggin witnessed all this in silent amazement. He had read a few books that took the purple-bloom view of art, but not sufficient to turn his brain, and at present his chief touchstone of merit in a picture was the two-foot rule. The Van Pothaus he had just seen sold for such a considerable sum was no larger than many works he had got at home, which he fully believed he had bought with

the rarest taste and judgment. He saw more lots disposed
of to buyers who had little knowledge of their own to guide
them, and who took the well-advertised character of the
late Sir Saffron Hill, as a guarantee in every way sufficient
for the value of the paintings. The Salamans family looked
on, bought nothing, and gained some useful information
about buyers. Mr. Huggin looked on, and thought he saw
his way, while gaining the reputation of a person of taste,
to work a wonderful field for profitable investment. He
bought a few more volumes upon the purple-bloom view of
art, which he read, and mixed up with his shop-view of
the subject. When he had settled down once more in his
northern city he was in as fit a state as any collector could
ever be to be tapped by a judicious picture-dealer.

VII.

When Eizak Sleman started in business, he showed
himself to be a picture-dealer by birth, as well as by
apprenticeship. He lost no time in fulfilling his mission.
This mission was to find an untapped innocent purchaser
of the highest class—a purchaser whom he knew to be
waiting for him—somewhere.

The promising buyers who had turned up at the sale
of the late Sir Saffron Hill's collection, had been secured
by his brothers, and other labourers in the same vineyard.
Lord Eikey Drummond had fallen to his father; and
though he felt that he could have made more of his lordship, the duty due from a son to a parent forbade him in-
terfering in their transactions.

This position drove him, in some measure, into the country ; and he tried a plan, well-known in the trade, which
had something of the prospecting-rod about it. He took a
small and well-assorted stock of pictures into certain lead-

ing provincial towns, situated in the midst of the landed
or wealthy gentry. As the drummer in attendance upon
the Punch and Judy show always beats a few notes upon
his instrument to draw the children to the nursery windows,
so did Mr. Eizak Sleman pitch his tent in each town, and
endeavour to draw out the local patrons of art, by a
travelling picture sale. He sometimes said the sale was
by order of the sheriff, which looked official. He sometimes gave out that the collection belonged to a gentleman
in the neighbourhood, whose pecuniary difficulties had become too great to be borne. This stimulated curiosity,
which brought an audience ; and it was rare, indeed, if the
auction passed off without something being sold at a handsome profit.

The enterprising picture-dealer pursued this plan for
months—the summer months—without meeting with a
promising victim. He had pushed himself, stage by stage,
far into the land, and had just concluded an unsuccessful
sale in a very dull, but substantial northern town. He
had retired, rather depressed, to his hotel, when he was
told that a gentleman wished to see him. The proper
couple had found each other at last. The gentleman was
Mr. Huggin.

VIII.

Five years soon flew by after this interview at the hotel,
and Mr. Huggin, to all appearance, had " bled " very freely.
His walls were covered with paintings from garret to cellar
—with " noble works," " delicious productions," " religious
subjects," and warranted " masterpieces." Mrs. Huggin
turned up her eyes when she looked at these treasures,
shrugged her shoulders, and said nothing. Women are so
odd. Mr. Huggin believed that the mantle of the late Sir

Saffron Hill had descended upon his shoulders; and as he had impressed his neighbours with the same belief, he was supremely happy.

Mr. Eizak Sleman often made his appearance at Huggin Hall with a quantity of luggage; and he was always welcomed by the proprietor. When he left, after staying a night in the mansion, he had seldom anything more than a carpet-bag to take down to the station.

" Blessed if ever I see sich a man as you," said Mr. Sleman to his innocent purchaser, over the dinner-table; " you know a sight more about pictur's than I do, a'tho' I've bin in 'em all my life !"

" P'raps so," returned Mr. Huggin, evidently gratified, " p'raps so; I generally understand anything that I give my mind to."

" You ought to be in my place," continued the picture-dealer, in a thick, hoarse voice, " an' I in yourn."

" I might fill your place, Mr. Sleman," replied Mr. Huggin, with pompous dignity, " but it doesn't by any means follow that you could fill mine."

" No more it don't," said the picture-dealer, suddenly convinced; " no more it don't. I'm no use to you, I can see."

Mr. Eizak Sleman's visits to Huggin Hall were always made to effect a sale, but sometimes, as a matter of policy, he attempted to re-purchase.

" You know Lord Eikey Drummond ?" asked Mr. Sleman.

" I've seen his lordship in public," answered Mr. Huggin.

" About that Teniers : he's mad a'ter it, an' don't mind three hundred pund."

" I'm sorry for his lordship."

" You on'y giv' me two, for it, yer know."

" Mr. Sleman," said Mr. Huggin, sternly, at this point, " I will not be talked to in this manner. My principle is to buy pictures, not to retail them."

Thus this pair went on for several years; Mr. Huggin " bleeding " freely—almost to the death—and Mr. Sleman fattening undisturbed upon his innocent purchaser.

IX.

The purple-bloom view of art had never taken an un-divided hold of Mr. Huggin; its influence had been shared with the lower feelings of the trader. Mr. Huggin was just as much a picture-dealer as Mr. Eizak Sleman; with this difference, that he trusted to " self-education," and " natu-ral abilities " to teach him his business. There are very few men in the coal and potato line who feel incapable of editing a newspaper; and there are very few editors of newspapers who feel incapable of managing a slate quarry. Mr. Huggin had more than his share of this enterprising confidence; and when he began to grow tired of the barren reputation he had established as a person of taste, he pre-pared his gigantic collection for the market without the slightest misgiving. The impression made upon him at the sale of Sir Saffron Hill's treasures had never faded from his mind, and Messrs. Crystal and Ransom were, of course, the gentlemen who received his instructions. From this moment the hitherto constant Mr. Eizak Sleman dis-appeared, and melted, for ever, into the broad bosom of the Salamans' family.

X.

There was something wrong about the first day's sale. The attendance was tolerably numerous, and many pictures were sold, but the receipts were ridiculously small, considering the expectations of Mr. Huggin. Perhaps Mr. Huggin's reputation was not so well advertised as the late Sir Saffron Hill's? Perhaps it would have been better if the 'collection had been sold as belonging to a mock baronet? The auctioneers were suspiciously—almost painfully—silent. Mr. Huggin glided busily about the room; and was much hurt to find that those who appeared to be professional picture-dealers abstained from rising beyond a very low bidding. Mr. Huggin prided himself upon being a shrewd, experienced man of business, and he thought he knew exactly what to do under the circumstances. He privately retained several sham buyers for the second day's sale, in order to support the market.

The first lot that was brought forward was an enormous piece of Chinese-looking art, that was said to be the masterpiece of the divine Bellini.

" Ten pounds," began the auctioneer.

" Thirty, forty, ninety, two hund'ed, seven hund'ed," shouted half-a-dozen shabby men, who leaped up one after the other, like so many Jacks-in-boxes at different parts of the room.

" Ten pounds, I say," repeated the auctioneer, looking sternly at the sham bidders, and going back to his starting point.

" Ninety, two hund'ed, six hund'ed, thousan'," exclaimed the same shabby men, leaping up as before.

" Gentlemen," said the auctioneer, with dignity, " it's very evident what this means; and I think we'd better close the sale."

There was much confusion after this, but no serious opposition to the proposal, and in half-an-hour the public had all left the place.

"Mr. Crystal—Mr. Ransom—sir—gentlemen," said Mr. Huggin, excited and humbled, in the auctioneers' private counting-house, "there's some mistake about these pictures—there is indeed!"

"Mr. Huggin," replied Mr. Crystal, in a tone of pity, "the mistake is entirely on your side. You have been grossly imposed upon in a way we can understand. Many hundreds of gentlemen have been so deceived before, and many hundreds will doubtless be so deceived again. Good morning."

The mist was blown away; the heavy dream was broken; and the poor picture-collector retired with his mocking treasures, to munch his bitter apple of knowledge in obscurity and silence.

PICTURE GAMBLING.

WE have now had about fifteen years of Art-Unions, or legalized gambling societies for the improvement of the people. It is assumed, in defiance of reliable evidence, that these institutions have been so generally beneficial to the subscribers, that a Book-Union may be profitably started on the same principles. The old currency fallacy that there is a vast difference between money and money's worth must somehow have got mixed up with the plan of these societies. What is heinous in Bride Lane, and illegal in Capel Court, appears to be praised in the Strand, and tolerated in Manchester or Edinburgh. To bet upon horses, to play at cards, to throw dice, or do any similar thing for the purpose of causing money to pass from one pocket to another, is not considered respectable, and is against certain Acts of Parliament. To attempt a distribution of twelfth-cakes on the Art-Union plan is to invite a police prosecution—as a certain Frenchman found to his cost during the last winter. A legalized lottery, or gambling society under distinguished patronage, must be sanctified by a motive strongly flavoured with social reform. The belly is not allowed to toss halfpence for its vulgar gratification; nor is the breeches pocket licensed to play at chuck-farthing, except in an indirect manner. These games can only be carried on under cover of pictures, statuettes, works of saleable art, and a professed desire to improve the tastes of the people.

We have so many Parliamentary committees on all kinds of subjects, and so many elaborate blue-books as the result of these committees, that it requires no very great stretch of modesty to ask for more. We want to see a return of all those families amongst the lower, middle, and the working classes, who have really retained their art prizes as household adornments. It may be that we are a little prejudiced against these Art-Unions—as much prejudiced, perhaps, as the House of Lords was during the last session, when it snubbed Lord Brougham on the question of Book-Unions—but we cannot get rid of an impression, founded in a great degree upon personal observation, that two-thirds of these Art-Union prizes are in the hands of the Jews. Instead of gracing the cottage of the labourer, or the parlour of the clerk and artisan, we fancy they will be found in mouldy pawnbrokers' garrets, or the sale-rooms of picture-dealing auctioneers. In one-half of the cases where they may be discovered looking down upon admiring families, it will possibly be found that their owners are not subscribers to the Art Lottery, but persons who have bought them as "job" pictures at sales. If the investigation be pushed a step further, the original winners of these art prizes will be found sitting within bare walls, having honestly disposed of the pictures or statuettes to raise money for meat, drink, clothing, tobacco, and potatoes.

Whatever the design of Art-Unions may be upon paper, and whatever the few really philanthropic members of Art-Union committees may mean in theory, these societies, in practical working, are little more than legalized clubs for gambling under restrictions. The prize is not a straightforward cash payment, as it was in the honest old lotteries, but a something which the winner takes away with a fine art blessing, and turns into money at a discount of fifty per cent. A working man subscribes his shilling, or his half-crown, as the case may be, and wakes up one morning to find himself the possessor of a two-hundred guinea picture. The work may not be worth half the money—it may not even have cost the society half the money, for these things are often very carefully managed by the Art-Union officers. It figures, however, in the list, as a two-hundred guinea prize, and its size, design, and subject are all out of tune with its unfortunate winner's habits, education, and dwelling. It is like the family-picture painted for the Vicar of Wakefield; there is no fitting it into the humble house, and it has to remain neglected in a rough outbuilding. A few weeks pass by, and when the novelty of the prize has a little worn off, and the neighbours turn their backs upon the show, the unfortunate owner begins to think of selling his property. Being unused to picture-dealing, he mechanically seeks the advice of some one connected with the Art-Union. He is not rebuked with that severity which he might naturally expect, seeing that there is no excuse for his winning an Art-prize unless he intended to keep it. His application is treated as an everyday matter of business, and he is dealt with in the hardest ready-money manner. His two-hundred guinea prize is pared down to fifty pounds, and two or three pounds are deducted for carriage and "incidental expenses." He takes home about forty-seven pounds sterling in hard cash, and the money is spent according to the taste of the family. A few coloured drawings, of a very low school of art, may be bought in the market town, just to keep up a recollection of the lucky lottery. As strong drink is sure not to be spared on such an occasion, let us hope that the Art-Union is not forgotten amongst the convivial toasts and sentiments.

We are sadly afraid that no result more hopeful than this can be shown for one-half of the Art-Union labours. Instead of being vast engines for improving the tastes of the world, these societies are only ordinary lotteries with inferior prizes. If gambling is to be legalized under one pretext, it may as well be legalized under another, and we have, therefore, not a word to say against the proposed Book-Unions. It would be more honest, however, to take down the false educational colours under which all these institutions sail, and to go boldly back to the system of cash payments. That public decency might not be suddenly shocked, and the many ornamental committees of these lotteries not be dissolved, the money might always be handed over to the winners with a sound moral admonition.

PANACEAS.

If I allowed myself to write one word against the age I live in, I should be nothing better than the blackest ingrate. Few of the commonest animals in creation are without some feeling of gratitude, and shall man—superior man—admit an inferiority to the beasts that perish?

It is a beautiful, a generous, a wealthy, and believing age. When I hear accounts of its increase of population, I say, Go on and prosper. When I hear accounts of its increase of wealth, I likewise say, Go on and prosper. The larger and richer the field, the better will it be for the reaper.

When I look around me at the world of the present hour, I pity the condition of those of my class (the class that is too wise to steal, too clever to work, and that has intellect enough to scheme), whose misfortune it was to live in the seventeenth and eighteenth centuries. I am filled with commiseration for my ancestors, when I think what ingenuity in those days may have been allowed to perish in silent neglect, or may have been rewarded in a very partial and inadequate manner.

I am the inventor of those three once popular names—the "Druids' Ointment," the "Druids' Lotion," and the "Druids' Pill." I lived for years magnificently upon those names; I realized a handsome fortune by them; and I sold

their copyright, though somewhat worn and tarnished, for
a sum that would open the eyes of any plodding, every-day
trader.   That copyright term has expired, the names
themselves have almost expired, and I am perfectly at
liberty to write as I now do.

First of all, I feel it my duty to record, in the most honest
and unequivocal manner, what that pill, that lotion, and that
ointment really were not.   The pill was not made of old
leather breeches, forty years behind the fashion, which were
rescued from the moths and rats of an old slopseller's warehouse, at a nominal price per ton, and chopped and ground to
powder by the aid of machinery.   The pill was not made with
equal mixtures of tan-dust, and gum Arabic (pronounced
"marrowback"), and the sweepings of a saw-pit.   It was
not made, on any occasion during my proprietorship, with
old felt hats of a past generation, discarded and "jobbed
off" like the aforesaid leather breeches.   Of course, I am
only answering for the medicine while it was in my hands,
and under my management.   I sold it, with all letters, testimonials, etc., on the seventeenth of July, eighteen hundred and fifty-four.   What it was in substance, though
still retaining the name, after that period I have no authority nor desire to state.   The lotion was not a very important, or much demanded division of my medicinal stock-in-
trade, and it was not manufactured by a combination of
Spanish liquorice and thin barley-water.   The ointment,
which stood next to the pills, and almost equalled them in
its sale, was neither rejected railway-cart grease, condemned
butter, nor the re-appearance of a bankrupt pomatum-
maker's stock, that had been bought for a mere trifle at the
assignee's sale.   Each and all of these stories about my
medicines were the idle fabrications of diners-out and
professional funny dogs, who often took the remedies in

full faith which they openly affected to despise. So have I known many noisy sceptics with a strong and secret superstitious belief in the coarsest and vulgarest of miracles.

Having described what the pill, the ointment, and the lotion were not, I can soon state, in a very few words what they really were. They were incapable of hurting a child. The flour which composed the pill, and the lard which composed the ointment, were the finest and purest that could be purchased in the market, while the lotion was nothing more than weak tobacco-tea, as any one ought to have discovered in a moment with the least sense of smell. A little jalap was sometimes mixed in the pills, to act as an aperient upon those whose faith required quickening.

These were slender materials, it would seem, with which to build up a fortune, and they would not have gone far without other things to help them. The first step of importance was to invent a taking title, and here I found, by experience, that I had been peculiarly happy. I sank all personal considerations, all the pleasure of being decorated with foreign orders and foreign diplomas (both of which are to be purchased in the market), all the delight of advertising my own name, and being known as the benefactor of my species. I stood, like Junius, the shadow of a shade, and gave up everything for the remote and venerable Druids. It was not De Jones's marvellous discoveries that were healing the awfullest of sore legs, purifying the most obstinately stagnant blood, and renovating the most shattered constitution. It was the pill that had been handed down from the dim old mystic days, when Stonehenge was a busy temple, and not a deserted wilderness; it was the ointment that had followed the pill, at a decent distance, and the lotion that had followed the ointment.

The next step was to impress these titles deeply in the public mind, a laborious and a costly proceeding that absorbed a considerable amount of capital. This capital was supplied by a gentleman—a kind of half banker—who had moral scruples about entering into a partnership to establish such a thing as a popular pill; but who advanced the cash as a loan transaction at a highly remunerative rate of interest. I know many fountains of capital, like this nameless gentleman, whose streams of hard money flow into many alleys and by-places, to the existence of which they profess to be utterly blind. In sowing this large sum of golden sovereigns broadcast, it required a firm faith in the credulity of the public to feel that it would ever take root, and yield back both principal and interest. It may not be good or wise to trust princes, but, in such a case, it is good and safe to trust the public. By repeating the same assertion, boldly and unflinchingly, day by day, year by year, you will find your followers and believers gradually increased. There is hardly a ragged crossing-sweeper in the London streets—the Salt Lakes of Utah are my witnesses—who might not declare himself the resurrection and the life, if not moved on by the police, and be secure of many adherents, who could follow him to the death. As to imagination, that quality declared to be so rare by the critics, and supposed to be entirely engrossed by a few favoured professional writers, there are thousands of people in the commonplace world who are drunk and mad with it; mountains of it that have never been ascended, or taken note of; mines of it as deep as chaos, that have never been explored. Spiritualism shows us something of it. Great Easterns are built by it to be the laughing-stocks of the practical few; Suez canals are carried out under its influence, and Spring-heeled Jacks are considered by those who sit under

its spirit to foreshadow the end of the world. A scarcity
of imagination, forsooth! Where? There may be a scarcity of the logical faculty, a failure in the crop of common
sense, but in Bedlam or out of Bedlam, in a Rotherhithe
hide-warehouse, or the Rainbow Library of the National
Museum, imagination is as plentiful as chick-weed or table-
ale. Knowing these facts and seeing these manifestations,
need any man, not a fool or a coward, hesitate for a moment
to cast his whole life, fate, and fortune upon the waters of
popular credulity, of popular imaginative faith?

In throwing out my bait to catch the sufferings of
humanity, I was careful only to angle for those that had
an extremely impalpable and fanciful existence. Neither
of my boasted and well advertised panaceas professed to
cure much that could be seen, could be weighed, could be
measured, or could be grasped. I confined myself to such
ailments as tingling of the ears, shooting of corns,
twitching of the nose, tickling of the throat, fear of suffo-
cation, flushing, blushing, hesitation, want of punctuality,
and loss of energy; spasms, unstrung nerves, heaviness,
sympathetic pains, lowness of spirits, want of ability to
play the piano, to compose a poem; want of money to
meet a bill; palpitation, shortness of breath; intellect
declining from intense study (of course from nothing else),
general derangement of the organic network, chagrin from
having walked out in an ill-fitting coat, or from having
missed an agreeable appointment; hydrophobia, flatulency,
singing in the ears, cramp in the foot, general functional
and secretory affections; horror of a postman's knock, the
hurdy-gurdy, the national debt, the bag-pipe or *corna
musa*; want of galvanism in the gastric organs; sacerdo-
phobia, languor, irritability, tendency to smash crockery
and abuse books, excitement, fear, distaste for society, want

of ventilation, ignorance and impatience of taxation, envy, hatred, malice, and all tanning, redness, and dryness of the system. These were the afflictions of the human frame which I laid myself out to attack with the "Druid's Ointment," the "Druid's Lotion," and, above all, the "Druid's Pill." I was once nearly extending my crusade against the enemies of the hair, the whiskers, and the teeth, but I wisely abandoned this project upon maturer reflection. The list of ailments I have given above presented a field quite wide enough to be cultivated with prudence, and afforded hopeful prospects of full employment. For one man who is really seized with a serious complaint, a hundred suffer from "lowness of spirits," "heaviness," or a "want of energy." Though I was bold enough to lay siege to the liver with no weak or trembling hand, I found that my best policy was to cling to the vaguest manifestations of indisposition. The cure of an awful case of sore leg, which I have before alluded to, and which I paraded, perhaps unwisely, in most of my general advertisements, was a reputed triumph of some medicine, name unrecorded, which was authenticated in a letter of thanks nearly a century old, written by the patient himself, the Earl of Plum-colour. This letter was honestly bought by me at the sale of a physician's effects, and as it spoke merely of "medicine" and "those pills," I had no hesitation in using it. The date was sometimes altered or modernized by the stupid printers, but that was not my fault. My panaceas professed to be strictly historical, and I felt that I had a perfect right to such an historical testimonial.

It was a difficult task this creation of testimonials, and one which had to be performed at the very outset. It divided itself into two sections; the collection of the real and local testimonials, and the composition of the sham ones. The latter was a labour requiring some literary skill, and I may be pardoned for feeling a little pride, when I say that I undertook it myself. The following are a few specimens, which I have selected with care, for the purpose of showing how works of fiction are largely used by your successful pill-sellers :—

FROM THE REV. JOHN JAMES, M.A.

" *Thorley Vicarage, Thorley-in-the-Hollow, near Fogmoor, Dec.* 3, 1846.

" SIR,—I should always feel that I had neglected a paramount duty, did I not hasten at once to acknowledge the benefits I have derived from your invaluable medicines. Before they were (providentially) introduced to my notice, I was a miserable man, incapable of any continuous work, either of a secular or a clerical nature. Whenever I began to eat, I felt a dryness in the throat, accompanied by shooting pains in the wrists, and a determination of blood to the head. Whenever I attempted to compose a discourse, I felt a melancholy slowness of ideas, and a sense of oppression at the chest. I am fourteen miles from a regular medical practitioner, and had not the very Rev. the Bishop of Galloway spoken to me of your remedies, I know not what would have been the result. After seven-and-twenty boxes of your excellent pills, I am (providentially) another man ; and I look upon my flow of spirits and sense of self-reliance as something truly marvellous. I shall be in town (*D.V.*) in the spring, and will endeavour to call and thank you personally. In the meantime you have perfect liberty to use this letter in any way you may think fit.

"JOHN JAMES, M.A."

" *P.S.*—Send me, by return, twelve more boxes of the

pills, and a quart of the lotion.   By rail and coach to Fogmoor, thence by carrier."

REMARKABLE CASE.

"SIR,—Left an orphan at an early age, I committed
the unspeakable folly of drinking freely at a street pump
when I was hot.   Well, sir, time rolled on.   An arctic
chilliness in winter pervaded all my limbs.   The sports of
childhood had no longer any attractions for me; the lessons
of learning and tuition filled me with loathing and disgust.
My appetite was ravenous; but what of that?   Half my
food seemed to go the wrong way.   I was troubled with
strange visions in the night, so much so that I dreaded the
approach of the hour at which, by my school regulations,
I was compelled to retire to my couch.   I pricked a blue-
ink picture of an anchor and a lamp-post into my left arm,
but they did not seem to afford me any relief.   The crisis
was approaching.   One day a turncock produced a little
hillock of water from a plug in the street, for purposes
best known to himself.   I danced round it like a red
Indian round a stake.   That night I was taken ill.   I
heard that it was hydrophobia!   .   .   .

"I draw a veil over my sufferings.   They told me I was
cured by your invaluable lotion and your more invaluable
pill, and I believe them.   For obvious reasons, sir, I conceal my name, but I shall be happy to answer privately
any questions.

"ED—GR P—O."

AN UNSOPHISTICATED TESTIMONIAL.

" The Original Rag and Bottle Warehouse,
Old Brewery Lane, Whitechapel,
March 14, 1847.

"Respected Sir,*—Now I'm on my legs again, and all
along of you, I hope that no offence will be taken if I do
the thing that's right. I might have been cold meat, if it
hadn't been for your pills; and all I can say is, here's to
you and the Druids in any kind of sociable drink. I don't
know who the last gentlemen may be, but they've done
me a power of good. If it hadn't been for them, I might
have gone on giving the fullest price for all kinds of
kitchen stuff, until I was brought to the workhouse and
the grave. But no says your pills, and cures me of
delirium tremens before I could smash a wine-bottle.
We've also cured our baby with the ointment; and we're
going to have a few friends to-night, to drown it in the
bowl. You may fancy I'm looking towards you, about
half after nine.—Your grateful servant,

"Joseph Ricketts."

FROM A HAPPY FAMILY.

" Warren Lodge, Upper Breedham, Suffolk,
May, 21, 1848.

"Gentlemen,—I have now taken your invaluable
medicine for nearly fifty years, and I fearlessly pronounce
it to be the best blood purifier and life regenerator ever
produced. My wife has taken it for about the same period,

---

* The style of this letter has been retained, but the spelling has
been altered and improved.

and she joins me in this testimony. My children (I possess nineteen) have taken it with the most beneficial effects, from as early an age as four days old, and they also join me in this testimony. My servants take it of their own free will, and I have been the happy means of introducing it very largely to my tenants. It is no uncommon thing to see our family-circle watching as anxiously for our monthly parcel of pills and ointment, as if it contained the choicest sweetmeats. I have no hesitation in saying that no household can be worthy of the name of an English home unless its chief members always keep it supplied with your invaluable remedies. I should not feel happy, I could not resign myself to rest at night, unless your old familiar boxes and bottles were standing on my dressing-table. Oh, sir, words are too feeble to express all that we owe to you! May you never be reduced to the necessity of taking your own medicines, is the sincere wish and prayer of

" GEORGE WARREN."

(*Here follow the signatures of Mrs. Warren and the nineteen children.*)

A BUSINESS TESTIMONIAL.

" 14, *Bolt Court, Mincemeat Lane,*
Sept. 26, 1849.

" SIR,—Your pills of 21st inst. are to hand, and in reply beg to state have given much satisfaction.—Yours respy.,

" WILLIAM SHARP."

AN OFFICIAL TESTIMONIAL.

(*Translation.*)

" *Junglbagdoor, Nov.* 13, 1849.

" SIR,—I am directed by His Highness Jamjelly Hobbardehoy, to state that he has derived much benefit from

your excellent medicine. Neither the pills, the ointment,
or the lotion were in the least degree damaged by the
violent change of climate.

"COOLEY CAWABS,
"*Private Secretary to His Highness.*"

A BLUFF BUT HONEST TESTIMONIAL.

"SIR,—If any man had told me twelve months ago
that I should one day be writing a testimonial for a patent
medicine, he would have found himself lying on his back
before he knew where he was. I don't like writing, much
less writing about physic; but you have a claim upon me,
and no man who has a claim upon Joe Rumble shall ever
say it wasn't paid.

"I was off my feed; there's no mistake about that.
Fresh air isn't everything. A man who's off his feed had
better make room for somebody else. To make a long
story short, you put me on my feed again; and here's
your letter to do what you like with.

"JOE RUMBLE.
"*Sayers Mills, near Four Oaks, Kent.*"

A DELICATE TESTIMONIAL.

"SIR,—You will pardon the liberty I take as a lady
and a stranger in addressing to you a few lines; but in
so doing I am only fulfilling the last wish of a beloved
friend, who, alas! has now gone to that 'bourne from
whence no traveller returns.' If you could have seen her
emaciated frame before she was induced to try your mira-
culous medicines, even you, sir, would have despaired of
producing any relief. We are fearfully, we are wonderfully
made! She took them, and what was the result? A

gradual restoration to those greatest of all blessings, health,
and (comparative) strength. She left them off, alas! by the
advice of her prejudiced physician, whom I will not name,
and what was the result? My poor friend sank slowly,
step by step, until the lamp of life—if I may be allowed
the expression—flickered in the socket, and finally—alas!
too finally—expired. It was a curious and affecting wish,
but she desired to be buried with the last neglected bottle
of your ointment [*sic* in MS.] by her side, and I need hardly
say that that wish was fully gratified. I have now performed my melancholy task; and I hasten to lay down the
pen. Though I have lost a friend, I have gained a knowledge of an invaluable medicine, which cannot prove otherwise than useful to me, wherever my lot may be cast.

" Lucy Croaker."

" *Hartful Lodge, St. John's Wood.*"

REMARKABLE CASE OF LONGEVITY.

(From the Cowshead Guardian.)

" August 4, 1853.

" Biddy Crumble, familiarly known as 'Biddy Hare-
lip,' the oldest woman in Sowash, and, in fact, in all Essex,
expired on Thursday last at the very remarkable and
advanced age of one hundred and twenty-four. She remembered distinctly the incorporation of the Glaziers'
Company, the foundation of the Marischal College, the
invention of Napier's Bones; and she has often heard her
grandfather speak of the great consternation which was
felt throughout the country when it was rumoured that
Julius Cæsar had landed in the character of an invader.
She preserved her good humour and faculties to the last, a
fact which may be attributed to her constant habit of taking

the celebrated 'Druids' Pills,'—a box of which was her
faithful companion night and day."

The other portion of my testimonial business, the collection of real and local letters of thanks, was intimately
connected with the appointment of agents. In organizing
this part of the system, I was compelled, in some degree,
to run on the lines laid down by my predecessors. The
rule, when engaging an agent (generally a chemist), was to
stipulate that he should find a certain number of real and
fabricated testimonials every year, and should answer all
letters of inquiry, if necessary, respecting those testimonials.
A sharp and clever agent would often obtain letters from
very respectable people, by persuading them that the medicines had really done them considerable good. When very
respectable people were scarce for this purpose, the same
active and intelligent agent was not to be foiled. A
credulous or impressionable old housekeeper or cook at a
neighbouring mansion would often develop, by proper
treatment, into a highly imposing referee. The first thing
to do was to give or sell this old woman a box of the
famous pills; the next, to convince her that they had
saved her from the grave; and the next, to get her to sign
a letter, written by the agent, stating very earnestly that
such was her firm belief. The general readers of this letter,
when it is published to the world as a favourable testimonial, never doubt but what " Mrs. Scullery, of Portico
Hall," is the distinguished mistress of the mansion. Any
letters that may arise from scribbling and inquiring sceptics
are, of course, taken in, carried by Mrs. Scullery in fear
and bewilderment to the active and intelligent agent, and
answered by that invaluable man in the most prompt
and satisfactory manner. What has been done for pills,

lotions, and ointments in this way can hardly be calculated.

Sometimes the most rapturous letters of gratitude poured in spontaneously upon my different agents, especially after my vigorous advertising had caused the panaceas to strike root in the public mind. On one occasion, an agent himself was positively bitten with a belief in these medicines, and was moved to preach of their virtues like an inspired prophet, the only difficulty being to keep his enthusiasm within reasonable bounds. As I before observed, there is no lack of imagination in the commonplace world.

Of my advertising system, it is hardly necessary for me to speak at great length. Everybody knows how the art of attaining publicity has developed within the last twenty years, though few persons will venture to predict the height it may attain in ten, fifteen, or twenty years to come. Some of our public buildings—not all—still sullenly refuse the tempting advances of the trading throng, but if they are cursed with the dangerous gifts of eligibility and position, it is almost certain that one day they must yield and fall. We shall rise up some morning in the clear summer air, and find that the bill-sticker's defiling hand has been busy upon the sacred, gloomy dome of Saint Paul's.

Of course, I employed people to speak carelessly but favourably of my panaceas in the bosom of society; engaged house-walls; occupied railway carriages and other public vehicles; hastened to secure favourable advertising positions in magazines and newspapers; and did all that every energetic advertiser is still doing, or has done before. I called art to my aid, and had an oil-painting, with countless engravings of the venerable Druid, Alceazar, the traditional discoverer of the medicines supposed to have descended to me. I beckoned to literature, and she obeyed my summons, by producing part of an historical novellette, whose chief design was to push the sale of the lotion, the ointment, and the pill. The author went on very well for about a dozen chapters, all introductory, and all discursive; but when he came to the interesting point, where Alceazar, the Druid, was represented gathering herbs on the exact spot where Salisbury Cathedral now stands, he unaccountably broke down. I know I could have done it better myself, if my business labours had only spared me the time. There were huge lumps of Ossian stuck in it, as large as a child's head.

The advertisements that were drawn up by my own hand were always turned, so I flatter myself, with some point and skill. A few short specimens may not be uninteresting :—

" THE PLEASURES OF THE TABLE.—Why should any man be debarred from partaking freely of those dishes which wealth or hospitality has placed before him ? How many thousands—nay, millions—live in a Tantalus-state of existence, seeing a tempting panorama of food passing before them which they dare not touch, or touch only to suffer from giddiness, flushings, and pains in the back ? All this is remedied by the 'Druids' Pill,' the 'Druids' Ointment,' and the 'Druids' Lotion.' Sold in boxes at 4s. 6d., 10s. 9d., and one guinea; and bottles at 18s., 35s., and 52s. N.B.—A considerable saving is effected by taking the larger quantities."

" THE WHITLOW SEASON.—Beware of this stealthy and dangerous complaint, which comes upon you like an avalanche. No one is free from it, the infant in the cradle,

the strong man on the mountain top, especially during the
Asiatic months. The only safeguards are the 'Druids'
Pills,' the 'Druids' Ointment,' and the 'Druids' Lotion.'
Sold in boxes at 4*s.* 6*d.*, 10*s.* 9*d.*, and one guinea; and bot-
tles at 18*s.*, 35*s.*, and 52*s.* N.B.—A considerable saving is
effected by taking the larger quantities."

"SOCIETY, HOPE.—No victims of unstrung nerves, heaviness, or tingling of the ears; no melancholy martyrs to tickling in the throat, hesitation, or languor, need any longer be
self-banished outcasts from that SOCIETY they are so eminently
fitted to adorn. There is HOPE and a certain remedy in
the 'Druids' Pill,' the 'Druids' Ointment,' and the
'Druids' Lotion.' Sold in boxes at 4*s.* 6*d.*, 10*s.* 9*d.*, and
one guinea; and bottles at 18*s.*, 35*s.*, and 52*s.* N.B.—A
considerable saving is effected by taking the larger
quantities."

It must not be supposed from all this that my
business-life was one of roses. I had my difficulties to
contend with. Some of my agents and testimonial-
makers took advantage of me, or tried to do so, as witness the following letter from one of my chief provincial
stations:—

"*Leepool, Dec.* 28, 1853.

"DEAR SIR,—As the end of the year approaches, I feel
it impossible to go on any longer at my present salary. I
have borne every disease you put upon me, and the consequence is, I am now being shown up in the 'Daily Cheru-
bim,' one of our local papers. I copy an epigram which
appeared last Saturday in the 'Poet's Corner.' (We ought
to have advertised in that paper):—

'Epigram

On Mr. J——s R—b—y,

Agent for the 'Druids' Pill,' etc.

'Affliction sore long time he bore,
And suffered not in vain,
Till Puffaway reduced his pay,
Which eased him of his pain.'

Besides this, the letters inquiring about the 'testimonials' are so numerous, that I shall have to get a boy to answer them; and, taking all things into consideration, I don't see my way clear under a hundred a year *for life*.

"James Ruby."

I did not comply with the demands of this letter, and many like it, by return of post, and it was fortunate that I acted as I did. The pill, the ointment, and the lotion received a shock, a few days afterwards, from which they never wholly recovered. The popular imagination and credulity that had helped me to my success were equally ready to turn against me. I am not surprised at this. When mobs are logical the millennium may be considered as ushered in.

It was shortly after Christmas that an old gentleman was found dead in an easy-chair. He was a short, stout man, a free-living man,—a man who abhorred exercise, and loved sleep. He had evidently been a good customer or patient of mine, for he was literally surrounded by the united panaceas, and the Druids' pill-box was lying open on a table near his hand. Reason pointed to apoplexy, but popular feeling connected his death in some way with the united panaceas. A thorough investigation failed to remove this besotted impression, and my medicinal property was enormously injured. I never attempt to argue with an excited crowd. Upon counting up my gains, I found I had done very well; and I therefore disposed of the injured copyright in the united panaceas to the first daring speculator who offered me a reasonable price.

SAWDUST PILLS.

local newspaper, which I am rather fond of :
n see the following tempting advertisement :—

            " SAWDUST GRATIS.

1000 sacks to be given away : apply at tl
——."

ost persons of an inventive turn of mind, w
ly read this announcement, would naturally t
s to discover what use they could make of s
is such a charm in getting a thousand sacks
not absolutely offensive, for nothing, that ma
ave doubtless obtained a quantity of this s
an idea that, like all bargains, it will come in
ne period. To these people I venture to throv
ble suggestion. As dolls are often stuffed w
mical material, why should not the human
with it? There are two ways of doing this—
physic; but as the human doll is ten times
s about the first as he is about the second, I
m him with this sawdust in the shape of pills.
e first thing required in this sawdust pill w
name, and that can be obtained from any
man who is clever in inventing titles. Th
will be the command of capital—from ten to
nd pounds; and courage to scatter it broac

advertizing this title. Put your trust in the credulity of
the great Anglo-Saxon race, and it will never deceive you.
No man amongst those leviathan quacks, who spend their
thirty thousand pounds per annum in advertisements, ever
had cause to complain of the intelligence of the public.
They planted the titles of their nostrums years ago in the
popular mind, and their businesses now go on like an
excellent clock, which only requires an occasional
inspection.

In mixing your sawdust pills, you will require one
ingredient that can make its presence felt to the believing
nostrum taker, and gamboge is the cheapest and most effective substance for your purpose. "Testimonials" will be
required to back up your advertisements, and these you
will have to procure from some "literary gentleman."
Real testimonials will flow in freely enough after a time;
and no wonder, in an age when respectable people rush
forward to testify that they have shaken hands with Homer
under a dining-room table. Still, you must not rely too
much upon these certificates, and as your business cannot
be conducted without the aid of literary talent, you will do
well to engage such talent from the moment of starting.
Your advertisements will have to be altered so as to hit
the prevailing feeling of the hour; and the following may
be regarded as a model in this respect :—

"WET WEATHER.

" The last spring and summer were almost unexampled
for the fall of rain, which has caused the rate of mortality
to be unusually high; and it is now, unfortunately, rendered higher by the dearness of provisions. From such
depressing influences diseases must arise, but, fortunately
for the humbler classes, Professor Puffaway has discovered

the means of averting or curing most disorders, especially
such as occur from poor or depraved blood. By Puffaway's
remedies that fluid is perfectly purified from all contamina-
tions caused by irregular living, unwholesome diet, foul
air, or insalubrious vapours. His medicine, and no other,
will regulate the digestive organs, and vivify generally every
corporeal, solid, and fluid."

In specifying what diseases you profess to cure with the
sawdust pill, be careful not to use any terms but what are
vague and general. Cling to nervous, imaginary, and digestive disorders, but never break into the province of the surgeon, or you may expose the weakness of your nostrum. Head
your advertisements—" To the Nervous and Debilitated"—
" A Boon to Nervous Sufferers"—" Bile! Bile! Bile!" or
" Bile, Wind, and Indigestion"—" The Sinking may be
Saved"—" Health and Happiness"—or, " By Her Majesty's
Royal Letters Patent." Get these " letters patent," and
the Government stamp—they cost very little—and they
will give an air of authority to the sawdust and gamboge,
which will be of infinite value. Whenever an epidemic or
prevailing disease appears—such as the Asiatic cholera,
for example—leap upon its back with your sawdust pill
without the slightest hesitation. Such diseases never last
for any length of time, and when they are gone you can
take credit in your advertisements for having expelled
them. You may sometimes find it of advantage to start
an opposition against yourself, or to come to some under-
standing about mutual abuse with an opponent already
existing. Old Dr. Gravesend is now engaged in a profitable fight with young Dr. Gravesend respecting the celebrated sauce of prunella; and it is marvellous that the
enterprising Doo Babby has never tried this expedient in
puffing the delicious prevalenta. If your sawdust pill is

.L.8.

ant will stand
vo shillings,——

			£
-	-	-	0
-	-	-	0
			0
-	-	-	0
-	-	-	0
			0
-	-	-	0
			0

itates about bl
t pill——of cour
im get some
pular pills of th
most notoriou
eral names of a
s——the prolific
sis of them al
xtract of colocy
l of linseed, oil
ves. They are,
sition with the
ed at the public
druggist in the
tibilious pills,
re highly silver
l in boxes at on
consist of sca
one pennywor

cochie, as it is termed, would make about two boxes. This may be considered a highly profitable nostrum, and I congratulate the oriental proprietor upon his valuable property.

Another set of pills consists of extract of colocynth, extract of aloes, Castile soap, and a little oil of cloves, and another set, called antibilious, is made chiefly of aloes, scammony, jalap, and gamboge, with a very small quantity of camomile. Another set that is labelled restorative, consists of about equal parts of gamboge and aloes; and the most popular set of them all, warranted to cure every disease, is composed of aloes, a vegetable matter like scammony or jalap, and soap.

Another set of the professedly antibilious division of pills is made up of aloes, scammony, gamboge, jalap, calomel, soap, and syrup of buckthorn. A very popular bilious and liver pill is made of aloes and colocynth; and certain well-advertised vegetable pills, credited with the most marvellous qualities, consist of aloes and cream of tartar; or gamboge, aloes, colocynth, cream of tartar, and a vegetable matter like horehound. The pills which are reputed to keep off death until the patient reaches twice the allotted age of man, are made of nothing more remarkable than aloes and a vegetable extract like colocynth. This simple compound has yielded one or two fortunes and a parliamentary membership, and is still a much more productive property than all the cardinal virtues put together.

The basis of all these pills, and many others, appears to be a common and cheap substance which is usually called bitter aloes; and upon this is built up a mixture of soap, scammony, jalap, colocynth, and frequently gamboge. Of all these substances, the last is by far the most dangerous, in fact, it is ranked amongst the acrid or hot poisons. In the United States (still amongst the great credulous

Anglo-Saxon race), where nostrums abound, perhaps, more
than in this country, it has been proved that calomel is at
the bottom of nearly all the cheap aperient pills. The
reason that gamboge has been selected by the quacks in
England as a principal ingredient of their antibilious pills,
is because of its great activity as an aperient. Nine people
out of ten believe in a nostrum all the more firmly the more
it prostrates them, and a strong mixture is accordingly
provided.

There is another class of pills which may be alluded to
—the stomachic, dinner, digestive, and tonic pills. They
are composed of aloes, ginger, rhubarb, ipecacuanha, and a
volatile oil, such as cloves or peppermint.

One tonic set consists merely of rhubarb and ginger ;
and another highly popular pill, which is supposed to be a
sweetener of the human system, is made of aloes, extract of
camomile, and a little oil of camomile. Another set is
composed of black hellebore, liquorice, turmeric, opium,
Castile soap, syrup of saffron, and oil of turpentine ; and
another, which, from its title, appears to have been invented
by the nobility and gentry, is made of aloes, mastic, red rose
leaves, and syrup of wormwood.

A third, and the most disgusting class of quack pills, is
the renal and gravel pills, which consist of soap and car-
bonate of soda. Two of the most notorious of these owe
what little activity they possess to the alkali of their two
ingredients. Another pill, put forward as a cure for hemor-
rhoids, consists chiefly of pitch.

Certain pills have been advertised very extensively of
late in the form of an appeal to nervous sufferers, from a
" retired clergyman," who undertakes to send the recipe
on the receipt of a single postage stamp. The prescription
generally sent upon application runs thus :—

"Alcoholic extract of ignitia amara, thirty grains; powdered gum Arabic, ten grains; make into forty pills."

This recipe is usually accompanied with a sincere and earnest hope that, under Divine Providence, it may be found to produce the desired effect. It commonly happens that no one can make up the prescription but the dispenser to the "retired clergyman," and another application has to be made, accompanied with two-and-sixpence in postage stamps, to obtain a supply of the pills. These pills have been examined, and found to contain no particle of the active principle of the ignatia amara, but their real ingredients were eight grains of gum, eleven grains of starch, and one grain of a greenish matter wholly inert. It is fortunate, perhaps, that the "retired clergyman" is cautious enough to send such a preparation, for if the pills containing the real ignatia amara were taken with any degree of indiscretion, it is very probable that death would be the result.

The stomachs of "nervous sufferers" and afflicted people need be strong, for train oil is often a principal ingredient in the common soap so largely used in mixing these quack nostrums. The speculator in the sawdust pills need not fear to venture, after wading through such a nauseous list as I have just given. His compound will at least have the merit of simplicity. The sawdust, which is to form the basis, can be invested with all the real and imaginary qualities of peruvian bark, and the gamboge by its activity will, as usual, prove the truth of this or any other assertion. If my sawdust pill project be not immediately seized, I shall begin to think that no enterprise is left in the country.

RASCALS.

THE biography of a rascal, if truthfully and briefly written, would probably show the same changes in families which we see in respectable society. A father and mother, living on the borders of what have been very affectedly called "guilt gardens," carry on the occupation of "duffers." The father is a tailor; the mother hunts about the drapers' shops for pieces of cheap cloth; the father makes up these pieces into showy garments; the mother pawns them at various pawnbrokers for the highest loans she can obtain for them—generally a little more than their full value. The pawn-tickets are sold separately or in bundles, most probably to play a part in another form of swindling.

If any moralist or teacher were to call these people to account for their occupation, they would consider themselves insulted. They regard themselves as traders making the most of a little capital. They think they are far better than some of their neighbours, and as good as most of them. The frauds of adulterating tradesmen, users of light weights, and sellers under false pretences in more exalted spheres of trade, unfortunately, seem to warrant their deceptive dealings.

What, by a stretch or tolerance, may be considered as being only sharp trading on the part of this father and mother, becomes, by a law of progression or divergence, rank swindling on the part of the son.

The son, made useful from necessity from time to time in pawning the clothes manufactured by his father, becomes familiar with deception. The different uses that may be made of pawn-tickets unfold gradually before him, and if his parents seek to keep this knowledge from him, with the usual keenness of childhood he arrives at it in spite of them. When he starts in the world to get his own living, he probably fancies he sees a way to profits far larger than his father's. Gathering tickets from other "duffers"— from pawners of duffing watches, duffing jewellery, and duffing cabinet-work; getting also a few made-up tickets from unscrupulous pawnbrokers who wish to sell their unsaleable stock at a good profit, he makes his bow to the public as a "struggling tradesman." The struggling tradesman has always pressing need of ten or twenty pounds to meet a bill, to extend his business, or to purchase a beneficial lease; he is always willing to give a five or ten pound bonus if accommodated with this money for a fortnight or three weeks, and to deposit property with the lender worth four times as much as the required loan. He offers one or two thousand per cent. per annum with excessive security, and advertises almost daily in various forms for tenders. That his advertisements succeed we are bound to believe, because of their regular appearance; and they generally take one or other of the following forms :—

"CASH £50.—£20 given for the IMMEDIATE LOAN of £50 for one week only. Security worth £200 (real, and convertible at a moment's notice) deposited.—Address, Alpha, Post-Office, Ludgate Hill."

"MONEY—£25.—A small manufacturer of ten years'

standing REQUIRES this SUM till the 30th instant. To insure
the punctual return, will deposit real security to treble the
amount, and pay £7 for the accommodation. Address X.,
Money Order Office, Blackfriars Road, S."

"A BONUS of £8 will be given for the use of £20 for
seven days. Security to the value of £100 will be deposited. Address Bonus, Manchester Street, King's
Cross."

This form of swindle has now been more or less practised for twenty years; and the somewhat greedy victims
who lend their money on bundles of pawn-tickets or sham
jewellery, tempted by the extravagantly high rate of
interest promised, can hardly be astonished when they
find that the security is almost worthless. When they
redeem the pledges, they ought not to feel surprised that
they have been throwing good money after bad, and are
left in possession of property made for pawning and
nothing else.

There are many schemes which the full-blown swindler
tries besides this money-borrowing business, and none
probably pay him as well as the sham " Loan Societies."
By starting on the assumption that one-half of the world
are fools, and that a large proportion of that half are
generally in want of money, he is able to extract the
largest amount of plunder with the least possible amount
of risk. Without the courage of the burglar or the
physical strength of the garotter, he arrives at far more
profitable results by merely dodging behind a screen.
Under cover of the " Good Samaritan Loan and Discount
Association," or some title likely to inspire equal hope
and confidence, he attracts unwary dupes from every
corner of the country. With a little capital, no scruples,
and a large share of low cunning, he has founded a

business which nothing seems able to destroy. Exposure
may follow upon exposure with little or no effect. Per-
sistent prosecutions may secure one member of the gang,
but another springs up directly to supply his place.
Victims wearied by paying "inquiry fees" which bear no
fruit, may be taught prudence in time, or may learn it
from heavier losses and the warnings of magistrates; but
still a fresh flock is always ready to be fleeced. Just as
the billiard-sharper seldom fails to find a ready listener
who believes him to be a clergyman's son just come into
possession of several thousand pounds, so the sham loan-
office keeper is seldom without believing applicants. A
certain number of weak but respectable people seem to
have formed themselves into a society for the encouragement of scoundrels, and we can therefore hardly wonder
that swindlers increase and thrive. It appears, from a
hundred cases brought forward in the course of the year,
that such swindlers have only to ask and to have. They
merely shake the boughs and the willing fruit drops into
their ready mouths. They enjoy an unwholesome security
because the law is uncertain, because prosecutions are ex-
pensive, and because people who have been swindled often
object to be paraded as dupes.

When the "struggling tradesman" buds into the
"capitalist," and becomes the manager and owner of a
sham "Loan Office," he generally derives his profits from
inquiry fees. He entertains no application for loans without a cash deposit to pay for all the supposed necessary
inquiries as to the respectability of the applicant, etc. As
two or more sureties are always demanded, this gives an
excuse for extracting more fees to pay for inquiries touching the securities, and it is almost needless to say that
these inquiries never prove satisfactory. The applicants

for loans are generally dismissed with letters declining their propositions with thanks, and they may think themselves fortunate if the swindle proceeds no further. Sometimes the capitalist, however, is encouraged to extract much more from his victims by promising the loan on receiving a prepayment of the first year's interest. This is greediness which brings him within the grasp of the law, and is almost sure to lead to the break-up of the office. A gang of "capitalists" of this kind was very recently exposed and convicted, but not before their members had swindled successfully for two or three years. They consisted of a laundress, a bill-sticker, a commission-agent, a quack who had once been imprisoned for eighteen months for swindling under pretence of curing deafness and diseases of the ear, and one or two other members equally disreputable. Their office was only a dilapidated tenement in a low neighbourhood, but they succeeded by reason of the uninquiring faith of their dupes, and their own bold and unsparing use of the best banking and commercial names. They advertised in country papers that post-office orders were to be made payable to Gurney, Lindsay, Twining and Co., and were gladdened by receiving thirty or forty communications a day. One letter, stopped by the police, contained thirty pounds sent up as payment of a year's interest in advance on an expected loan of five hundred pounds, and many other letters were intercepted, which showed how easily people might be defrauded of their money.

The thorough swindler is heartless enough in his management of these sham loan offices, but he thrives upon other swindles which are even more heartless. He preys without remorse or pity upon a peculiarly helpless class—that large, struggling, needy, and believing body

who are always seeking employment. A new occupation,
or a new invention, is often used by him as a new mask,
under cover of which he carries on his frauds. The sewing machines seem to have been the last invention which
the swindler has made use of. He puts an advertisement
in one of the morning papers headed, "Highly advanta-
geous to young ladies in search of employment," in which
he sets forth that the advertiser, who carries on an extensive business, will teach applicants the art of using this
machine, and obtain them profitable work when they
become proficient, for a fee of half-a-guinea. The applicants, mostly needy females, scrape up the necessary fees,
pay them over to the supposed thriving tradesman, attend
at his office, see three or four cheap machines at work for
a few days, at the end of which time the machines and their
swindling owner disappear together. Hundreds of shops
in faded or half-developed neighbourhoods seem to exist
only as empty traps, to be occasionally baited by swindlers
of this description.

The most common swindling appeal to the pressing
wants and scanty purses of females seeking employment,
comes in the shape of a " Registry Office "—a parlour fitted
up as a general business agency web in which to catch the
poor flies who are seeking for situations. These offices are
found more or less thriving in every quarter of the town,
but particularly in neighbourhoods where the population is
dense and has to fight for its living. The proprietors of
an agency office of this kind generally fix themselves on
some terrace of fading respectability, where they herald
the approach of that decay which gives up mansions to
small brokers and cheap photographers. They put a black
board outside the house where the delusive registry is to
be established, and on this they paint the words, "Adver-

tising, Registry, and General Business Agency Offices."
This board, with a table, a couple of chairs, and a desk,
placed in the front parlour or reception room, constitutes
all the "plant" of the office.

The first thing which the keeper of this place does is to
buy regularly two or three of the newspapers most noted
for their miscellaneous advertisements, and to copy on slips
of paper all those announcements which relate to vacant
situations. The names of the persons advertising are carefully omitted from these copies, the object being to attract
applications to the "office" and to extract fees. These
slips of paper are pasted on the black-board, in a column
headed "Vacant," and are made to appear as if they were
original applications for servants sent to that particular
"Registry."

When applied to by a person willing to accept one of
these situations, the keeper of the office charges a fee which
varies from sixpence to half-a-crown, according to the look
of the applicant. In exchange for this payment, the
address of the employer is given, and that is all—a piece
of information which might have been learned from the
newspapers. If the fee has been made large enough to
entitle the applicant to the first suitable situation which
may come to the knowledge of the office-keeper, a few
stamps for postage are demanded to cover letters to employers. These letters are often written, because they
help to advertise the office, and often lead to a few genuine
applications from employers for servants, which mix well
with the borrowed advertisements. Advertisements con-
cerning "businesses to be disposed of," "apartments,
warehouses, and shops to let," "articles lost or found,"
and "servants wanting situations," are also freely borrowed
or stolen. In some of these offices an extra fee is charged,

which binds the office-keeper to pay for the insertion of one special advertisement in a leading London newspaper, if he fails in obtaining a situation for the applicant within a week. He keeps to his contract by inserting the advertisement, but, by making it sufficiently general, and having the answers addressed to the office under initials, he makes it satisfy a dozen applicants to whom he may be bound in the same way. The whole system is based upon fraud and deception. It is as heartless and cruel as that other system by which applications are encouraged for posts long filled, though formally advertised as open, that a few joint-stock directors may keep up appearances, and seem not to have favoured their friends. By both systems the time and money of the poor are recklessly wasted, and false hopes are held out to those who are already sick with hope deferred.

THE POOR MAN'S MONEY-LENDER.

THE pawnbroker is necessarily the poor man's money-lender, regard him as we may, and, if he charged a fair and moderate rate of interest, he might often be of great service to his customer. Where, as in many instances, his business is conducted according to the provisions of the Act of Parliament, and proper caution is exercised by him in the reception of property—no one has any right to blame the individual, although the system is open to censure. Where, however, as is too often the case, the pawnbroker exacts far more than the legal rate of interest —where the few provisions of the Acts of Parliament— which are much more in his favour than in that of the depositor—are constantly and systematically evaded, these abuses press very heavily on the poor. It is a notorious fact, that in all the poorer and more degraded neighbourhoods, the pawnshops and marine-store dealers abound most and flourish.

Pawnbroking in England is in private hands, but in France it is in the hands of the State, who derive a revenue from it, which is used for charitable purposes, and protect the poor from the impositions, heavy rates of interest, and sacrifices of property, which they constantly have to endure here. The careful and precise manner in which the managers of the *Mont de Piété* act before they grant a loan, effectually prevents that institution from becoming what the pawnbrokers and marine-store dealers too often are in this country—encouragers of thieves and receivers of stolen goods. The French thief knows his business too well to confide his spoil to the care of the *Mont de Piété.* The French law throws its protecting shield over the property of the subject by rendering the disposal or pledging of stolen goods difficult; whilst in this country it is too often the direct interest of the pawnbroker to shelter crime from detection, as much as possible, in order not to have to give up booty to its rightful owners. Perhaps it is not too much to say that if there were no pawnbrokers, dolly-shop keepers, or marine-store dealers, or, if they were under a more strict and genuine supervision, there would be an immense diminution of theft in England.

The *Mont de Piété* receives no pledges from any pawner who cannot bring distinct proof of his identity. In most cases the managers insist upon seeing the receipt for rent, which often enables them to stop a tenant in furnished lodgings from pawning his landlord's property. Many articles are pledged by agents, who are responsible for all representations made on behalf of their employers. The French laws for preventing the sale of stolen property are very severe. The French dealers in gold, precious stones, and other valuable articles, are bound not to pay for the purchase of such property anywhere but in the houses of the sellers, after making due inquiry of the neighbours and the house-porters.

The pawnbroker in England does not confine his attention only to money-lending. In poor neighbourhoods he keeps a shop where unredeemed property appears to lie for sale, but which is, in fact, a warehouse for delusive bargains. This shop is a store-house for articles of the com-

monest description—Birmingham guns, pistols, tools of
defective metal or finish, jewels of bad quality, imitation
gold, and generally all kinds of manufacturing failures and
deceptions. The pawnbroker, owing to his reputation for
getting things at less than half their value, can always
obtain a better price for such articles than the ordinary
trader. In rich neighbourhoods, the pawnbrokers have
other shops for the sale of spurious antiquities—cracked
china, yellow Carrara statuary, and dusky oil pictures.
Not long ago a man was taken before the magistrates for
stealing a large bronze figure while it was acquiring the
market signs of venerable old age. This figure—a modern
cast of a certain value—had been put down a sewer, that
the foul gases might give it that mouldy "patina" tint so
much sought after by art-collectors; and afterwards it was
exposed on the roof of a house to relieve it from an unpleasant odour. While it was taking the air in this position, it was carried off by the thief, whose examination only
taught art-collectors another of those lessons which they
never seem to profit by.

Many of the large pawnbrokers derive an income from
deposited plate and jewels by lending them to persons for
dinner-parties and balls. An assistant is often sent to
watch the plate in the disguise of a head-waiter, and he
generally lingers in the hall until her ladyship has done
with the jewels. In some cases, the borrowers give full
security for these loans, and then all such precautions are
of course rendered unnecessary.

The substance of those parliamentary regulations under
which pawnbrokers are supposed to conduct their business,
may be stated in a very few words. When the amount
lent on any pledge exceeds forty shillings, and does not
exceed ten pounds, the legal interest is fixed at the rate of

fifteen per cent. per annum. On pledges below forty shillings, twenty per cent. per annum is payable, and these charges include all claims for warehouse-room. When the pledges are redeemed within six days beyond the expiration of a month, only one month's interest can be legally charged; when not more than thirteen days have elapsed, only one half-month's interest in addition to the month's can be demanded, and the second month's full interest can only be claimed when the term has exceeded the first month by fourteen days.

The pawnbroker is bound to keep books giving a description of goods pledged, the name and address of the pawner, and to give a ticket with full particulars, for which he receives a sum varying from one halfpenny to fourpence, according to the sum advanced. The pawnbroker is forbidden to buy or take in pledge unfinished goods, linen, or apparel, and when he breaks this rule he is liable to forfeit double the amount lent, and to restore the goods to the owners. He is allowed to sell unredeemed pledges by public auction at the expiration of twelve months, after advertising in some newspaper his name and address, the number of the pledge, and the month in which it was deposited. As a small check upon this power, the pawners are allowed to give notice to the pawnbrokers in writing not to sell the pledges for three months beyond the twelve.

The pawnbroker is ordered to keep an account in a book of all prices brought at such auctions by the unredeemed pledges, and to return any balance remaining after deducting the interest and expenses of sale. He is bound to allow the pawners to examine this account on payment of one penny. He is not allowed to purchase pledges that are in his custody, nor to take pledges from persons under

twelve years of age or from intoxicated persons. He is
also ordered to exhibit in a public part of his shop a list of
the legal rates of interest, an account of what tickets and
memoranda are to be delivered free of charge, and the
expense of supplying a new ticket for a lost one.

From these provisions of the Act of Parliament, it will be
seen, that the poor man's money-lender obtains fifteen and
twenty per cent. interest, besides the amount paid for
tickets, on loans for which he has a far better security
than that often given for money advanced at five per cent.
The pawnbroker fixes the amount he is willing to lend—
seldom more than one-third of the marketable value of the
pledge tendered; and where the loan exceeds ten pounds
it is advanced on what is called an agreement, written on
stamped paper, which gives the pawnbroker the right of
sale or of keeping the goods for the sum lent, and of
extorting as much interest as his own greed and the necessities of his customer will allow. As loans of this character are not under the control of the Act of Parliament,
the pawnbroker is not compelled to show his books, nor
to give any information in case the goods have been dis-
honestly acquired. He can dispose of them in any way
he may think fit, within the terms of his agreement, and he
may almost snap his fingers at the rightful owners. In
most cases of fraudulent bankruptcy the above is the mode
in which the property of the creditors is often disposed of.
A case occurred some years ago in which a woman who had
started as a jeweller, defrauded several manufacturers and
diamond-merchants by pledging their goods, as soon as
they were obtained, to one of these receivers. Every
difficulty was thrown in the way of the creditors who
wanted to get a sight of the property, only to ascertain whether it was worth redeeming. No pawnbroker

can honestly pretend that he believes there is nothing wrong when a tradesman continually pawns his stock and never redeems it, or when goods are carried almost direct from the warehouse to the pawnshop without the " private marks " of the wholesale dealer even being torn off. There are too many auctioneers and "job-houses," of apparent respectability, who deal largely in these dishonest " bargains," but the pawnbroker encourages such frauds far more than any other tradesman.

The legal rates of interest ranging from fifteen to twenty per cent. (in France the rate is fixed at twelve per cent. per annum, with one-half per cent. for valuation) are not always high enough to satisfy the poor man's money-lender. In far too many cases the pawnbroker will cheat his ignorant and needy customer with an arithmetical juggle. On a pledge of three shillings, for which the legal rate is three farthings a month, and for twelve months sevenpence-farthing, he will often exact ninepence, which he reckons in the following manner:—Interest on 3s., $\frac{3}{4}d.$ per month, multiplied by 12, equal 9d., which sounds correct, but if calculated properly would stand thus:— Interest on 3s. for twelve months at twenty per cent per annum, $7\frac{1}{2}d.$ This nefarious practice, which is called "taking the long interest," although it enormously increases the pawnbroker's profits, may only rob the poor man of a trifle, but trifles are an object to that suffering class who have to supply their pressing wants with the proceeds of three-shilling pledges. Two or three pence may only represent the value of a loaf of bread, but a loaf of bread may often represent a life snatched from the arms of death, and one disgraceful case of starvation less to be recorded by the Great Registrar-General.

There used to be a certain class of informers who kept

the pawnbrokers to some degree in check, and though a
vile and unreliable body, they were not altogether useless.
The pawnbrokers, however, soon bribed these amateur
detectives into silence with annual presents distributed at
Christmas. The plan of these informers was to pledge
articles and to redeem them at·the end of the month and
six days. The pawnbroker, having got into a habit of
cheating, would mechanically charge the illegal two
months' interest, thus putting himself into the hands of
the informer, and being compelled to effect a compromise.
At one period there was nearly a dozen of these informers,
who each had a regular annuity of one or two guineas
from three or four hundred London pawnbrokers, but now
the magistrates have very properly discountenanced this
spy-system, and it can scarcely be said to exist.

Many pawnbrokers, when an article has remained in
pledge a few days beyond the twelvemonth, will take one
penny per month (supposing the sum lent is three shillings),
thus fining their poor and ignorant customers thirteen pence
on the false ground that the article has been forfeited.
When an application of this kind is made for an article, a
more serious imposition is often practised. The article is
privately examined, and if it promises to yield much more
at a sale than the money lent upon it, with interest and
overcharges, the pledger is told that it has been sold. As
the pawnbroker rarely lends more than the third of its
market-value on any pledge, the loss to the pawner by this
imposition is very great. Many pawnbrokers adopt this
plan of dealing when articles have been left only a day
beyond the twelvemonth. Sometimes when the article
pledged is an old family relic, one of those tokens of
affection, the saddest of all pledges, which no money could
replace, it is natural for the poor applicant to express

much anxiety for the loss. This anxiety is too often observed and traded upon by the unscrupulous pawnbroker, who offers to try and re-purchase it from the imaginary buyer. If his offer is accepted, as it generally is with eagerness, he charges two or three times the money lent for his supposed trouble, and fresh pledges are often brought in to make up this payment.

Although the Act of Parliament forbids them to take more than a month's interest, supposing one month and six days to have elapsed since the pledge was deposited, yet in too many instances the full two months' interest is exacted, with extras. The interest-tables fixed in the shops are often placed where they cannot be easily read, and too many of the pawnbrokers' poorer customers are not accustomed to difficult reading.

Many pawnbrokers in poor neighbourhoods each deliver from fifteen hundred to two thousand pledges on a Saturday night—some even deliver them on a Sunday morning —and on these pledges the overcharges of interest reach a very considerable amount in the course of the year. Four to five pounds a week has been pilfered in one house in this way by the master and his assistants, the money being put into a box which was emptied late on Saturday night, and which was honestly called a "Robbery Box." Of course, it is needless to add that the assistants have a certain share of this plunder given them by their employer to encourage them in further sharp dealing.

Another very common and shameful fraud on the poor is the practice of exacting an extra sum for professing to take particular care of any article. If a new Sunday coat or a silk dress is brought to the pawnbroker this extra sum is demanded for putting it in a separate drawer. The money— twopence or threepence a week—is often readily paid for

this supposed advantage, but the coat or dress is rarely
better treated for the payment. All these exactions—
though trifling, if taken separately—amount in the aggregate to a large sum. A man who pledges his coat, a
woman who pledges her dress every Monday, and takes it
out again every Saturday night or Sunday morning—and
pawners of this character may be numbered by thousands
—will pay a frightful rate of interest in the course of the
year, often far more than the amount of the loan. When
money is lent upon furniture, a heavy rate is often charged
for warehousing, contrary to the spirit of the Act of Parliament, and warehousing is often charged for a bed, a
demand that is thoroughly illegal.

The regulation which orders the pawnbroker to take the
name and address of the person pawning, and to give a
ticket specifying all particulars, is constantly evaded. As
a general rule, the pawnbroker merely asks the name of
the pledger, and puts down any address that passes through
his mind. When pressed upon this point, he says that he
generally knows his customers too well to require such a
register. The experiment has been recently tried of sending round a perfect stranger to about twenty of the largest
houses in the trade, and in no instance was the address
asked for, nor any inquiry made. In one case the pawnbroker put down "Fleet Street," without asking a question.
None of these pawnbrokers could have known whether the
goods tendered were stolen or not. The pledger went
unknown and remained unknown; and the articles were
taken in without the slightest questioning. It is true, that
if they had been stolen, the pawnbrokers would have been
compelled to give them up, and so it appears to be against
their interest to take in stolen property; but it must be
remembered that they only disgorge on conviction of the

thief, and have therefore a strong motive to prevent detection as much as possible. Even if one case be discovered, there are probably fifty that go undiscovered, while by the system of agreements, before alluded to, the pawnbroker gets rid of all liability, except that incurred by ordinary purchasers of stolen property.

The numerous instances in which poor needlewomen have been punished for pawning goods entrusted to their care to make up, proves that the rule which forbids the pawnbroker to take in unfinished goods, linen, or apparel is constantly broken. Not long since, a clerk in a wholesale house was detected in robbing his employers of several pieces of silk and velvet, and he confessed that for five years he had been stealing and pledging these goods, and that he had rarely been asked any questions by the pawnbrokers. He invariably produced the goods from under his waistcoat, and he had habitually pledged them at five or six shops, tearing up the tickets. The merchants who had been defrauded wrote to all the pawnbrokers, giving a description of the goods, and offering to pay half the sum advanced, but they only got back a very small portion of their property.

The regulation framed to compel the pawnbroker to sell unredeemed pledges at the end of twelve months, if not requested in writing by the pawner to hold them for three months longer, and to hand over any surplus to the pledger, and to allow an inspection of accounts on the payment of a penny, is a rule that is broken in the most bare-faced manner. By the system of "knock-outs"—much exposed lately—and other means, the pawnbroker often succeeds in defrauding his ignorant and helpless customers. The "knock-out" system is an auction-room combination—a conspiracy doubtless in law—by which a sale by auction is reduced to an empty ceremony. The pawnbroker and his friends agree not to bid one against another, while one is instructed to buy for the rest. After a few bids for the sake of appearances, the lot is knocked down to this bidder at a nominal price, unless there is much unusual competition in the room, and the second or real auction takes place later in the day at a tavern, where the pawnbroker and his disbanded confederates really bid against each other over the dinner-table. The difference between the price realized here, and the price which the article fetched at the auction-room goes into a general fund, to be divided amongst the conspirators. Of course, the first, or auction-room price, is the one which is registered for the inspection of the pawner, should such inspection ever be demanded. If this price seems too high, it is immediately lowered, and entered in a duplicate book, which is kept entirely to show to inquirers. The auctioneers invariably refuse to give any information, and such frauds are therefore perpetrated with impunity. The poor pawner is robbed still further by being charged with a fancy commission on the sale, supposing he should ever come forward to claim his withered surplus. The pawnbroker pays five per cent. to the auctioneer for selling the goods, or rather for allowing his room to be used for a " knock-out" combination, but the poor pawner is charged fifteen per cent. on the price realized at the auction-mart.

The numbers of children of tender years, and of staggering drunkards, who may be seen at certain hours on certain days coming out of the greasy side-entrances of pawn-shops, are proofs how little the regulations of the Act forbidding the encouragement of such customers are regarded. The pawnbroker professes to know that the children are authorized by their parents to pledge ; but the

Act is very precise on this point, and much harm is done to the children by encouraging them.

The pawnbroker, with all his keenness, is occasionally deceived by swindlers. Not long ago a cask of wine was received as a valuable pledge, which turned out to be only water with a bladder of wine inserted in it. Beds have been taken in before now with children inside them, and parcels of gloves, only made for the right or left hand, have been pawned as pairs, and bought back by a confederate of the pawner for a mere trifle. The man who preys systematically upon the innocent pawnbroker by pledging articles made up for pawning and nothing else, is called a " duffer," and the term is often applied to the articles he pledges. As soon as a particular tool is superseded by a new invention, and consequently becomes almost worthless, the duffer will send it round to the pawnbrokers; and, by the aid of male and female agents, will succeed in getting rid of a large quantity before the pawnbroker hears of the change in its value. Sometimes the duffer appears in a more distinguished shape; and we have heard of an aristocratic pledger who pawned and redeemed a really valuable jewel several times, until the pawnbroker's confidence was gained, and then tendered a spurious copy of the property, which was accepted, and never reclaimed.

When an unscrupulous pawnbroker has a few articles in his possession on which he has lent, by mistake, more money than they would fetch in a sale-room, he revenges himself on society in a peculiar manner. He ties these articles up in separate parcels, and pawns them to himself at fancy prices. The tickets made out for these goods are then entrusted to a duffer, who gets part of his living by selling pawntickets in public-houses. The duffer receives a large share of the money which he gets for these false tickets, and the unfortunate buyers, after going to the shop, paying the interest due, and looking at the pledges, of course decline to redeem them. They sell their tickets for what they can get, and other buyers go through the same unprofitable ceremony. By this plan, which breaks the rule forbidding him to buy pledges in his custody, the pawnbroker often gets three or four months' interest paid to him in a week, which more than counterbalances the losses he often sustains from duffers.

It may be gathered from the foregoing statements that most of the legislative rules intended to regulate pawn-broking are systematically evaded, and that the poorer classes pay most extravagant rates of interest for loans upon personal property. Half the impositions pointed out could often be plausibly explained away as clerical errors, even if poor men could afford the time and money to set up as prosecutors. The law may be impartial, but it cer-tainly is not cheap, and prosecuting is a luxury only reserved for the rich.

The trade of pawnbroking, as at present carried on, reflects no credit either upon lender or borrower. The pawnbroker works under an evil reputation, and the pawner slinks to borrow money on good security, as if he was going to rob a till. If capitalists, seeking for safe invest-ments, and philanthropists, trying to benefit the poor, were to turn their attention to model pawnbroking, they might found a *Mont de Piété*, without the intervention of the State, that would be a most beneficial institution in the squalid neighbourhoods of our large cities.

PEACOCKISM.

We are always ready to preach to the lower orders; to lecture them upon the vices of dirt and rags, and the folly of intemperance. We too often shut our eyes to our own faults, while pointing out those of our poorer neighbours. Cleanliness may be so stretched as to become a vice, dress may exhibit as much personal recklessness on the part of the wearer as rags; and there may be as much intemperance in indulging in certain bonnets and shawls as in beer-bibbing and gin-drinking.

Peacockism in dress has increased to an alarming extent of late years, fostered by the bold fulness of a recent fashion; and I am sorry to say that the ladies are the chief offenders. There is no such creature in England as the human male peacock. The bird who mates with the female peacock appears to belong to a totally different species. He boasts of no plumage—especially of late years; of no covering that can be considered very costly or attractive. His hue is chiefly confined to black, or brown, or drab, and economy seems to be studied quite as much as elegance. His trousers, or leggings, are only about sixteen shillings a pair; his coats about two or three guineas each; and everything he wears is in the same proportion. His evening dress is so contrived that he might appear in it for years, and no one be aware of his slender wardrobe. His "walking suit," at two pounds four shillings, is a leveller of all class distinctions. No men have certainly hit Toryism so hard as the new race of cheap tailors.

How different is it, however, with the human peacock proper—the female mate of this somewhat dingy bird! She lives, apparently, only for her plumage. Take that away from her, and life seems no longer to have any attraction. This plumage may be gaudy, or not, according to her taste, but it must always be costly and luxurious, and made with little regard to her position in the world. In proportion as her means to pay for these feathers diminish, her desire to obtain them seems to increase. The same may also be said of her power to obtain them, for credit is seldom given more freely than when it is recklessly demanded. Here is a part, and a very small part, of an account, amounting to nearly £3000, recently proved against a lady by a West-End milliner in the London Court of Bankruptcy :—

	£	s.	d.
Court dress of gold and white lace, and train of brocaded gold, silk lining, embroidered glacé skirt, additional glacé, and flounces of gold	55	10	0
Lace tucker	0	18	0
Pink roses and leaves	1	5	0
White and silver wreath and Brussels lappet	4	14	6
Dressing four dolls	12	12	0
Brussels lace cap, pink roses and brown leaves	4	14	6
Point lace cap, lilac and pearls	11	11	0
Making train into dress, silk linings, stiff net blonde, and pearls	11	9	0
Pair Venice point sleeves	4	4	0
Pair of lappets	8	8	0
Point lace	10	10	0
Green brocaded moire-antique dress, pink ribbon, fringe, and tassels	19	19	0

White blonde bonnet, with pink roses	.	.	4	4	0
Renovating bonnet	.	.	.	.	0	18	0
Black lace bonnet, velvet leaves, roses, and white					
flowers	.	.	.	.	.	3	18	0
Black lace fichu, lilac ribbon	.	.	.	1	15	0
Re-trimming evening tulle dress, stiff net and					
black velvet	.	.	.	.	.	5	18	6
Carmelite mourning dress	.	.	.	3	13	6
Scarf, with lace	.	.	.	.	.	5	15	6
Black moire-antique morning-dress	.	.	13	15	9
Glacé mantle, with lace	.	.	.	.	12	12	0
Point lace parasol	.	.	.	.	18	18	0
Venice point flounce	.	.	.	.	84	0	0
Rose point bonnet	.	.	.	.	14	14	0
Point lace trimming for velvet dress	.	.	36	15	0
Nine yards Brussels lace flouncing	.	.	28	14	0
A Brussels lace square	.	.	.	.	31	10	0
A black lace ditto	.	.	.	.	31	10	0
Three ditto flounces	.	.	.	.	31	10	0
Pair Brussels lace sleeves and lace for body	.	4	4	0
Pair Lisle lace sleeves, with white satin	.	4	4	0
Pair Mechlin sleeves and lace for body	.	.	5	5	0
Venice point lace	.	.	.	.	13	2	6
Covering parasol handle with lace and silk	.	12	12	0
White glacé parasol with French lace	.	.	10	10	0
Brussels lace handkerchief	.	.	.	6	6	0
A steel spring hoop	.	.	.	.	2	2	0
Brown velvet mantle, Maltese lace and trimmings	16	16	0
Black velvet goat sable something	.	.	73	10	0
Mantle of brown velvet, and trimmings	.	16	16	0
Drab and blue cloth coat, steel buttons	.	.	8	8	0
White blonde mantilla	.	.	.	.	15	15	0

The human peacock, as we see by this melancholy record of folly and waste, will sometimes be decently happy in a plumage valued at four or five pounds sterling; at others she will be fretful under a plumage of thirty pounds,

and only supremely contented when it represents nearly a
hundred pounds. Much will depend upon the "society"
she is keeping, and the rivals she meets; for peacockism
has its leaders and its followers, its struggles and its con-
tests, its hungry ambition and its gnawing envy, the same
as any other field of emulation. When it takes the form
of a race for notoriety between two fashionable peacocks
of equal daring, it is difficult to say what combinations of
grace and extravagance may not be effected. Jewels may
be the weapons selected if the peacocks are middle-aged,
or some new material from Lyons adorned with precious
yellow, dusty lace, if they are a little younger. Lace is a
favourite adornment of the fashionable peacock. She
collects it, as people collect old china, or rare engravings;
and when she orders a collar at thirty pounds, or a hand-
kerchief at fifteen pounds, upon three years' credit, she
calls that "making a good investment of her capital."
Whatever suit of plumage a fashionable peacock may
array herself in, it is her unalterable rule never to appear
in society with it more than once. Society is only composed of a certain number of birds, who each, in their
turn, become the centres round which the others revolve.
It never seems to have struck these fashionable peacocks that
they are parts in a living, moving, breathing kaleidoscope,
and that an infinite variety of effects may be created by the
same colours, and the same pieces. They change their
plumage at every movement of the glass, in ignorance of
this principle, and often annoy each other by producing
the monotony they are laboriously seeking to avoid.

If nature provided the feathers of these birds, there
would be nothing more to say, but nature, in this case, has
left this duty to the milliner.

The fashionable milliner is able to carry on her business without cash payments. The sole *nexus* between man and man (according to Mr. Thomas Carlyle) is not required between woman and woman. The fashionable milliner lives by giving and taking credit. She dresses up her peacock dolls, and seems only to ask that their names shall appear upon her books, and their appearance shall do her justice in the world of fashion. She thinks nothing of trusting a distinguished peacock with feathers to the extent of four, six, or eight hundred pounds sterling, and for any period within the statute of limitations. If the peacock is very bold, or very distinguished, indeed, this mark of trading confidence (as we have just seen) may be extended to some thousands sterling. When one capital is exhausted, the fashionable milliner " calls up " another, and her call is seldom uttered in vain in the ear of her " wholesale houses." Brilliant as the plumage of the West may seem in the height of the peacock season, the feathers are nearly all the property of dingy streets in the city.

The fashionable milliner sometimes provides her peacocks with jewels, and assumes the character of a buyer as well as a seller. The way in which the peacock borrows money is a lesson to all students in finance. Her first step is to select bracelets, necklaces, and brooches to the amount of a hundred, or a hundred and fifty pounds, and to wear them, on a few occasions, when she goes into society. Her second step is to tell her milliner that " she positively hates the sight " of these jewels, after a few weeks, which causes the milliner to offer to repurchase them at half their nominal value. Her third step is to accept this offer, which brings her fifty or seventy pounds, while the jewels still stand against her at the usual term of credit. Her old feathers—the dresses she has worn two or three times—she often deals with in the same manner, and either converts them into ready-money, or a payment off her account. This is a clever way of raising a loan, and concealing its ruinous character under the cover of a sale; but sometimes the fashionable peacock is much more straightforward in her dealings. She has her I O U's, and her bills of exchange, if the fashionable milliner is willing to discount them, and the spectre of " sixty per cent." appears in the boudoir, perhaps quite as often as it does in the smoking-room. She sometimes speaks of her " marriage settlement," when, she enters upon these transactions, and laments that her " dividend-day " is so long in coming round. It may happen that this marriage-settlement and dividend-day have only an imaginary existence; though they serve, for a time, to keep off the demand which the male peacock must eventually pay. Sometimes no such agreeable fiction is offered or expected, and money being freely sold to the female peacock, is paid for by the male peacock (if it is ever paid for) under the disguise of " velvet trimmings," or " Honiton lace extras."

Though money is thus often extracted by the fashionable peacock from the fashionable milliner, it is very rare, indeed, that the process is allowed to be reversed. The fashionable milliner is so schooled into a fear of losing her " connection," that she is afraid to refuse credit to any member, hanger-on, or dependant of the " great families," and afraid to ask for even partial payment, years after the credit has been given. She is taught to believe in secret cliques of united peacocks, who combine to resent any insult that is offered to their species. A demand for money is such an insult, and dunning is looked upon as a mortal offence. What are creditors for (as the hero remarks in the " Game of Speculation ") but to give credit? The vulgar tradespeople must wait. If they decline to do this, they must take the consequences, and these consequences are sometimes threats to pay. When the fashionable peacock produces the money under these circumstances to " close the account," the fashionable milliner is taught to believe that from that hour her business will begin to decay.

The fashionable peacock, however, has seldom the power to play the tyrant which she affects to possess; and she is more often bound hand and foot in the fetters of the milliner. Her feathers are generally procured without the sanction of that dingy male bird whom she calls her husband, and all her ingenuity, and that of her confidential servant—her lady's-maid—are exercised to keep from him as long as possible, the knowledge of the liability hanging over his head. Perhaps his eyes ought to be opened by the sensation his wife is making in the peacock-world, and by the appearance of his infant son, aged ten months, attired like Richard the Third, and his eldest son, aged seven years, dressed in silk velvet and jet bugles, like Hamlet the Dane. If his eyes are opened by these things, and his will is strong, the growing peacockism of his household is speedily and effectively checked. The feather-money of his peacock-mate is not only granted, but its outlay is carefully watched, and its produce is periodically surveyed. Few of these dingy male birds have the intelligence, industry, and courage, however, to see and do this, and the milliner is left undisturbed to adorn the peacock in any plumage her taste and extravagance may select.

When the fashionable milliner receives instructions to " cook " the bill whose delivery can no longer be delayed : to turn the account of one costly garment into two that are not so costly; to place that to the children's charge which ought to go to the mother's; and to keep back one-half of the amount to be rendered at a future period, she begins to feel that this peacock-customer is, in some degree, in her power. A gentle hint that money must be had, and an affected reluctance to apply to the dingy male bird, are generally found to bring a little of that precious metal to the surface, whose appearance is so extremely rare. In some cases even this promising process is known to fail, and, upon inquiry, it is then often found that the dingy male bird, behind the screen, was careless of his peacock-mate's accumulating plumage, because he felt in that state of chronic insolvency which no law is able to cure.

The principle that high profits must be made to cover high risks applies to all businesses, and to that of a fashionable milliner amongst the rest. It is under the practical operation of this principle that good debtors are compelled to make up the losses sustained by the bad ones. The ultra-peacockism of the present hour is remarkable for being built upon credit—a blind, unwavering credit—that asks only to hear the rumble of a carriage, and to catch a glimpse of a footman's plush. The gaudy bubble can never burst while credit remains as it is, because no pressure is ever likely to be applied. The loss, if any, is not felt so much by the fashionable milliner, who seems to suffer as she feeds her peacocks, for the peacocks really feed upon one another, the bad upon the good. The dowdyism that does pay, and the moderate peacockism that can pay, together are the great supporters of that ultra-peacockism, which never did pay, and never will.

CHEAP DRESS.

THOSE who are fond of seeking for facts on which to found disheartening generalizations, might easily find them, to all appearance, in the cheap dress of the day. Of course we are not alluding to the dress of the ladies. That has attained a degree of luxury which makes matrimony one of the largest financial undertakings in the market. We are speaking only of the humble dress of the male sex, which seems almost to have reached the verge of workhouse cheapness. While the ladies are flaunting in costumes which are denounced from the pulpits of unfashionable churches, the men have descended, step by step, through every degree of cheapness, until they have altogether deserted the old fashioned five-guinea coat for suits which look passing well at half the money. They cannot be strictly said to have clothed themselves in sackcloth and ashes, but they certainly go as near the penitential style, in some of their tourist garments, as decency will allow. The days of "guid braid claith," as Robert Fergusson, the poetical progenitor of Burns, puts it, are as much things of the past as the days of hair-powder, patches, and satin breeches. Materials which at one time would have been considered only fit for hearth-rugs now form the favourite walking-dress in the most refined cities.

Such a radical change in the foundations of dress was

sure, sooner or later, to affect the minor articles of clothing, and we can hardly, therefore, feel surprised at the rise and popularity of paper collars. There is nothing like a shrinking modesty about these articles, and those who sell them. Paper collars are boldly exposed in the shop-windows, in every variety of shape and colour, side by side with false cuffs, sometimes made of the same material, and waistcoats which are all front and no back. To those who remember the decent reserve which was always maintained, both by buyer and seller, about an old piece of harmless deception, popularly known as a " dickey," there must be something almost recklessly brazen in this new mode of dealing. The " dickey," or false shirt-front, was a thing generally purchased in the dusk of evening, with a variety of excuses made by the purchaser about a pressing appointment. The shop-keeper, on the other hand, was usually ready with a few assuring remarks about the convenience of the garment as a makeshift, and the impossibility of always being prepared for everything. The purchase and sale were generally conducted in a private part of the shop, with as much ceremony as often accompanies a transfer of contraband articles.

Paper collars, paper cuffs, " Agathon vests," butterfly neckties, constructed to show every atom of their surface, and neither to go round the neck, nor to dip down the chest, though all as deceptive as the old " dickey," are evidently not ashamed of their character. The way in which they are bought and worn doubtless gives them this confidence. Their slinking predecessor was the makeshift of the few, while they are the favourite adornment of the many. We have seen a noble duke in a paper collar, and a barrister of some position putting on a pair of cuffs in a railway carriage, on his way to Brighton to dine ; but these were probably exceptions. The great consumption of these articles evidently rests with " Young England," and Young England seems rather proud than otherwise of its taste in clothing.

The influence of small articles of dress on the character of their wearers is a subject which has never received its proper share of attention. We should like to take a young man of fair average moral qualities and test him with purple and fine paper, and then with purple and fine linen. It would be curious to see how far his self-respect would be increased when he knew he had nothing upon him which professed to be what it was not, and how far that self-respect would be lowered when he felt that his adornment was more showy than solid. There may be natures so wanting in sensibility, or so philosophical, that they feel no more pride when their cravats go all round their neck, instead of merely sticking on their chests, and no more self-satisfaction when their white shirt-cuffs really represent a white shirt, instead of false gauntlets to a dingy woollen covering. With people so disposed we, of course, can have little sympathy, because, while multitudes of men are compelled to herd together, the art and morals of dressing are worthy of a little study. If old Howell prayed in very dissolute times, as he tells us he did, when putting on a clean shirt, we may rest assured that there is something more in a clean shirt than meets the eye. We have known people to be singularly affected by some ornament or new article of clothing, worn under the dress ; and we have seen a man's appearance of respectability surprisingly increased by dressing him in a pair of drab gaiters. These are facts which ought not to be despised by any inquirer into the springs of human action. A man may dress himself in a variety of make-believe articles without any moral degradation, or his nature may become subdued to what he appears in. It all depends upon whether he uses these articles as conveniences or deceptions; and the frank, open way in which they are bought and sold would seem to point to the first course rather than to the second. As long as all these contrivances are constructed more for utility than display there is, perhaps, some guarantee that cheap dress, a good and wholesome thing, will be used more than it is abused.

TEACHING OUR GRANDMOTHERS.

THE homely proverb which gives a title to this paper is very old, but the spirit which gave rise to the proverb is older still. The desire to teach our elders to suck eggs is not the birth of an age, but of all time. It came in with human nature, that most ancient of conquerors, and it will probably go out only with the light of the world.

This time-honoured desire to teach everybody their business, especially in this country, shows no signs of decay. If anything, it is a little too full of life. It has cropped up in a governmental shape, and has given itself the title of Social Reform. It has cropped up in an official shape, and sits snugly in museums and departments to encourage commerce, manufactures, and the arts. It has cropped up in a philanthropic shape, and would like to board, lodge, and educate in a peculiar way nine-tenths of the whole human race.

If the governmental passion for teaching everybody their business could be fully gratified, we should have inspectors of everything at every street corner, and no man would be required to think for himself. There would be an inspector of shirts, whose duty it would be to see that all the buttons were in their places, and that the fronts were properly starched. There would be an inspector of shaving-water, an inspector of slippers, and another inspector to see that the bed-room candle-sticks were in proper order. Barriers, with comfortable official dwelling-houses attached, would be built at the end of every street, and no person or thing would be allowed to pass these barriers without examination and an official order. Every man's pulse would be felt and tongue examined every morning by travelling doctors, before he was allowed to go to business, or to start on a journey. Every city would be turned into a huge barrack, and every man in it would be treated as a soldier on duty. The food for breakfast would be fixed by official order, and also the hour and dishes for dinner and supper. The complaint about cold mutton would be no longer a table-squabble between man and wife, but a thing to be filled in on an official form, and sent in to a particular department. Sheets of folio foolscap with a margin would be in demand at every turn of existence, for without them no protest could be officially brought before the constituted authorities. The hour for going to bed and putting out the light would be fixed as it was in the curfew days, or as it is fixed now on board ship in the docks. Producers and consumers would not be allowed to trade together on their own terms, but as it is now between cab-drivers and cab-hirers, water-sellers and water-buyers, gas-sellers and gas-buyers, the price which one should give and the other should take would be settled by an army of inspectors. The area-bell, the street-door scraper, the knocker, the chimney-pots, and the letter-box, would all be under the charge of a staff of sub-inspectors. No bread, nor wine, nor beer would be eaten or drunk before it was tested, and perhaps analyzed by a government officer. Births, deaths, and marriages would all be regulated by a state department, and no child would be allowed to come into the world or go out of it without giving three days' clear notice to the managing secretary.

All this over-government would be carried on under a professed wish for the people's good, and there would not be wanting believers in the perfection of the system. It is astonishing how much management, how much curbing and reining, some people can bear. We need not go to a despotic state for supporters of officialism : they give a sanction to the encroachments of the few on the many in places where liberty is supposed to have made its home.

The popular mind can hardly complain that it is occasionally taught to suck eggs, for it is just as ready to act the teacher whenever it can get a chance. Take half the letters written to newspapers, which get into print during the parliamentary recess, and they will all be found trying to teach many of us something we have already learnt. We may even pick out a large number of leaders published during the " dull season" which strive to do the same work in a much loftier way.

There is that question about hotel charges, sometimes called the hotel nuisance, for the sake of variety, which is always raised at the stagnant period. A particular line of business is taken ; its price lists are criticized, its arrangements are examined, and its conductors are called up to be lectured by amateurs. One amateur tutor settles the price which ought to be charged for food ; another explains the terms upon which all kinds of wine should be served to the public ; another fixes the price of bed-chambers and sitting-rooms ; another lays out a plan for the management of the servants, and another turns his attention to the subject of wax-lights. Some of the tutors make no suggestions for improving the business under discussion, but only object to the manner in which they find it conducted. One man relates his experiences, then another does the same, and then a third comes forward to prove that he has been the worst treated of all. One traveller complains that he could not have peacocks' tongues in all places at the price of pickled whelks. Another orders prawns when they are out of season, in a town many hundred miles from the sea, and is surprised to find that they are a shilling a-piece. Another man expects strawberries as large as pincushions to follow him wherever he goes, at a cost much below the current charges of Covent Garden Market.

All these facts and wishes are brought before the silent hotel-keepers, who never trouble themselves to answer. Their silence is looked upon as a proof of guilt. A new universal scale of prices is accordingly drawn up for their guidance, in which everything is to be supplied at very low fixed charges, regardless of seasons and differences of position. A broad average is struck between all the taverns, inns, and hotels in the country, and they are all expected to subscribe to the same rules. It is almost need-less to say that they pay no heed to these lessons and sug-gestions, but conduct their old business in their old way. Those who look through a file of newspaper correspon-dence on this subject, signed "Viator," "Bonâ Fide Tra-veller," or "Mungo Park," as the case may be, will see the same old hotels abused in 1864, as were abused in 1851, and abused on the very same grounds. Where they have improved, the great increase of travellers has been the chief cause, enabling them to accommodate numbers at a decreased cost. The letter writers have had nothing to do with the improvement, although they may fancy they have, for prices are not regulated by pens, ink, and paper. If any man is dissatisfied with the charges of a trading neighbour, his course is very simple. Instead of teaching his neighbour to suck the particular egg, let him act as if no such egg were in existence.

The passion for teaching everybody their business has taken an eastern direction since the American war has dammed up the flow of cotton. This is a remarkable instance of an attempt to instruct our grandmothers. Here is a country loudly exhorted to grow cotton which has been growing it for three or four thousand years. Deputations from Manchester cotton-consumers—a class who are popularly supposed to know what free-trade means—are sent out to Indian cotton-growers to stimulate production. This is on a par with the proceedings of some of those official organizations whose professed object is to encourage manufactures, commerce, and the arts. The seller is thought to be no true judge of his own interests, and is therefore lectured on this head by the buyer. The order of nature is reversed—the world is moving backwards—the blood is flowing the wrong way, the buyer is running after the seller, and not the seller after the buyer. The producer is told how he ought to grow the plant, how he ought to gather it, how he ought to clean it and prepare it for the market. The buyer tells him all this, and travels many thousands of miles to teach him. There is only one difficulty in the way of the well-meant lesson—the producer has been taught before. His ingenuity has been stimulated by the hope of gain, and his resources taxed to the utmost, almost before the new teacher was born. India had its position fixed in the cotton market more than a quarter of a century ago, and no deputations from Manchester mill-owners, temporarily forgetful of the laws of trade, are likely to advance this position one jot. The most singular part of the whole business is, that the deputation goes to the dearest market, but not to buy. It talks, but it makes no offer to ship. The cotton bales are stored up in the Indian warehouses, but the teacher has no instructions to move them. He wants cotton—at least, he believes so—but not *that* cotton. He tells the Indian how he may grow a better material—at least, he believes that he tells him; but the pupil knows he is listening to nothing that he has not heard before. The cotton produced is the best Indian cotton; there is no real prospect of producing a better article; the best Indian cotton will not do for Manchester until the mills are completely starved out of their American supply, and so the Indian bales remain lodged as before in the Indian warehouses, and the deputation, after leaving many instructions with its grandmother, slowly withdraws.

While the consumer is thus teaching the producer his business, officialism is tenderly watching over both. Trade has always been the favourite child of government departments, a precious treasure to be watched over, dandled, coddled, and spoilt, to be always kept in leading strings, as if it had never shown any power to run alone. The child is made to pay pretty heavily, too, for all this unnecessary nursing, for Government is not so charitable as many people suppose. It can give nothing, because it possesses nothing, and what it distributes with the right hand it must first have taken with the left.

Officialism has seldom shown itself more watchful and encroaching than in connection with what are called industrial exhibitions. After the great international display of 1851, it believed itself ordained to perform a great work. It first persuaded itself and then it tried to persuade the public, that all our commerce, fair as it seemed to the eye, was rotten at the core. We are told that the art of designing had never fallen to such a pitch of vulgarity and coarseness; that there was no taste, properly so called, throughout the country; and that unless some great efforts were made we should lose our position in the markets of the world. The engineering skill and enterprise which had spanned broad rivers and pierced high mountains; the manufacturing energy which had given employment to millions, and had changed swampy villages, like Manchester, into huge toiling cities; the artistic feeling and conscientiousness which had given us such manufacturers as Wedgwood; and all the qualities which yearly provided the statistical wonders for the Board of Trade; were to perish miserably, unless officialism were allowed to take the reins. The fly on the chariot-wheel thought that the coach could only be moved by its puny force, and it warned the sleeping passengers in time. Artisans, manufacturers, merchants, and traders, however, paid little heed to the warning, and went on much as they did before officialism taught them how to suck their eggs. If they were successful, they were rewarded with profits; if they were unsuccessful, they were punished with loss. Self-interest kept them in the way they should go, without the help and assistance of half-instructed guides.

Officialism, having thoroughly satisfied itself, however, that commerce could not walk alone, and having secured the Exhibition surplus of something like two hundred thousand pounds, prepared an elaborate scheme for a great Industrial University. It prevailed upon the government of the day to join in the scheme, and to provide an amount of money from the public purse almost equal to the Exhibition surplus. Never, perhaps, was molly-coddling proposed on such a gigantic scale, or a less scrupulous attempt made to rob a neighbour of his business. The Society of Arts was the originator of the Exhibition, the creator of

the surplus, and the earliest existing society formed for
teaching our grandmothers to suck their eggs. In the
middle of the last century it had done all that the Manchester men of to-day are trying to do in "stimulating
production." It had sent out commercial missionaries to
the West Indies, and had scolded children for destroying
acorns, and so stinting the supply of oaks. There was
scarcely a branch of trade to which it had not made un-
practical suggestions in carrying out its plan of encouraging commerce, manufactures, and the arts. Of course,
amidst a heap of folly, it contrived to do a little good, for
no institution, however false may be its basis, or weak its
management, can be wholly bad. It struggled on year
after year, with varying success, and was not as robust in
1849 as it was at its birth. The Exhibition of 1851 saved
it from death, and so far may be said to have repaid its
father; but still the Society had as much claim to the
surplus as the Royal Commissioners had, though it was
not in a legal position to secure its rights. To increase
its annoyance, the rival body, which had retained the
money, proposed to apply it in starting an opposition
business, and the Society was only saved from this additional insult by a change in the plans of Government. The
British Parliament refused to sanction the removal of the
National Gallery of Pictures from Charing Cross to South
Kensington, and so destroyed the only object which the
Government had in view when they agreed to a partnership with the Exhibition Commissioners. The official union
was at once dissolved after this parliamentary decision, the
Government taking the South Kensington Museum as
their share of the capital, and the Commissioners taking
the Kensington Gore estate as theirs. The great university
scheme for teaching our trading grandmothers was given

up, and the Commissioners turned their attention, like sensible men, to the improvement of their land, but not before their ridiculous pretensions had done as much harm to industrial exhibitions as the greatest enemies of those displays could desire.

Officialism is not in the habit of hiding its light under a bushel, and therefore when it has done anything which it thinks tolerably successful, its friends soon spread the news of the triumph.

As much stir is made about a petty museum, a loan of a few casts or models to a provincial school of design, or the opening of a feeble exhibition of art in the suburbs, as if officialism had discovered the Philosopher's Stone, or the Elixir of Life. We hear of these triumphs in a variety of ways, but generally through complacent official reports, drawn up by believers in the divine right of coddling, and printed upon public paper at the public expense.

When trading enterprise makes its mark in the same field—which it does every day and every hour—it must not look to official pens to record its praises.

Officialism has no sympathy or connection with any other shop. It looks coldly upon any traveller going along the same road. There is a place in London which is a creation amongst Art exhibitions, and yet officialism has probably never heard of it. I allude to the Canterbury Music Hall in Lambeth Marsh. It has been worthily patted on the back by several admiring journalists, and one has called it the "Royal Academy over the Water." It was built in 1851, as the leader of a new school of music-halls, designed to supplant the old tavern concert-rooms and the public-house "harmonic meetings." The building was framed with some architectural pretensions; sculpture was used as part of the decorations; the ventilating arrange-

ments were well planned, and the comfort of the visitors
was secured in every way.   The music performed included
many popular songs—both comic and sentimental—some
of them being those classical lyrics which the world will
never let die; but the chief feature of the evening was a
selection from an opera, rendered by a very efficient company of singers, with a chorus and instrumental accom-
paniments.   Under this head some of the best works of
the best masters were given, night after night; and so
energetic were the conductors in getting opera-scores from
France, Germany, and Italy, that the quiet, orderly working men and women who formed the chief visitors of the
Canterbury Hall, heard many works of foreign musical
composers long before they were brought out at the Italian
Opera Houses.

After some few years of successful management in this
way, the proprietors added a side-hall to their building,
and this they fitted up as a gallery of modern pictures.
Well lighted, well supplied with works by many of the
leading Royal Academicians, and with a printed catalogue
of the paintings, this gallery was a great and refining
attraction to the visitors.   The Exhibition, for its size, was
as good as any average May display at the Royal Academy,
with the additional advantage of being open at a time
when working-men could go and see it.   The admission
charge to the hall, concert, and picture-gallery, was sixpence.

Such was the Canterbury Hall, Lambeth; and such, I
am happy to say, it is now, with its glory and success un-
diminished.   Those who know the neighbourhood in which
it has sprung up—the "gaffs" and coarse, greasy theatres
of the "New Cut"—will rejoice to see such wholesome
amusement provided for the factory-workmen and their

wives, who form three-fourths of the local population. The educational influence of such a place can hardly be over-rated, although it is created by mere trading enterprise, acting in an obscure corner of London. If officialism had been the father of this music-hall and picture-gallery, we should have been called upon to bow down and worship the whole scheme, including a long line of official managers, with enormous salaries. Every blue or green covered official report would have alluded to the place as a great instrument for regenerating the masses. As it is, the temple of social improvement is left to announce its own attractions, and we find it, as we wish to find everything, without an official guide.

THE JOCULAR MIND.

FOR some years past we have been entertained by a knot of small wits, who take unto themselves the title of social satirists. Their ambition seems to be satisfied when they have ridiculed the cut of a man's coat or a woman's gown, or the rude boor who uses his knife with salmon. They make no pretension to reform the human heart, to check vices, or to teach principles; they are content if they can pry into the kitchen when the mistress's back is turned, or can get just such a glimpse of life as must be familiar to most footmen and housemaids. They lift the veil from many struggling households, and show us how much of the plate is really silver, how much is electro-gilded, and how much is borrowed for state occasions. They tell us which sofa is stuffed with horse-hair, and which with straw; how many times the muslin dress of the eldest daughter has been washed, and the silk dress of the hostess turned or dyed; how much the port-wine has cost, and how many bottles there may be in the cellar. They seem to have a horror of nothing except economy and prudence, and bow down and worship that showy elegance which is often based upon credit. They speak contemptuously of all London neighbourhoods that are not prominent in the "Court Guide," and give them sweeping general characters, which are drawn entirely from imagination. It is not surprising that such satirists generally love a Lord, and cramp themselves up in stuccoed dwellings on the borders of a fashionable district.

In every bushel of chaff there is a grain of wheat, if we only take the pains to seek it, and the social satire with which we have been feasted for the last twenty years, may not have been entirely useless within its proper limits. Although it has, doubtless, helped to foster that extravagance of living, which is one of the greatest vices of the present time, it may have kept a few weak people from striving after a false appearance. If these people, however, had had the courage, dash, and ingenuity to rush into debt, they might have made their coveted display, and have escaped the lash of the censor. The social satirist, looking no lower than the surface, with all his occasional affectation of depth, would never have been shocked by anything not offensive to " good taste." No hole could have been picked in Redpath's coat until the morning of his arrest for forgery, and the admiring social satirists who dined at his graceful table must grieve that such a faultless patron of art is now a condemned convict. The money he stole from vulgar shareholders was spent with so much aristocratic judgment, that, according to the teaching of social satire, some retired soap-boiler ought to have been transported as his substitute.

This open, avowed preference for elegant wrong, and contempt for inelegant right, is peculiar to much satire which has lately aspired to lead public opinion. It trades upon a few parrot-phrases, eked out with a few well-worn, caricature signs, and shows us how much is made of a little wit by satirists who have neither invention nor principle. If the faded dress which is turned and patched, and worn with a self-satisfied, would-be distinguished air,

is such a target for these terrible satirists, how is it that
they constantly adopt the same old forms of ridicule, which
must be as familiar to their public as the loaf on the
breakfast-table? There is surely much here of patching
and turning, of wearing thread-bare, of keeping up appearances. The stock-in-trade of our professional satirists can
be held upon a platter, can be counted on the fingers. It
consists of a few deceptive tricks, and a few dressed-up
puppets that were never instructive, and have almost
ceased to be amusing.

One favourite caricature with the jocular mind is an
exaggerated Jewish nose. No one can tell exactly when
this caricature was first used, or what it precisely means;
but it is a sign or symbol that is worked very vigorously
against the Jewish race. Some people look upon it as a
punishment for usury, forgetting that lending money at
high rates of interest is not confined to the Jews, and that
there must be two persons to every usurious transaction—
a borrower as well as a lender. Other people regard it as
a punishment for giving out slop-work at low prices, forgetting that labour is the best judge of its own value, and
that masters have about as much power to raise wages to
some sentimental height demanded by a few enthusiasts,
as they have to raise the tide a foot higher all over the
world. Sometimes the huge curved nose is varied with
another symbol—three hats, stuck one upon another, on
the top of a venerable hermit's head. This is a sign which
is held to speak volumes by those versed in the language
of caricatures. It proves that sixty per cent. is too much
to charge bankrupt young noblemen on accommodation
bills, and that no shirt ought to be given out to any sempstress at less than three shillings the hour. It is astonish-

ing how liberal your social satirist can be when he is dealing with the property of other people.

Another favourite caricature with the jocular mind is the red nose, and the protruding stomach. By some process of reasoning, not apparent in the caricature, these signs of a not very graceful humanity, are held to prove more than a volume of laboured writing. A man with a red nose cannot be a true patriot or a noble-minded hero, as we are all expected to feel when we look upon the picture. A man with a prominent stomach is not fit to form an opinion on any public question, as we are also all expected to feel when we look upon the picture. A man with a red nose and a prominent stomach combined is a monster capable of any crime, and devoid of all generous sympathies.

Another favourite caricature with the jocular mind is the Quaker's broad-brimmed hat. It appears so often, and is so universally understood to be a symbol of hypocrisy, that there is hardly any occasion to describe it. Its mere outline proves that the wearers are an inferior race, treacherous, selfish, and not to be trusted. It often covers the heads of men called Mawworms, and we all know precisely what a mawworm is. We have never, perhaps, met one in private or public life, but we should know him in a moment from his portrait and description. To be forewarned is to be forearmed, and the mawworm cannot be too often described. He is a slimy villain. His hair is sleek, his eyes are small and blinking, his face is coarse, he has two if not more chins, and a habit of folding his hands and turning up his eyes when speaking. His voice has a peculiar snuffle that is considered to be indicative of great seeming piety; and his limp white neckcloth, and greasy black clothes, give him the aspect of a preacher. He is fond of holding forth upon theological subjects—of improving the occasion, as it is called—and he is nearly always speaking of a future state, when his mouth is not filled with buttered muffins. Sometimes he has been known to commit forgery, if it suited his purpose, and he is always trembling on the verge of some hideous crime. The most remarkable thing about this extraordinary creature, according to his artists and historians, is, that he never takes the slightest pains to conceal his real character. He walks, talks, dresses, and behaves in such a peculiar way, that no one can fail to take him for a mawworm. He can be recognized a mile off by his melancholy victims, and his hypocrisy, so it seems, might be discovered by a child.

The jocular mind has a hundred other favourite caricatures of men, women, and things, that are equally remarkable for their fancy character. Whole nations are treated in the same way as classes or individuals, and we are favoured with caricature pictures of national characteristics. We all know when we see a plaid check that a Scotchman is the wearer, and that that Scotchman represents a thrifty, pushing, prudent, crafty race. No Scotchman was ever seen clothed in any other patterns than checks or plaids, or was ever improvident, drunken, or disorderly. The statistics of Scotch whisky consumption, and the dens of Edinburgh and Glasgow, may seem to disturb this theory, but the caricaturist never stops his pencil for social facts or figures. He persists in drawing all Yorkshiremen cunning, all Frenchmen frivolous, all Englishmen bluff and honest, and all Irishmen jovial, for no other reason than because they have been drawn so for years, in defiance of much evidence showing the falsity of the pictures.

If these caricatures were only the amusements of an idle hour, there would be little occasion to analyze them so closely, but they often profess to be something more than this. The public jester now is not content with the character of a mere jack-pudding, but sets up as a guide, philosopher, and friend. He wishes it to be thought that his mirth is not without a motive, and that the cap and bells may be made an instrument of public instruction. He follows in the rear of more serious and recognized leaders, and instead of pulling a droll face, and singing a comic song, he discourses upon politics, currency, and the law of nations. The buffoon, like many other people, wishes to figure as something which he is not, forgetting that the form in which he is compelled to appear is not adapted for public teaching. A caricature never proved anything, no matter who drew it, and it is nearly sure to be a flatterer of popular prejudice. To test the value of much of this jocular teaching, it is necessary to search the pages of its books for the best part of a century. When the press was fettered, and the pent-up thoughts of millions had no free vent in words, the caricature did its work coarsely, but tolerably well. As the press, however, grew in strength and freedom, the necessity for allegory ceased, and caricatures became more decent as they grew more feeble and scarce. In whatever form, however, they appeared, whether pictorial or literary, whether humorous or scanty, they were never found to be a day in advance of public opinion. They reflected all the ignorance, all the prejudices of the hour, just as they do now, and made their pupils more ignorant and more bigoted by feeding them upon false types of character.

The rule adopted by the caricaturist, if he acts upon any rule, is to degrade the present, the age he lives in, and

the men who are active and prominent in it. No man is a
hero to the caricaturist until he has been dead a century.
When dead, he is exalted or respected in the same uninquiring way as he is degraded while living. Judging from
what we read and see every hour, we may imagine how
Luther would have been ridiculed by our present jocular
teachers. His face would have been too coarse, and his
stomach too large, to make the Reformation more than a
sectarian sham. The fine, old, crusted Mawworm caricature would have been put upon the table, and we should
have been asked to regard it as a portrait of the Reformer.
Melancthon might have fared better, being a more presentable man; but Luther would have been measured
round the waist, and found wanting in elegance. The
smart "leaders" that would have been written to prove
that the movement was a low, vulgar conspiracy and riot
—a daring innovation—a revolution got up to please the
rabble and strike at " the existing order of things"—would
have been as plentiful as blackberries. Smart leader-
writers and jocular caricaturists would have pulled well
together in this matter, shaken hands in the streets, dined
together at the clubs, and quoted each other on the mutual
admiration principle. About half an hour before the
Reformation became a great fact, they would have con-
gratulated themselves and the country on their victory
over dangerous "demagogues."

There are other great events in the world's history that
would have been treated in much the same way by the
short-sighted caricaturist. Every man who has ever done
any real work, has always had to break through the crowd
of jibbering apes who tried to stop his progress. He has
met them in shoals, as the knight in the fairy tale met an
army of grotesque monsters, who tried to drive him from

his duty. The moment, however, the enchanted palace is broken into, and the good work is done, the whole of these monsters either melt into thin air, or turn into an alley of gold-laced lacqueys, who struggle which shall be first in bowing to their new master.

The whole art of being jocular seems to be based upon a few mechanical rules, suited to the meanest capacity, requiring no mental strain, and to be learned with ease in an idle hour. By these rules we shall find that there is something excessively funny in debt, and that there is no more amusing picture to be drawn than a young man lighting his cigar with writs, and mocking a companion weak enough to have paid a tailor. A sheriff's-officer, with a great-coat and a thick stick, is always looked upon as a safe mirth-provoking sketch; and the humour of a man standing up in a battered hat, with his pockets turned inside out, has never been half exhausted. The same jocular rules teach us that all middle-aged ladies are divided into mothers-in-law and old maids, the first being stout and imperious, and the second thin and vinegar-faced, with a strong determination to conceal their real age. The great rule, however, of the jocular code is the one which decides what trades and professions shall always be considered ridiculous. Tailors, of course, are awarded a leading position in the list, and after them come butchers, doctors, lawyers, with a host of others. In applying this rule to any occurrence which we may wish to put in a ridiculous light, it seems that we have merely to mention the trade of the person we want to humble. A case occurred very recently in which this rule was applied with distinguished success. A certain prime minister went down to the town which he honours with his Parliamentary patronage, to go through the empty ceremony of being re-elected. He

stood upon the public platform in the usual old, consti-
tutional way, inviting any criticism from his constituents
on his past career, and professing to be ready to answer
any troublesome questions. A certain butcher, who shall
be nameless, not being aware that these fine professions
were not meant to be tested, and that the old rough theory
of questioning your member, when you can catch him, had
been given up in practice, applied to the noble candidate,
in an open, public manner, for a little explanation on
points of policy and conduct. The butcher was answered
in a way that told him he had done a very impertinent
thing; and the smart leader-writers and caricaturists took
their tone from his lordship, and badgered the poor tradesman for many weeks afterwards. It was not pretended
that he had no right to put the questions; that the questions were not sensibly put; or that the minister was
without reproach. All this would have involved that
serious argument and patient investigation so distasteful
to the jocular mind; so the easier course was adopted of
harping upon the word *butcher*. No one who examined
the question as put by the small wits of the day, could fail
to perceive how absurd it was for a butcher to question a
prime minister, and that butcher, too, a provincial butcher.
The fact was conveniently forgotten, that a provincial
brewer had once made himself king of England; but small
wits and their smaller followers have wonderfully short
memories.

The evil resulting from the false types of character
which popular caricaturists palm upon a trusting world, is
seen in the security given to real rogues and vagabonds.
While the public are amused, for example, with that highly
fanciful picture of the Mawworm class, the real Mawworm
—a slim, elegant hypocrite—is enjoying himself unnoticed.

The false picture acts very much like that preconcerted cry of " Stop, thief!" which is often got up by artful criminals to draw off the attention of the constables. A Mawworm, such as we may observe any hour in our popular literature, or in caricature pictures, would stand about as much chance of succeeding in his villanous design, as a thief would of robbing a house if he knocked at the street-door in the middle of the day, and candidly announced himself as a notorious burglar.

COMIC DISEASES.

No mad ass is now baited for the intense enjoyment of gentility and fashion; no bull is now turned loose with fireworks; no dog is now roasted alive, or allowed to fight; no rats are killed; no badgers are drawn; no cocks are allowed to spur each other into eternity; the prize-ring has fallen into contempt; the turf is rapidly following in the same direction; the four-in-hand club has just revived —the mere spectral shadow of what it was—and Hockley-in-the-Hole is buried for ever from the public and admiring eye.

There is an Act of Parliament (so I am told) which effectually provides for the legal protection of dumb animals; and there is a society (so I am also told) whose task it is to see that the act has something more than a mere passive existence.

With all these aids to improve our superficial humanity, and to regulate our conduct to the brute creation, it will naturally be supposed that we are a nation of gentle beings, who have given ourselves up entirely and unreservedly to the study of the fine arts, which has softened our conduct to a wonderful degree, and is never likely to allow us to become brutal. Never was a greater delusion indulged in by a too credulous nation. We have transferred our brutality, not destroyed it; and where it before found an inferior field for its operation in the bodies of the animal creation, it now gloats, without a blush or a twinge of conscience, upon the painful infirmities which afflict poor suffering humanity.

Medical men have a method of classifying diseases; but their catalogue of miseries—their hand-book of pain—their index of suffering, is anything but perfect. They can tell us what are epidemics, what are endemics, what are pulmonary complaints, what are acute, and what are chronic disorders; but they are no guide to that small but important division—the Comic Diseases.

No one, except farce-writers, low comedians, and comic artists would believe what an intensely funny thing disease can be made in the hands of a man who thoroughly understands his audience. Sea-sickness (not so much a disease as a passing complaint), if properly handled, is better than all the wit of Swift and all the humour of Smollet. Whoever failed to get a laugh from the picture of the stout man, with the rueful countenance, staggering across the deck towards the side of the vessel? Whoever thinks of women and children lying helplessly in a close and filthy hold, when he is enjoying the humour of a faint gasp for Stew—ard?

People have died under this funny complaint, upon long voyages, but they were evidently persons of very defective stamina, bent upon making themselves disagreeable to their fellow-passengers.

Cholera-morbus, as exhibited through its outward symptoms of violent stomach-ache, is always a safe card to play upon the comic stage, when the dialogue begins to flag, and the interest of the situation has to be kept up by what is technically known as a little extra business.

Listen to the conversation (sometimes rather animated)

morning after the per-
author and the manager
exercise of the pruning-

an to the company gene-
. the second act !   What

his pen ; but the stage-
onstrance.
ian in a decided tone,
st the wings, upon the
t without my stomach-

theatre, taking courage
manfully for his gout,
;h the audience on the

ɔ cut my gout."
rt, Mr. Gills," replies the

ʃ it," returns Mr. Gills,

lown ; it interferes with
a don't get much out

lmost shouts Mr. Gills.
nd had heard the shouts
ɪon kicked me violently
- so."
r at this point, " I think

ɪger, " let it stand ; but

"Oh!" says Mr. Gills, with an air of affected resigna-
tion, "if you touch that, I'd better resign the part."

"It's too long," says the manager, firmly.

"Do you think so?" mildly inquires the author; "we
may prune the dialogue a little, but the situation, in my
humble opinion, ought to be preserved."

The situation is preserved, as a matter of course, and
without prying farther into the council of the green-room,
we can easily imagine what it is. Given a tea-urn, and a
gouty man upon the stage, and it is required to know what
a popular dramatist will do with them.

The gouty man, stout, red-faced, helpless, testy, and
much padded about the legs, will be wheeled on in a
chair by the comic servant, and fixed at the breakfast
table. A tea-urn will then be brought in, foaming like a
brewhouse copper, and placed upon the table, when the
comic servant will withdraw. After a few seconds taken
up with speaking, and the business of the table, the gouty
man will find the water dripping rapidly from the tea-urn
upon the worst of his two lame legs, which it is totally out
of his power to move.

The gouty man cannot reach a bell, and he knocks
violently on the floor with a thick stick, the audience in the
meantime roaring with delight, when they are made fully
aware of the humour of the position. After a most un-
warrantable delay, the comic servant makes his appearance
with anything but signs of pity and contrition upon his
countenance. He pretends to be nearly bursting with half-
concealed laughter, at which the audience shout in sympathy, and when he condescends to recover his speech, and
addresses his afflicted master, who is suffering from a painful disease, most painfully aggravated by the consequences
of his gross neglect, instead of asking pardon, as in duty

bound, he says, in the tone of an injured and unappreciated servant: "Well, sir, if I don't give satisfaction, I'd better leave!"

If the stage is a faithful reflex of the manners of the time (and we are bound to consider it so, according to the highest authorities) we have small reason to congratulate ourselves upon the improvement in our humanity. Putting feeling out of the question, we may naturally ask what there is about gout which renders it so intensely, and so pre-eminently comic? Small-pox, fevers, and broken limbs are never served up to amuse an audience, although the whole put together can scarcely equal the pain and helplessness represented by gout. The pleasures of the table are falsely fathered with the disease, although many more desperate cases come from workhouses than from palaces. Gatherers of comic material have either advanced too far in the province of disease, or have not penetrated far enough. There may be a wide, a fruitful, and a comparatively untouched field yet open to them, for mirth-provoking purposes. Rheumatism has many phases that might be rendered amusing in the hands of a master. Indigestion has been largely used; but bilious fever is still virgin soil. Ague and yellow jaundice would be effective in their dramatic manifestations, and are perfectly novel to the English stage. Consumption has been well-worked on its sentimental side; but there must be a comic aspect if diligent searchers will only seek it. The plague has been represented to a British audience with very equivocal success, but the persevering dramatist should not be disheartened by a single failure. Even the gout, well-used as it is, is not entirely an over-worked mine.

Why do the leading wits of the age linger idly at

the half-way houses of death, and not push on their journey to its legitimate conclusion? If disease can be made funny, why not the last scene of all? Death is not always strutting in its dignified poses; and many· men have left the world with something marvellously like an anti-climax.

HAPPY DOGS.

THERE is one benevolent institution in London, of recent origin, which really diminishes pain on one side, without increasing it on the other, and which does not undermine the self-reliance of those who are taken to it as a refuge. It contains no labour, housed, fed, and clothed at the public expense, and employed in manufacturing door-mats and fancy baskets to the derangement of trade in its district. It presents no population difficulty that cannot be solved with a tub of water. We are speaking of the Home for Lost and Starving Dogs at Holloway. It can hardly be said to attract the class it is intended to benefit, for, great as the acknowledged sagacity of the dog may be, the home can hardly reach that sagacity by advertising its comforts in human newspapers.

This charitable refuge for lost and starving dogs is now a permanent London institution. It has lived through all the doubt, difficulties, and ridicule which attended its birth. It owes its existence to a benevolent lady at Canonbury, who started by befriending a few stray dogs, and giving them a home in her own house. As their numbers increased the difficulty of keeping them in a private dwelling grew greater, and a gentle local agitation was got up to enlarge the sphere of the charity. The Home was established by these means in October, 1860, and its motto is, "I cannot understand that morality which excludes animals from human sympathy, or releases man from the debt and obligation he owes to them."

The Home is now no hole-and-corner institution, managed by one or two amiable enthusiasts in a back street of the suburbs. It has four lady patronesses, three of them being ladies of title; it has a committee of seven ladies and four gentlemen, and its honorary secretary is a clergyman. At present it has nearly fifty annual subscribers, and another fifty donors of all classes whose names are published; and the following address is put forward to the charitable public :—

"Persons walking through the streets of London, or of its suburbs, can hardly fail frequently to have seen lost dogs in a most emaciated and even dying state from starvation.

"The committee would willingly hope and believe that no one who is capable of appreciating the faithful, affectionate, and devoted nature of the dog, can have seen any of these intelligent creatures in that state without feeling an earnest wish that there were some means established for rescuing them from so dreadful a death, and restoring them to usefulness.

"The object of this institution is to give humane persons an opportunity to relieve so much misery.

"The parent Home is now established in Holloway, and all persons finding dogs in the state above described. are entreated to convey them to it, and all persons losing dogs are requested to apply at once to 14, Hollingsworth Street, St. James's Road, Holloway.

"In proportion as the funds will admit of it, receiving-houses will be established in all parts of London, from which dogs will be conveyed to Holloway."

This address may sound to many people like a parody

of an ordinary appeal on behalf of a reformatory, or some'
refuge for lost and repentant outcasts. If Dean Swift had
written such an address in his chapters upon the Yahoos,
no sense of fitness would have been outraged; and yet, for
all this, the charity is founded on a sound principle. It
begins precisely where the Society for the Prevention of
Cruelty to Animals leaves off; and we are not surprised
to find the rooms of that association placed at the disposal
of the dog committee, and Mr. Middleton, the secretary,
undertaking to receive subscriptions and donations.

The Home at present consists of three cab stables, in a
yard at the back of the house before mentioned. A man
is engaged to take charge of the animals, to answer the
questions of applicants who bring dogs or claim them, and
to keep the necessary record of incomers and outgoers.
When a dog becomes a member of this happy family, his
name (if he has one) and his breed are entered in a book
under a particular number, a tin ticket, with a corresponding number, is hung round his neck like a locket, and he
is provided with a place in a certain trough, basket, box,
cage, or tub, according to his temper and his bodily health.
Take the dogs altogether they are tolerably well-behaved,
and wonderfully like human beings under similar circumstances. They are dirty, and require to be washed; they
are diseased, and require to be cured (or killed); and they
are hungry, and require to be fed. It is a melancholy fact,
and one not at all peculiar to animals generally, that the
most worthless dogs have the largest appetites, and make
the most noise. The keeper knows about a dozen of his
large-headed, thick-limbed, gaping, shambling pensioners
by the title of the "wolves," and, to use his own words,
"they are a precious sample." They form the "dangerous
classes" of the Refuge; they do nothing but eat and yell,

are never likely to be reclaimed, and belong to that large family of gift dogs which people never will look in the mouth.

Within a period of four months about 170 have been taken in. 100 of these have gone, some having been given away (the Society does not sell dogs), some having been reclaimed by the owners, and some having died, leaving about 70 now in the Home. Only one Newfoundland and one King Charles spaniel have found their way to the Refuge. The majority of the animals are " rough dogs," answering to regular street tramps, Scotch terriers, mongrel "tykes," and a few fighting dogs. The ladies on the committee must be rather astonished at the infinite varieties of the dog as registered in the Society's books ; and even at the appearance of a few of those square-headed, black-nosed, red-jawed bull-terriers, who creep into the Refuge, like broken-down prize-fighters, too old to earn a living in a professional way. Some of the inmates are flabby, blinking, weak-minded animals, who seem contented with their position, and utterly incapable of supplying their daily physical wants without the aid of a master. They form what we may call the idiot ward of the asylum. Others are knowing, experienced street dogs, not unwilling to be housed and looked after during the winter months, but who, with the first signs of summer, will get away if they can, to trot along the roads with their heads downwards, to slink into butchers' shops when no one is looking, and to be chased out between the legs of the passers-by with something very like a rump-steak in their mouths. Some of these dogs were brought in during the two severe months of December and January, a period when the incomers far exceeded the outgoers. This helps to show that the dog-refuge does not differ very materially from many other refuges.

The charity, like all other charities, has had difficulties to contend with, and has made mistakes at its commencement, which it has since rectified. It had a consulting surgeon to look after the dogs, after the fashion of more ambitious charities, but now the manager is the doctor to the establishment. The difficulty about giving the animals open-air exercise has not yet been got over, simply because the society have not yet sufficient funds to purchase a piece of land in or near London.

The chief imposition practised on the society comes in the shape of old, glassy-eyed dogs, brought by boys who have grown tired of these animals. If we want to see real cruelty to animals, we must go amongst children. When an old dog has been worn out in playgrounds or in plunging for pieces of wood in ponds and canals, its youthful owners and tormentors often try to dispose of it at the Refuge. The manager, however, is prepared for these applicants, and also for those dog-fanciers who endeavour to own animals they have never lost. The following are the rules and regulations of the society:—

"1. Any dog found and brought to the Home, if applied for by the owner, will be given up to his master on payment of the expenses of its keep.

"2. Any dogs lost by the subscribers and brought to the Home, will be given up free of all expense.

"3. All unowned dogs, after they have been in the Home for some little time, will be given away; but, as this is a charitable institution, it is hoped that all who can afford it, will make a donation towards the expenses of the Home, in proportion to the value of the dog selected.

"4. To prevent dog-stealing, no reward will be given to persons bringing dogs to the Home. The committee hope that, to persons of ordinary humanity, the consciousness of having performed a merciful action will be a sufficient recompence.

" 5. It is intended, as soon as suitable arrangements can be made, to have a place especially prepared for the reception of dogs belonging to ladies and gentlemen who may wish to have care taken of them during their absence from home.

" 6. None but governors of the institution shall be eligible for the committee, or vote at any meeting of the institution.

" 7. A donation of five pounds constitutes a life-governor; and the yearly subscription of five shillings and upwards, an annual governor of the institution; and any lady or gentleman collecting small sums to the amount of five pounds, will be considered a life-governor."

The subscriptions, donations, and collections, if small, flow in from all quarters, some coming from Ireland, and different parts of the country. They represent an income of about £90 for four months. Scarcely half-a-dozen subscribers appear under such fancy titles as " Pompey : an old pet ;" " Puff : a pet ;" " Jacob Faithful ;" " Billy ;" and " A lover of dogs ;" the rest giving their names and addresses in a bold and spirited manner. Public entertainments in aid of the Refuge have also commenced; and Mr. William Kidd has given one of his " gossips" under the heading of " The Dogs' own Benefit Night."

So far, the Refuge appears to be popular and well managed ; but the committee is not altogether of one way of thinking. Some, perhaps the most humane portion, insist upon placing all the animals in the Refuge on an equal footing, and object to any dog being destroyed, rejected, or given up as incurable. Others, perhaps the most practical members, see the necessity which exists for

checking the increase of the " tykes ;" the " rest ;" the standing balance which " eats its head off," never moves on, and
becomes surplus dog population.   Here the old workhouse
difficulty, with hopeless paupers, is reproduced on a small
scale, with animals performing the parts of men.   How it
will be got over, time alone will show, and the dissension,
if the practical party carry the day, may probably cost the
society a few subscribers.

The one objection to this charitable refuge is, that it is
always trembling on the verge of absurdity.   Its whole
proceedings can hardly be so managed that they shall not
appear to be a parody of institutions for the relief of human
suffering ; and it is only by a process of reasoning that we
become its friends and supporters.   The society stands
upon firm ground when it claims the dog as the devoted
companion of man ; and it is assailable only in details—
never in principle.   The *reductio ad absurdam* argument is
easily brought to bear upon these details, and it is just as
easily employed in the defence of the society.   Adopting
the London tradition, that all stray dogs are converted into
sausages, it can soon be shown that the Home must have
an effect upon that particular trade, by cutting off the
supply of the raw material.   From this we jump to the conclusion that all opponents of the dog charity must be connected with the sausage interest, or must have a large
capital invested in the pork-pie business.   We have much
pleasure in placing this argument at the service of the
Society.

UNHAPPY DOGS.

THERE is a common proverb which tells us to give a dog an ill name and hang him. We have complied with one part of the request, but not with the other. We have given the dog one of the most terrible of names—that of hydrophobia—but we have not exterminated him. Liverpool lately made itself ridiculously notorious by the massacre of some six hundred dogs, but its example has fortunately not been followed by any other important city. The dog, in spite of the fearful imputation which hangs over him, and the panic-stricken brutality of the Liverpool police, still holds his place as the most cherished companion of man. He is suspected by police authorities, and muzzled by Act of Parliament in England and France with different degrees of ingenious cruelty, but he is still the chosen friend of old and young. The children find in him a toy which perpetually renews its freshness; and mothers, as Doctor John Brown truthfully puts it, find in him a perpetual infant. He is not allowed to work—also by Act of Parliament—but he relieves his restless idleness by becoming the guardian of property. He has even survived a tax —also imposed by Act of Parliament—which is not, however, collected with very severe regularity, if he is wise enough not to bark at the tax-gatherer.

With so many excellent institutions, some of them

founded for his special benefit—with a Society for the Prevention of Cruelty to Animals, and a Home for Lost and Starving Dogs, which has lived through all the false ridicule showered on its birth, it seems a pity that some authoritative inquiry has not been instituted before this as to the reality of what is called hydrophobia. No disease to which doctors ever gave a name has been surrounded by so many vulgar errors, and the belief in it which exists in the popular mind may be placed on the same level as a belief in witchcraft. One by one, nearly all the supposed characteristics of the disease have been given up by medical men, and yet they are still articles of faith with the majority of the public. Nearly every week, during the occasionally hot months of summer, we are called upon to read " another case of hydrophobia." How many cases of this kind are reported every year it is impossible to say, but probably many hundreds, and yet the last report of the Registrar-General contains the following remarkable statement :—" There was only one death from hydrophobia in the year." Are we to believe the official record, or the village doctors? If real cases of this kind are so rare, where do such medical men get that experience which can alone qualify them to certify that a patient dies of hydrophobia? Though the name of the disease implies a horror of water, and a horror of water is now known not to be a distinctive sign of hydrophobia, the name is still retained. Though people really suffering from this affliction—call it by what name we will —are known not to foam at the mouth, not to go on all fours like an animal, not to bark, not to fly from drink, not to be relieved if the dog recovers or is brained, as usual, by a ready butcher, all these signs are duly recorded. Whether such records are the result of a distempered imagination, a foregone conclusion, exaggerated hearsay, or careless observation, it is impossible to tell, and where so much doubt exists we may be pardoned for trusting only to science. Science tells us that a so-called mad dog does not foam at the mouth, that he is generally afflicted with a burning thirst, that his ferocity is only shown in an inclination to bite dogs, and that he is exceptionally kind to his human companions. We have even been warned to beware of excessive affection as one of the recognized signs of his approaching madness. The question of dog-madness—or rabies, as it is technically called —being caused by thirst in hot weather has been put to the test of experiment. Dogs have repeatedly been tied up in the so-called dog-days, and kept without water, but though they have died under this privation, they have shown no signs of rabies. Their martyrdom was cruel, but it has not benefited their species. The "distemper"—a common disease with dogs, which is easily cured by a few hours' confinement in the dark—is nearly always confounded with madness. If a dog walks with his tongue out in July and August, or runs with moderate speed in a straight line, or turns round, or does almost anything except keep out of sight, he is at once proclaimed mad by the popular voice, and his brains are dashed out in a frenzy of excitement. This is not cruelty—for the dog has no kinder friends, a little dog-fighting excepted, than the lower classes—but gross, honest ignorance. July and August are the two months of peril for the dog, because the public and the police authorities have so willed it; though it ought to be known that April, November, and December can show three cases of so-called dog-madness for one in the hottest months. While this disease is so obstinately associated in England with hot weather, it is curious that South America, the East Indies, Egypt, and Equatorial Africa should be free from hydrophobia. We leave professional medical writers to explain this evident contradiction.

It strikes us, as it must strike any impartial observer, that the dog has been far from fairly treated in this matter. There is undoubtedly a disease which attacks human beings, and which shows itself in such signs as inflammation of the windpipe, gullet, or stomach, accompanied by a choking sensation, to relieve which the patient coughs, perhaps somewhat peculiarly, and certainly desperately. This cough has been magnified into a bark, not, we are afraid, without early medical sanction; and a French writer on the subject has even tried, not very successfully, to convey a notion of it by musical notation. The attempt to connect the dog with this painful and sometimes fatal disease is too often made by questions which lead up to a foregone conclusion. If not recently bitten by a dog, he is asked if he was ever so bitten, and there are few people who could not fancy they had received such a bite at one time or another. A question like this will naturally act upon the imagination, the commonest faculty possessed by mankind, and then the hydrophobiac symptoms will probably begin. A case is recorded of a maid servant who is said to have died of the disease merely from seeing her mistress vomit while labouring under hydrophobia, and another in which a dying young man recovered when the dog which bit him was brought into the room and shown to be perfectly sane. Such cases will show what imagination may do for the growth of hydrophobia; but why should the dog be alone saddled with the responsibility of this terrible disease? If medical works are to be relied upon, a cat, a pig, a cock, a rat, a duck, and a badger, can all propagate hydrophobia; and horses, apes, camels, bullocks, bears, and monkeys are held, when rabid, to possess the same dreadful power. The knowledge of this ought to relieve the dog from some share of odium, though we should be sorry to see the other animals condemned without better evidence. The horse is comparatively safe, because he costs more money than the dog, but even he has been accused of giving his master the glanders.

This question of hydrophobia always turns up at least once a year, to be discussed with more or less doubt and prejudice. Some little time ago " Blackwood's Magazine " promised a series of articles on this subject. The first, evidently written to support the old foregone conclusion, was published, but the rest never appeared, being stopped, we presume, by an exhaustive reply from Mr. Moy Thomas. It would have been well if the series had been continued, for the more discussion we have the better. Here is a disease of some kind which has been popularly fathered upon the dog, though nearly every creature can produce it, so we are told, except canaries and infants. We have something like authentic records to tell us that it has been caused by the bite of a man, and one case is narrated in full detail by Dr. Le Dulx in the fifth volume of the " Transactions of the Batavian Society." The name of place and date are duly given. After stating that on the 17th of March, 1789, information was laid before the court of justice that a man named Van Vliet, " a writer," had stabbed himself in a fit of madness, the learned doctor continues :—

" The court proceeded to the place without delay, attended by the town-surgeon, Lombart, where they found the patient, by direction of the surgeon attending him, bound, and in strong convulsions, particularly of the eyes. The family being interrogated as to the origin of his com-

plaint, related that, four or five days previous to the act,
the patient had a quarrel with a friend, which proceeded
to a furious scuffle; when his antagonist, finding himself
not a match for the patient, in a moment of rage bit him
in the arm. The wound was bound up in the usual way,
without the least idea being entertained of the dreadful
consequences which a bite, thus made, in the heat of
passion, was capable of producing. Three days after this
happened, the patient was attacked with fever; but still no
particular regard was had to the wound. The surgeon who
attended, observed that he was in a state of continued
delirium; that he had a great antipathy to every kind of
medicine, and, in particular, a strong aversion to water.
On the fourth day, the surgeon, on entering the apartment,
found him stabbing himself with a knife. With some difficulty they seized and bound him down upon a sofa. On
the town surgeon being sent for, he offered him a spoonful
of water, which he refused; but on being told it was *gin*,
he endeavoured with great difficulty to swallow it. When
a glass of water was presented to him, the most ghastly
spasmodic convulsions were observable in his face, and
over his whole body, accompanied with such a degree of
terror, that he exclaimed, '*Water, oh! Jesus have mercy
on me!*' His terror increased on wiping his bloody hands
with a wet napkin, when, in convulsive agonies, he called
out, '*Oh! God, water!*' Perceiving clearly that hydrophobia had supervened from the bite received in anger, we
resolved to treat him accordingly; but he died in the afternoon of the same day."

We are also told that this disease may be produced by
eating beech-nuts. If beech-nuts will play us false like this,
what shall we think of truffles? When no bite of any
animal can be had, and beech-nuts are out of reach, there is

what is called spontaneous hydrophobia, spoken of by Mr. Samuel Cooper in his "First Laws of the Practice of Surgery." Dr. Watson, who had a long and extensive practice both in private and in the hospitals, never met with more than four cases of hydrophobia, one of which arose from the bite of a cat, and another from the slightest bite of a sane terrier.

The great John Hunter tells of a case he had heard of, where "twenty-one persons were bitten by a mad dog," only one of whom became affected, "and he," as the doctor sneeringly remarks, was "not the first nor the last, nor the most lacerated." He adds, "Little more of this disease is known than was known a thousand years back; and if any medicine had been given to these people we should have said we had found a specific that succeeded in curing twenty out of the twenty-one."

Mr. Youatt, the well-known writer on dogs, certainly believed in hydrophobia, but his experience hardly sustains the popular opinion as to the fatal and communicative character of rabies. He says:—"My hands have been repeatedly covered with the foam of rabid dogs, and I have been bitten by them much oftener than I liked."

When an animal so faithful and necessary to man as the dog is found labouring under a murderous imputation, which is based upon such very slender and conflicting evidence, it is surely only just and humane to call for a calm and scientific inquiry. We have left off burning witches, but we have still a vast capacity for superstition, and perhaps this belief in dog-madness and its consequences may be equally degrading.

AN OFFICIAL MYSTERY.

THE British Museum is full of wonders, which every Englishman believes himself familiar with. We have all some recollection of sneezing amongst Egyptian mummies; of laughing at images which were gods in New Zealand, but which are walking-sticks in Great Britain; and of trying to admire a small portion of human leg on a platter, represented in stone, which we have been taught to consider a splendid relic of Grecian sculpture.

If any person speaks of the great building which contains these rarities, we call it a "wonderful place;" if he speaks of the rarities, we call them a "wonderful collection." We are not generally aware, when we apply these terms, that the Museum is more entitled to claim them than we probably imagine.

The chief and comparatively unnoticed wonder of the British Museum is the fact that it is closed for nearly half the year, excluding Sundays, and excepting the library. It is a marvel not catalogued or explained in any history of this national institution, why the "public" should only be admitted on Monday, Wednesday, and Friday, and on Saturday afternoons, and should be turned away by a policeman, an armed soldier, and a lodge-keeper, all day on Tuesday and Thursday, and on Saturday mornings. The British sightseer must be a very formidable character, when he requires at least three forms of authority,—the civil, the military, and the official,—to keep him out of what is really his property. For nearly a month every year the place is entirely closed, during which time the policeman, the soldier, and the gatekeeper may snatch a holiday. This month, which is made up of different periods and days, may be set aside for the painter, the carpenter, and the charwoman. We only guess this. There is no " blue-book" on the subject, as far as we are aware; and we are only part of the general " public."

With regard to what is done within the building during the two days and a half every week on which the " public" is turned back, we are equally at a loss for information. We have our suspicions, and they point to a little " sky-larking." We cannot believe that this splendid building is used to cover any criminal proceedings,—such as coining, forging, or private distilling. We cannot believe that any of the Museum curiosities are like the conjuror's mechanical tricks, requiring hours of preparation for minutes of exhibition. We think that the games of " push-pin," draughts, " ring-taw," and cribbage may be freely indulged in, combined, perhaps, with a little boxing, fencing, and leap-frog, or hide-and-seek amongst the sarcophagi. We are led to this conclusion because we are bound to believe that a certain number of attendants are always on duty, and we never hear that any of them become lunatics or suicides. The Museum must be a dreadfully dull place on these Tuesdays, Thursdays, and half-Saturdays.

If we are wrong in all these surmises, we can soon be set right : a free admission on the " off-days" would clear up the mystery. We are not " artists," and refuse to go in under cover of this fiction. We can apply for and accept no ticket or privilege without candidly stating our object.

Such ticket or privilege has been refused us under these circumstances, and we may, therefore, assume that the "authorities" are opposed to investigation.

There was a time when these authorities, these eight-and-forty mixed and irresponsible trustees, with their faithful acting-officers, might have defended the sealing up of the so-called British Museum for more than one half of the working year, by referring to the necessity for keeping the building clean, the contents in perfect order and preservation, and the "students" private. This time,—this fine, old, crusted, Tory, obstructive time,—has long since been swept away by Radical institutions like the South Kensington Museum. In this latter exhibition the public is admitted every day in the week, every week in the year, of course excepting Sundays, Christmas-day, and Good-Friday. It is not found that dirt, disorder, and destruction prevail at South Kensington, although the hours during which it is open throughout the year are *four times as many* as the similar hours at the British Museum. It is true that a small admission fee of sixpence is demanded at South Kensington on the three "students' days" of the week, which are Wednesdays, Thursdays, and Fridays; but then the South Kensington Museum is largely self-supporting, while the British Museum is formed and maintained out of the taxes. Private collections may be left, and have been left, to both institutions, but these are not sufficiently numerous or important to alter the character of either museum. Deducting the paying days at South Kensington, we shall still have twice as many free hours of opening as at the so-called British Museum, more conveniently timed, it may be, for the general public. The practical operation of such an exclusive system in the old Tory institution of

Great Russell Street is to destroy one-half of this great national collection. Property is only valuable when it is used, and only a name when it is idly hoarded. Putting it arithmetically, and assuming the contents of the British Museum to be valued at a hundred millions sterling, the result is precisely the same, whether you take away one-half of the time during which you exhibit the collection, or one-half of the collection you have to exhibit. Fifty millions sterling of property exhibited during the whole working year is equal to one hundred millions sterling of property exhibited only half the year.

The mingled folly and injustice of this British Museum mismanagement is not altogether extended to the British Museum library. There is a reason for this. The library is largely used by "literary men," and literary men have pens and organs with which to enforce their claims. The present freedom, long hours, and six days a-week of the British Museum library were not voluntarily granted by sympathizing trustees and officials to an intellectual and refined class, they had to be fought for like any other popular right. There is no reason why books and prints should be treated as something different from specimens and antiquities. They both convey instruction ; but that is not the question. They both belong to the public, and the public ought to enjoy them. The library is tolerably free to every "studious person," as the trustees phrase it, and many novel-readers, devourers of "improper" books, and epicures in English *de*-composition, appear to be included under this title. As friends of free museums we are not about to complain of this, but of a certain inquisitorial authority claimed by the chief librarian, under the sanction of the trustees, to look over the work or study of every reader. When a man has applied for a "library ticket" in the prescribed form, has given the usual professional or householder reference,

and has obtained the sacred privilege, he naturally ima-
gines he can refer to any of the national books for any purpose short of mutilation. He is quite mistaken. The proprietors of two respectable trade journals have lately tried
the question. We know that mere trade journals are very
vulgar things, they are not "literature," they are not meta-
physical, they are not even genteelly topographical. It is
difficult to sympathize with their objects ; far more difficult
to stand up as their champions. The conductors of these
two journals wished to compile two *trade directories*, a
dreadfully utilitarian task, with nothing of poetry, obscurity, or mysticism about it. They went to the British
Museum library to collect materials, because they found
there the only complete set of trade directories in the whole
kingdom. They complied with the Museum regulations,
procured their tickets, began their work, were overlooked,
and finally expelled, without appeal, by Mr. Panizzi and the
trustees, because they did not come under the category of
"studious persons." It was not pretended that their
labour was of a nature to injure any existing copyrights;
the managers of the great hotbed of "paste and scissors"
authors could hardly say that; but they were not "studious
persons." Utility had marked them for her own, and the
chief librarian must cast them out. The managers of the
British Museum library (under the compulsory provisions
of the "Copyright Act," by which a copy of every work
published in the United Kingdom must be deposited in
the Museum library by the publisher before a copy can be
legally sold), are determined to gather the only perfect collection of trade and general directories in the country, and
then prevent English tax-payers from using them. The
story is new, and perfectly true, and calculated to eclipse
that of the "dog in the manger."

The legislature sometimes condescends to speak of British Museum reform, when it can spare time from the squabbles and complications of universal government. Without going into the vexed questions of official salaries, and the sub-division of contents, there ought to be no rest on the part of *domestic* politicians, until a collection of untold value ceases to be shut up for half the year, and the library is no longer the gilded plaything of those who appear to have forgotten their real masters.

THE COTTON FAMINE.

THE heavy distress which is falling upon Lancashire and those portions of Yorkshire, Derbyshire, and Cheshire which come within the cotton manufacturing district is now the talk of the world. Few right-thinking men can prevent its black shadow flitting across their minds, and haunting them like the wailing of sick children, or a corpse in the next room. Their sympathy with such distress refuses to be hemmed in by poor-law barriers, because they see in it nothing of professional mendicancy, or the pauperism of a degraded population. They know that a heavy blow has fallen on a self-reliant, almost a defiant body of men, who from childhood have been used to comfort and independence. They know that a class who would starve rather than beg are now standing sulkily at silent street corners, or lounging idly in stagnant market-places, stripped of all their little savings, and reduced almost to the level of workhouse parasites. They know that this misery is endured without murmuring, for the sake of a great principle. A blockade is respected which could be broken through like a cobweb, and a great moral example is set to all powerful nations. If the dreaded winter now close upon us should show half the endurance on the part of the poor which is hoped for, and half the liberality on the part of the rich which is sought for, the force of this great moral example will be increased a hundred-fold. The cloud, as usual, will have a silver lining, and starving Lancashire will be as impressive in its misery as it has ever been in the days of its greatest prosperity.

The statistics of cotton-working—an industry which in its sudden growth and importance is one of the world's wonders—have often been collected with pride and eagerness ; but now the task of gathering such facts and figures is laborious and depressing. This is no time, nor subject for so-called graphic writing ; for highly-coloured pictures of that distress which may be seen in the gloomy, stony-hearted streets, or of that less obtrusive want which hides itself away in the dull, red-brick houses. This is no time for engaging suffering families in conversation with the sole view of recording their words, and enlivening a cold but well-meaning report with snatches of dramatic dialogue. All those who have hovered on the borders of the distress—and no mere literary eavesdroppers can do more—must have felt that only one duty was required of them ; to aid the distress funds in every way by gathering and sifting facts, and setting them before the public as simply as possible.

The population of the cotton-working district may be taken roundly as 3,000,000, and this includes about 380,000 operatives. Of this later number at least 200,000, or more than one-half, are at present entirely out of work, or doing work that will not support them. An operative can live on three days' work ; he has had to do so before now when the markets were glutted, as they were in 1847, but he can hardly exist on a shilling a week. The average earnings of each worker in a family are from 9s. to 10s. 6d. a week in good times. His rent of 3s. or 4s. a week for his little stone-floored house is, of course, seldom paid in such times as these ; it accumulates as a debt against him, or it is given to him by the kindness of masters who happen to be his landlords. Much is given in this way which makes no show in the accounts of the various funds. One holder of house property at Blackburn, nominally worth £20,000, is now receiving scarcely any income from his rents ; and many more such cases may be found throughout the district. One large millowner has lent his workmen about £3000, to enable them to tide over the evil hour, and out of this more than £1000 will certainly never be returned ; others prefer to keep their work-people entirely during the pressure of the distress, rather than see them hanging hopelessly about town-halls and soup-kitchens. Many are working their mills at a loss to give employment to their work-people. While it is important that every local and general fund should be well supported by those who are able to give, such facts as these cannot be too generally known when the conduct of the masters is called in question. Self-interest alone, without any higher motive, will impel employers to keep their operatives together, and this can be done much better by individuals than through the agency of a committee.

The funds at present raised by subscription may be roughly stated at £150,000, and of this amount Manchester contributes £28,000, Liverpool £30,000, the Lord Mayor's fund £50,000, and the Landowners of Lancashire, under the head of the Bridgewater House Fund, £40,000. Landed property in the cotton-working district, according to a reliable estimate, has increased five-and-twenty per cent. in value during the last ten years.

The towns that have already made application to the different funds for relief are shown in the following table, which gives some interesting details about their condition and prospects :—

Town or District.	Population.	No. of Mills.	Working Full Time.	Working 4 or 5 Days.	Working 3 Days.	Working 2 Days or under.	Out of Work.
				SHORT TIME.			
Ashton-under-Lyne	34,500	86	1,327		7,279		2,100
Blackburn	63,125	127	7,088		6,635		13,321
Bollington	5,447	7	1,200		115		859
Burnley	35,766	100	...		5,705		4,978
Belmont	1,009	3	...		205		117
Broadbottom and Charlesworth	3,402	7	70		252		1,550
Chorley	15,013	21	1,562		1,416		1,311
Crompton	7,952	59	15		1,516		1,107
Dukinfield	16,000	16	54		1,278		4,703
Glossop	11,000	19	1,016		5,514		203
Hyde	17,190	20	910		6,059		1,558
Heaton-Mersey	2,900	1	107		183		214
Hurst	6,220	4	191		1,115		464
Livesey	3,887	12	130		802		2,292
Manchester and Salford	440,478	380	31,907		19,474		15,702
Mossley	4,545	16	1,014		2,186		1,115
Macclesfield	27,172	3	...		...		200
Oldham	72,334	160	4,568		8,467		9,345
Padiham	5,404	22	580		600		34
Preston	82,942	70	6,581		8,597		11,610
Rochdale	50,000	93	561		5,009		8,364
Royton	7,500	21	434		917		1,163
Ribchester	1,357	1	48		139		100
Ramsbottom	7,400	25	1,160		950		438
Stockport	54,861	67	2,620		8,853		6,494
Stalybridge	24,806	22	1,614		6,379		2,351
Stacksteads	5,000	15	150		650		1,410
Shuttleworth	3,000	11	86		181		211
Tonge cum Alkington	5,500	11	217		557		750
Tentwistle	7,000	15	470		2,736		632
Wigan	37,675	25	80		500		9,350 1 factory all out
Walton-le-Dale	5,257	5	...		...		1 factory all out
Catterall	765	1	...		...		350
Millbrook	1,500	1	...		800		350
Wilton	2,291	2	177		38		712
	1,071,785	1809	65,107		107,398		94,818

Mr. J. W. Maclure, the energetic Secretary of the Manchester Relief Committee, to whom I am much indebted for much valuable information, writes to say that £50,000 have been already raised and spent in Manchester, Blackburn, Preston, Wigan, Stockport, and four or five other towns, independently of all that has been done by private charity.

The weekly loss of wages in the district is now at least £100,000, and this loss will probably be increased during the winter to £150,000 a week. At the lowest estimate, the sum required weekly to support the unemployed operatives at the rate of two shillings a week per head, will before Christmas exceed the ordinary poor-rates by £30,000. One Manchester gentleman, who has considerable means of judging, estimates that when the distress reaches its height, it will cost £100,000 a week to keep the unemployed from starvation.

Mr. Farnell, the Government Poor-Law Commissioner, now reports, after an elaborate analysis of the accounts of twenty-four unions, whose population is usually employed to a great extent in the manufacture of cotton, that 140,165 persons are now in receipt of parochial relief, although in the corresponding week of last year the numbers were only 42,054. This shows an increase of 98,111 persons receiving parish relief, all of whom are able-bodied workmen, workwomen, and their children.

The rates to meet this distress will probably be from three to five shillings in the pound, and this from the poverty of many of the ratepayers, will increase the burden on those who can pay to seven or eight shillings. The operation of Mr. Villiers's Relief Act will do little to mitigate the severity of the pressure of the rates upon the class immediately above that of the operatives, inasmuch as no one parish can claim assistance from the other parishes of the union until three shillings in the pound has been spent on the poor, nor can the borrowing powers be exercised until an amount equivalent to three shillings in the pound on the assessment of the whole union has been collected in addition to the borough and other rates; and, lastly, the county cannot be called upon to contribute to the relief of any particular union until five shillings in the pound has been actually spent upon the poor of the union. A very high authority estimates that in many cases it will be necessary to levy six shillings in the pound before three shillings can be collected; and the same authority admits that these clauses so far neutralize the action of Mr. Villiers's Bill that most probably the borrowing power will rarely, and the County Rate-in-Aid clause never, be put in force. It may appear that three shillings, or even six shillings in the pound, is not a large sum to be spent upon the poor; but the real question is the proportion that the future rates will bear to those of former years. In some cases the average rates have only been about eight-pence in the pound, and the call will therefore be four or five times as much as the usual rates. This, when the insolvent ratepayers are deducted, will leave a rate eight or ten times larger than the ordinary demand to be paid by those who remain solvent.

A deputation from Birmingham, appointed for the purpose of collecting information regarding the extent of the distress, and the claim of the operatives for aid from that town, have reported fully and ably on these and other points, and they earnestly urge the inhabitants not to act as if they doubted the charity of the north, but to do all in their power to soften the sting of a great and undeserved calamity.

Speaking of Stockport amongst other places, they say, "In a population of 57,000, a diminution of £7500 has already taken place in the amount of weekly wages. Two-thirds of the deposits in the Savings' Bank, representing probably the whole of the savings of the cotton operatives, have been withdrawn. The small shopkeepers are unable to give credit any longer. One man stated that he had

£100 worth of debts which he never expected to recover. The pawnbrokers are full, and have ceased to lend. The inhabitants of the district have already themselves subscribed and distributed £4000 in addition to the contributions from a distance, which is equivalent to more than £20,000 from a town of the size of Birmingham. Yet the real troubles have scarcely commenced."

The operatives of Lancashire are sometimes better, but never worse, than fellow-labourers of the same standing in other parts of the country. Their savings are small and soon exhausted, as they are accustomed to rely upon a steady demand for their labour. The children in the cotton-working district have a well-known value in good times—a power of earning money, which they exercise to the fullest extent. They are sturdy, self-confident, and a little self-indulgent, but few people can blame them for the last failing. Now that adversity has fallen upon them, their rugged, untameable spirit sustains them in their troubles, and prevents them sinking into abject alms-seekers. Professional beggars, especially in Manchester, have not been slow to seek an expected harvest in the name of Lancashire distress, but the real operatives make no flaunting display of their want. Crime has decreased throughout the district, though drunkenness has slightly increased; the latter probably owing to a falling off in physical strength on the part of the drinkers, and the well-meaning but mistaken hospitality of companions who are working on full or short time. Every cotton town I have passed through shows the same melancholy picture of enforced idleness. The atmosphere has an unwonted clearness; the roaring of engines is missed; there is more clanking of clogs on the stony pathways in the afternoons, and the most honest, hard-working men and women who loll in doorways, or squat in groups by the roadside, have that skulking look which always marks a want of occupation.

Amidst all this misery and stagnation one question constantly arises—When will relief come? How long will this material of our great staple manufacture be wanting? When may we hope that this terrible dearth, which for the first time in the world's history has attached the ominous word "famine" to a want which is only in its consequences a want of food, may cease, and England once more reckon Lancashire among the most industrious, peaceable, and orderly of its manufacturing counties? The question is one of vital importance, not only to Lancashire, but to all England, and not only to the present but to future time. Every economist will tell you of the terrible mischief of lowering for any length of time the standard of comfort and decency in a large section of the population. It is this standard alone which determines the numbers of the people, and the condition in which they live. If the steady mechanics of these parts, whose rooms before these "hard times" were always clean and neat, and not without tokens of their owners living in some degree above that state in which life is absorbed in a struggle for mere food,—if these people had been content to sink into filth and misery, such as may be seen in many quarters of all great cities, there was nothing to prevent them but their own prudence, stimulated and supported by that self-respect and taste for comfort and decency, which was the average spirit of their class. Weaken this spirit, or obliterate it for a time, and it is impossible to say how much of it may be found remaining when the better day comes. Misery loses its repulsiveness like other things by familiarity. It has a constant tendency to perpetuate itself in new generations, who necessarily imbibe their ideas and habits from the scene in which they are reared. There can be little doubt that the proverbial misery of weavers originated in the enormous influx of French refugees during the great religious persecutions in the south of France; and a sudden increase in the supply of labour which sank the weaver's wages so low, and steeped them so completely in wretchedness, that they have never yet recovered from their original misfortune. Even the great inventions in machinery, though inestimable blessings to all classes, have not always been unattended with this unfortunate drawback, as we see with the stockingers of Leicester. The depression which a sudden loss of wages brings to an industrious people who are unable to turn to other employments, is, indeed, always more or less attended with this effect; and it is, therefore, a matter of incalculable importance that the Lancashire people should, as far as possible, be encouraged to keep up their spirit. This can, of course, only be hoped for on the assumption that they may look soon to resume their daily life of independent industry.

What are the chances of supplies? It is singular how little sound information can be obtained on this point. In the United States very accurate and extensive agricultural statistics have always been collected and published, both of the Northern and Southern States. There the amount of land sown, and extent of the crops of cotton, corn, and maize in each year, have always been familiar to persons interested in such matters. In no other cotton-growing country, however, does such a system prevail. In India, that vast continent of political and social darkness, nothing is known. We can but suppose that rumours of the high prices prevailing last autumn may have reached some of the native cotton growers, and that some may have been induced to sow a greater breadth than usual. Whatever

may be said of the apathy of Indian cultivators, there can
be no doubt that the ordinary instincts of self-interest are
no more wanting in them than in other people. The
6,000,000 of bales rashly vouched for by Lord Shaftesbury
as already existing in India, and waiting for speculative
purchasers, are clearly visionary. The enormous rise in
the price of cotton in Bombay, reported by recent mails,
would assuredly have brought them ere this from their
lurking places in spite of mountains and bad roads. In
countries nearer to the United States, and more susceptible
to the influence of news from thence, it is more reasonable
at present to look for a large increase; and it is really
wonderful how vast an extent of territory exists in which
cotton *may* be grown. The cotton zone may be roughly
said to comprise one-third of the habitable globe. From
Virginia to Paraguay, there is no spot on the two great
American continents where cotton cannot be grown. The
entire continent of Africa, including Madagascar, is cotton
land. The south of Spain, Italy, Greece, Turkey in Europe,
Asia Minor, Arabia, Persia, Turkestan, India, Thibet, China,
the Indian Archipelago, and the whole continent of Australia
north of Sydney and Swan River, are equally suited to the
cultivation of this plant. If we take a map, and mark the
places where it is generally grown for export, we shall
find that they form but a few insignificant spots upon this
vast belt of cotton-growing country. There is scarcely one
of these places having access to seaports, where a planter
who had been sharp enough to grow cotton, or if he was
already a cotton grower, to extend the area of his operations this year, would not at present prices be enabled to
obtain a splendid profit. Happily the cotton crop does not
require very long preparation. It is not like hops or vines,
necessary to plant and wait for several seasons ere the

plant will produce its fruit. Except in Algeria, where, we
believe, it is customary to look to the second year for the
best results of a planting, the cotton bush is almost everywhere cultivated as an annual. This, at all events, is the
custom with the American growers, hitherto the most successful cultivators of cotton in the world. It is, indeed,
usual with them to prepare their land in November, when
they plough and harrow down, and subsequently throw the
soil into ridges to experience the beneficial effects of the
winter frosts; but the actual sowing does not commence
till March or April, and when there is any frost lingering
about is even deferred as late as May.

A very interesting experiment lately ventured on by the
United States Government, of which I have just obtained
information, shows how quickly cotton may be produced if
the season is not allowed to pass wholly by. It will be in the
recollection of most readers that, in the autumn of last
year, an expedition was fitted out by the Federal Government, for a descent upon the coasts and islands of South
Carolina. As regards the islands, no resistance whatever
was offered. The planters fled to the mainland, having
destroyed what property they could, and taken with them
their cattle, furniture, agricultural implements, and the best
of their slaves. When Commodore Dupont took possession
of the islands, he found that a number of slaves, composed
in great part of old people, women, and young children, and
amounting altogether to 10,000 persons, had been left
behind. Crops of cotton just fit for picking being left
standing in the fields, the Government determined to set
to work such of their number as had been used to field
labour—in all about 3800 persons—to gather in the cotton,
as free labourers working for trifling wages. They thus
successfully gathered more than 110,000 pounds of fine

sea-island cotton, some of which has been sold for about
three shillings sterling per pound. These sea islands, as is
well known, give the name to this peculiarly beautiful
variety of American cotton. It always bears a high price,
although, from its being more difficult to cultivate and less
productive per acre, it is not generally considered peculiarly
profitable, and the demand for it is of course not extensive.
It being impossible to neglect these 10,000 negroes, who had
shown themselves remarkably docile and patient under the
direction of their new employers, some philanthropists in
Boston and Philadelphia urged upon the Government the
necessity for setting them again to work; but this time
not in picking only, but in cultivating a new crop. No
step, however, was taken. It was not until March of this
year that the philanthropists succeeded, and not till the
beginning of April that they actually went to work upon
the ground. Everything was most unpromising for the
experiment. It was already late in the season, and no
preparations had been made. They were wanting in implements, in ploughs, and in horses; few of the superin-
tendents sent from the North had ever seen a cotton plant
growing in the field, and some of them had no practical
knowledge of agriculture. They were strangers to the
country, the people, the usages, the climate, and had nothing
to depend on but their goodwill for the work, and the cheerful
alacrity of the blacks. Lost time, however, was soon re-
gained. Fourteen thousand acres were brought under
successful culture; and, more than a month ago, an intelligent gentleman, appointed to reside in the islands, and
watch the progress of the cultivation, reported that the
crops were " in an advanced and satisfactory state, needing
little more than a few weeks of ordinary fair weather to
insure a liberal harvest."

If results like these may be achieved under such conditions, by cultivators who started on their business for the first time only at the end of last March, it is clear that we may reasonably hope that a considerable increase in the cultivation will have taken place this year in most countries which have been accustomed to export any quantity at all. It cannot be said that as late as last March any rational man could have a doubt that a cotton crop, if in ordinary times remunerative, or even nearly remunerative, must this year be profitable in the highest degree. Theorists and unprofessional speculators may talk of the danger of the great cotton crop of America being suddenly let loose to flood the markets of the world, and rob the new competitor of his expected prize; but the self-interest of practical cultivators, to whom judging of market prospects is a daily habit, must have taught them better. Of what is going on in that sealed country we know little; but while cotton bonfires have been blazing wherever the Northern armies have penetrated, we may be sure that cotton growing has almost entirely ceased to be a part of the agricultural industry of the South. Compelled to be entirely self-supporting, her available labour, or so much as can be spared from military duties, must long ago have been turned entirely into other channels. To produce food and clothing, and arms, evidently taxes all her energies. Her 10,000,000 of people, including her soldiers, have been clothed from head to foot in cotton; and this consumption, necessarily lavish where the article is so abundant, and the waste and destruction of war, must already have made considerable inroads into the 3,000,000 bales of 1861. In February last, or let us say in March, it was quite certain that no crop would be grown this year. It is impossible to doubt that the planters of Brazil and Guiana, and other parts of the great cotton-growing countries of South America, were fully aware of these facts; and they must be singularly unlike all other human beings if they have not to some extent endeavoured to profit by them; nor can there be any doubt that Egypt, Algeria, the West India Islands, not to speak of the new cotton districts in Africa and Eastern Australia, will contribute considerably to relieve the markets.

It is consolatory to know that we cannot now be many weeks before we come to some solution of this problem. In the United States, if the season has been forward and favourable, the cotton-picking will commence in July; but if backward, the first general picking will be delayed till August. Successive pickings take place—the wool is "ginned," that is, cleared of seed, packed in bales, and sent to market at once; and it is with the planters a maxim, that by November the crop should be all baled and sent to market.

These facts are, of course, applicable to similar climates; but in India the times of sowing and picking are altogether different. From that country we can look for no relief until the spring of next year. The sowing season in India commences generally in June, but is prolonged till July or August in some parts. The crop matures about the beginning of February in some cases, but as a rule, the picking extends through March, and frequently into April. The speculators of Bombay, who, according to the late advices, had bid Surat—which sells in ordinary times for 3d. or 4d.—up to 1s. 2d. a pound, are assuredly keeping their eye upon this time. All things considered, it undoubtedly appears to be an advantage that the Indian crop is sown not in the spring but in autumn; for the Indian growers were probably not thoroughly aroused to the subject before the recent extraordinary rise in prices in their own markets.

Readers who derive their information solely from writers who pen diatribes upon the "apathy" of mill-owners, and their neglect of Indian cotton, must be under the belief that it is an entirely new thing to seek in India for relief from pressure in the markets for American cotton. This, however, is altogether a mistake. India has always acted as a sort of reservoir for supplying us in times of partial dearth. Even in ordinary times it has been usual for us to draw one-fourth or one-fifth of the whole amount of our enormous consumption from that country. It is curious, indeed, to observe how regularly and surely this safety-valve has acted. It may be safely said that the mill-owners have always obtained from India just so much of that cheaper but inferior kind of cotton grown by the Hindoos as the British public were willing to clothe themselves with. Any one who has ever walked through one of the busy shopping streets in the poor neighbourhoods in the suburbs of London, must have observed at inferior linen-drapers' and hosiers' shops, lengths of cotton cloth manufactured from it; which are always distinguishable for their bad colour, and the black specks which abound in them, and which are the chief features of bad quality. In ordinary times, not even the extraordinary cheapness of $3d$. a pound has induced our mill-owners to use more than the average proportion we have mentioned; for they are well aware that they would have no sale for it beyond that. In 1852, for instance, we consumed 1,789,100 bales of American cotton, at an average price of $5\frac{3}{8}d$.; while of Indian cotton, which was sold during the same period at an average of $3\frac{1}{4}d$., we used only 221,500 bales. The simple truth is, that if American cotton can be obtained at a reasonable

rate, our comparatively well-clothed and comfortable classes
will not wear Indian. But let the American cotton crop
even partially fail, and the *facts* are altogether changed.
In 1856, for instance, when the average price of the latter
rose to 6*d.*, the imports of East Indian rose to 463,000.
More striking still, in the following year, uplands having
reached an average of 7¼*d.*, East Indian rose to 5⅜*d.*; but
notwithstanding this rise, we imported of the latter the
enormous quantity of 680,000 bales, or within 60,000 of
one-half of the entire quantity of American cotton imported
into Great Britain in that year! After this, who shall say
that our manufacturers have neglected to avail themselves
of Indian cotton?

I have for some years devoted earnest attention to this
subject, and I am compelled to say that I have long come
to the conclusion that the Southern States of America have
hitherto held the market, not in consequence of any
" apathy" in mill-owners, shippers, or growers, or any failure
in the ordinary laws of supply and demand, but for the
simple reason that, on the whole, the balance of advantage
in production has been in their favour. Of course, the
activity of commercial enterprise, under the stimulus of
the present extraordinary range of prices, may help us to
discover some place having equal advantages, either in
climate, soil, labour, existence of capital, or means of communication. Hitherto, however, it must be confessed that
no such place has been found—I mean no place which could
compete with the United States, under ordinary circumstances; for, of course, their advantage may be not very
great, though sufficient to secure to them almost the
monopoly of the markets of the world; and, in this case,
while the war lasts, we may be supplied even by countries
which could not compete in ordinary times, at a scarcely

perceptible increase in price. No other theory than this could, indeed, possibly account for the facts. Just as the East Indian indigo has beaten Brazilian and the indigo of every other country from all the markets of the world, so has American cotton sprung up and flourished until, within sixty years, it has spread itself into the markets of the globe. The cheapness of slave labour alleged by some, denied by others, cannot, whether true or false, be the cause; for slavery exists in Brazil, once a great source of our supply, and yet Brazilian cotton is in ordinary times now scarcely known in our markets. No special affection for Southern planters can be supposed to have captivated the hearts of Liverpool or Manchester. The Liverpool broker cares not whence you bring it; he will take the staple in hand, examine it, pull it out, and tell you its price per bale to a fraction. It may be even said that our trade with America is conducted at a disadvantage, which tends to discourage us from seeking our cotton there. The disadvantage is the difficulty of paying for our imports with British goods. With a tariff always restricted, even before the recent changes, and designed to encourage the native manufactures of the very articles which form the staple of our exports, our merchants have never been able to sell in the United States goods to the amount of more than one-half of our purchases. In 1860, the last year before the war, the raw cotton alone purchased by us of the United States, was worth more than £30,000,000 sterling, the corn and tobacco another £7,000,000, while the whole amount of our purchases of that country, reached a total little short of £45,000,000. Against this, we sent them goods of the declared value, in round numbers, of £23,000,000. The balance is, of course, somewhat less than it appears, the exports being estimated before carriage, the imports after carriage, when, of course, they have become more valuable by all the cost of transport. The balance, however, after all allowance, must be considerable, and must be settled by shipments to other countries, against which bills are drawn —a circuitous mode of payment, which is always burdensome to the country standing most in need of the other's products. The barriers set up by the Americans against the admission of our manufactures, operate, in fact, as obstacles to our purchases, yet these obstacles appear to have had little effect.

No greater mistake can be made than to suppose that American cotton has been unduly favoured, either by prejudice of manufacturers against other kinds, or by apathy of governments. I am convinced that a dispassionate inquirer would come to the conclusion that the late East Indian Government honestly laboured to destroy the Southern planters' monopoly. I have now before me a solid volume of reports and documents connected with the proceedings of the East India Company, in regard to the culture and manufacture of cotton wool in India, printed by order of the East India Company, as long back as December, 1836, which abounds in valuable information on the subject, and which is not superseded by the volume published under the directions of the Supreme Government in Calcutta in the present year. Seventy-four years have elapsed since the Company resolved to give every possible encouragement to the growth and improvement of the plant in that country. They were, it must be remembered, subjected to no pressure from our manufacturers at that period, when our cotton manufactures were comparatively insignificant. Yet the Government exported to India screws for making bales, and distributed seeds throughout the peninsula. It seemed natural that India should supply us with cotton. It was cheaper there than anywhere else. It had been cultivated in Hindostan from the time of Alexander the Great, and probably from still more remote ages, and the quantity already grown there each year was believed to be greater than the production of the remainder of the entire globe. From that time, the East India Company never lost sight of their project. They again and again offered bounties on production of better qualities, gathered reports from all the collectors, and had information and practical instructions printed and distributed wholesale. They have even granted drawbacks both of internal and port duties, to encourage the export. In 1813 and 1814, they brought, at Government expense, a number of American planters to the country, with New Orleans saw-gins. It has indeed been suggested that these men, who all reported unfavourably on the attempt to grow improved qualities for profitable sale, were actuated by a determination to discountenance the project. It requires, however, but little knowledge of human nature to decide that this is improbable. English shipwrights and even English cannon-founders work well enough for the Czar. In all human beings there is a natural desire that the work they are engaged in shall succeed, and secure them the reward of their zeal, which is in the average sufficient to defeat the instincts of such far-seeing patriotism as is here insinuated. Besides, in 1813-14, New Orleans planters must have been endowed with something like prophetic spirit if they foresaw the future importance of cotton-growing to the United States, or the present vital necessity of the supply to Great Britain; for at that time, instead of 3,000,000, the Americans produced only about 200,000 or 300,000 bales; and England, instead of consuming, as at present, two millions and a half, consumed only about

200,000 or 300,000 bales, of which not one-fourth came from America. As late as 1840, the Company employed Captain Bungles to make a tour in the Southern States, and to procure information, seeds, agricultural and mechanical implements; and once more they imported skilled American planters. Soon after this they instituted experimental culture on a very large scale in all the three Presidencies. Among the latest steps taken by them was the gratuitous distribution of two hundred American cotton saw-gins among the three Presidencies, and the offer of a prize of £500 for an improved cotton dressing-machine adapted to native use. Then we have the life-long efforts of private persons, like Mr. Shaw in Dharwar, enthusiastically devoted to the improvement of Indian cotton. Even our war with the United States, when American supplies were almost entirely cut off, only brought Indian cotton into increased use as a makeshift; the proportion used sinking again immediately on the termination of the war. It must be remembered, too, that not only India, but all our possessions, including the West Indies, South Africa, etc., have up to a very recent period been offered a standing premium to compete with American cotton in the differential duties in favour of our own possessions. Still American cotton has held the market, growing yearly with astonishing rapidity. Is it possible then to doubt, however we may wish it otherwise, that up to the present time no place has been found capable of producing cotton of equal quality at the ordinary prices of American—for that is the question. Both in India and Brazil it is said that bad roads impede supplies; but there are large cotton districts in both countries near the sea, and other districts traversed by railways. As to India, the peculiar system of land tenure has been complained of; but this grievance, though

a real one, has certainly not prevented the cultivation of
indigo, opium, or even Assam tea, from reaching a condition of extraordinary prosperity. The late Dr. Royle,
whose extensive knowledge of Indian fibres was no less
notorious than his enthusiasm in favour of Indian products,
confesses that the Indian climate is unfitted for the production of such qualities as we receive from America.

The attempts to improve the cultivation and preparation of Indian cotton may produce some approach to improvement. The active search for new cotton fields; the
experiments now in operation in Natal, in Queensland,
Guinea, Algeria, and other places, may bring permanent
changes: but the use of American cotton has extended
itself under too many disadvantages for us to expect that
it will be soon displaced. It is not improbable that, on
the termination of the civil war, we may in a few seasons
see it again resume something like its old position. The
fact is humiliating; but it is pleasant to think that our
great trial will not wholly have been lost. Cultivators
throughout the globe will have had their minds directed to
the subject; many will have acquired a practical knowledge
of the cultivation which they had not before; all will have
been taught to look to a rise in the price of American
cotton as a signal to ridge up their land and prepare to
sow cotton-seed. The cultivation is, fortunately, very
simple—may be taken up, abandoned, and resumed, with
great facility, and even with advantage to the soil in the
change of crops. The Southern planter lays out the bulk
of his cash in "niggers;" little capital being wanted for
anything else. Give the world notice only in March that
you are likely to want cotton, and any quantity can be
grown against the fall of the year. Private enterprise is
not quite so stupid as some people would have it.

NEEDLEWOMEN.

THERE may be some few occupations followed by women whose hardships have escaped notice, but needlework is certainly not amongst the number. In its various forms, from the stitching of a coal sack, or a pair of fustian trousers in Shoreditch, to the construction of a gauzy court dress as large as a balloon in May Fair, it has received every attention from poets, journalists, and philanthropists. No branch of woman's labour has given birth to so many poetic wails, so many parliamentary investigations, so many letters in the newspapers, and so many suggestions by individuals and private committees.

A quarter of a century has glided by since its most painful features were dragged into the light, and still it continues fruitful of public scandals. If a young woman commits suicide by throwing herself into the river, if a middle-aged woman is found starved to death in a garret or a cellar, if another young woman—more delicately nurtured—is found dead, poisoned by bad air, over-work, and over-crowding in a West End sleeping-loft, the world is never astonished to hear that they were all needlewomen. The name of sempstress is so associated with misery, poverty, and oppression, that such an end is nearly always expected from such an employment.

As usual where very low wages necessarily prevail—

the result of the market being thoroughly glutted with
labourers—the employers are abused for not doing impos-
sibilities.   It is so easy for a mass of clamorous and indignant people to ask somebody to benefit somebody else, that
the request is always loudly made.   Most "charitable suggestions" which appear in the public prints at a time of
great popular excitement on some social question have this
peculiarity, and it is therefore hardly surprising that they
are seldom attended to.   Some of these suggestions or
demands—such as calling upon a particular employer to
pay a sentimental rate of wages for the production of some
article of universal consumption—are made with the most
wonderful obstinacy, stupidity, and regularity.   Though it
may be shown, over and over again, that the employer is
utterly helpless in such a case, that he has no more power
to raise the rate of wages than to raise the tide six hours
before its time, he is still asked and expected to do it.
Because he remains passive, he is abused and pelted with
hard names; is called an oppressor and grinder-down of
the poor, and is pointed at in every way as a fit object to
be sacrificed to popular indignation.   In some cases he is
driven to withdraw his capital from the hateful business,
which diminishes the fund that finds employment for the
workpeople; in others he is driven to encourage the invention of machinery which largely displaces labour.   Since
the "Song of the Shirt" created its nine-days' sensation,
and the hundreds of articles based upon it did all they
could to cause a mutual hatred between employers and
employed, the sewing machine has been perfected and
adopted in every needlework establishment.   Like all
machinery, it has benefited the general public by cheapen-
ing the cost of production, and, in doing this, has rudely
but wholesomely compelled thousands of half-starved nee-

dlewomen to seek other employments. It has enabled one
active worker to stitch, hem, fell, bind, cord, gather, and
embroider with a speed equal to ten ordinary sempstresses,
on materials varying from the thinnest muslin to the
thickest cloth.

Public attention, however, is not so much drawn at the
present moment to the miserable needlework slavery of the
East End as to the condition of the dressmakers and milliners at the West End of London. The recent death of
a young dressmaker at one of the most fashionable court
milliners, has caused so much public excitement and discussion that the whole vexed needlework question has been
re-opened, and a royal commission has been appointed to
collect evidence and make a report. The readiness with
which these commissions are now granted, contrasts
strongly with the obstructive policy formerly adopted by
governments. Very little action, however, is now taken on
the recommendation of such commissions, and they seem
to be granted with a view of shelving troublesome subjects.
If they ever answer the purpose of their promoters, it is by
the publicity which they gain for their collected evidence
and reports in the various newspapers. In 1842 one of
these royal commissions disclosed the hardships and sufferings which thousands of young women and girls were then
enduring from overwork and overcrowding in dressmaking
establishments. The evidence then taken led to the formation of an " Association for the Aid and Benefit of Dressmakers and Milliners," which still exists at New Bond
Street, under the management of Miss Newton. The pre-
sident of this Society is the Earl of Shaftesbury, and
amongst the vice-presidents is the Right Hon. W. Cowper,
M.P. The committee of ladies still includes, amongst
many others, the Dowager Duchess of Sutherland,

the Duchess of Argyle, Vicountess Sydney, Vicountess
Jocelyn, Lady Ebury, and Miss Burdett Coutts. The chief
objects of the association are—to establish a provident fund
and a registry of workwomen and employers; to afford
skilful medical attendance to the young women at a very
trifling expense; to promote an improved system of ventilation in the workrooms; to induce ladies to allow sufficient
time for the execution of orders; to afford pecuniary assistance to deserving young persons in cases of temporary
distress or difficulty; to induce the principals of dressmaking and millinery establishments to limit the periods
of actual work to twelve hours each day, and to abolish in
all cases working on Sundays. The abolition of Sunday
work has been chiefly due to the exertions of this association, but long hours of employment are still customary, and
the "season" is still as exacting as ever. In 1855, a bill
was introduced into the House of Lords by Lord Shaftesbury, for limiting and regulating the hours of work in the
London millinery establishments, but this was very wisely
rejected by a committee of the House, who reported against
it after taking evidence. It was felt that a short-hour bill
to limit the time-contracts between full-grown, thinking
young women and their employers, would be a well mean-
ing but mischievous and ridiculously inoperative piece of
legislation. The principle of the Factory Act, on which
this bill appeared to be based, was not to prevent men and
women working overtime, but to prevent them selling the
excessive labour of their children. As an attempt will probably be made next session to revive this bill, it is as well
at once to state this honest objection to it.

The needlewomen of London, if we include all those who
are partly as well as wholly dependent upon needlework
for support, number at least one hundred thousand: the

acknowledged sempstresses form nearly fifty thousand of this total, and twenty thousand of this fifty thousand may be classed under the head of milliners and dressmakers. Out of this last twenty thousand, not more than one-tenth, or two thousand, in-door needlewomen are spread amongst the employers in the West End and the circle around it. These workpeople may be divided into assistants, improvers, and apprentices, and they are distributed in the average proportion of about five residents to each house of business. The very centre of the fashionable circle, however, where the cream of the cream of "court milliners" is found, is far more thickly planted with these "young people." Twenty, thirty, forty, and even sixty in-door needlewomen are found in each of these leading establishments, and here it is that the root of the overwork evil really lies. The area is remarkably small compared with the whole field of needleworkers. The houses may number about twenty, the workers may number about five or six hundred. We are not prepared to assert that no instances of overwork and consequent physical suffering can be found outside this narrow circle, nor that millinery and dressmaking is the most healthy of all female sedentary employments.

Overwork is too common in all businesses where the rate of wages is low, and the results of prolonged sedentary occupation are too notorious, to warrant such an assertion; but inasmuch as the whole trade of millinery and dressmaking is not now upon its trial, we may be pardoned for merely looking at what is immediately before us. The recent lamentable death of a young needlewoman at the West End occurred in one of the most fashionable houses of business, and the outcry that has been raised has been about the system pursued in those few houses. That system is soon explained. " The girls in the large London houses" (so says an address lately issued by the Committee of the Ladies' Sanitary Association) " are, with a few exceptions, thoroughly respectable. Character is required by the managers, and is maintained in their establishments. This is a great point, for many of them [the young women] are orphans, often well educated and well conducted, to whom character is dearer than life. In a good house of business they are able to secure protection. A girl is usually sent to the business at the age of thirteen or fourteen, and bound for about three years. A premium of from twenty pounds to fifty pounds is paid on entrance, and she receives board and lodging during the time of her apprenticeship. At the end of that time she becomes an ' improver' for one year or more, receives her board and lodging, but is still dependent on her own resources for her other wants. By this time her little capital is generally exhausted, and she begins to earn a salary varying according to her abilities from twelve pounds to fifty pounds a year." This is a fair statement of this part of the case. " Talent," as it is called by the employers, that is, extraordinary taste, judgment, or power of forcing sales, is of course paid for much more liberally, and salaries varying from sixty pounds to one hundred and fifty pounds a year, with board and lodging, are frequently given to these valuable " hands." The in-door workers are paid just as much during the slack time, from September to March inclusive, as they are for the busy time, or " season," from April to August inclusive. They are allowed holidays varying from a fortnight to three months, during which time they receive their salaries, though, of course, they board with their friends. Much importance is attached, and perhaps justly, to the family protection given to these in-door workers, but the fact is overlooked that uncontrolled liberty is allowed them every Sunday.

The out-door wórkers, who, it may be unjustly, are regarded as a lower moral class, either take the work away to their lodgings, or work for stated hours in the house each day, coming in the morning, and going away at night, like clerks or warehousemen. Their average wages may be twelve or fourteen shillings a-week, and they are generally stronger than the in-door workers, probably because they work for shorter periods and get more exercise.

During the " season," from April to August, in the area we have named, that is, in the houses of the twenty chief " court milliners," it may be taken for granted that the in-door workers, not always including the younger apprentices, are kept at close labour for fourteen or sixteen hours a-day for many days together. " Taking the year round" (says a fashionable court milliner, who gave evidence before a Committee of the House of Lords, touching the system pursued in her own establishment), " I should think the young people work twelve hours a-day, because I give three months', or six weeks', or a month's holiday to every one. To show that ours is a business solely for the season, I am glad to give holidays, because I have nothing for the young people to do out of the season. The nature of our business is different to any other ; being a business of high fashion, the whole of that business must be transacted in five months, and we have to keep the establishment the rest of the year without paying our expenses. If it were a question of ten or twelve hours labour a-day all the year round, that would answer our purpose much better than the present arrangement, because everybody would live out of the house, and we should have no one to keep when we have no work to do. As it now is, we pay enormously for talent, as much as sixty, eighty, and a hundred pounds a-year for the first talent, and keep it six months without doing anything scarcely, in order that we may have it when we want it. It is impossible to say exactly the number of hours we work : at times the young people come into the work-rooms at nine, and leave at four or five; at other times they come at seven and leave at ten. From seven to eleven are the longest hours that any one works in my house, except on the occasion of a Queen's drawing-room, a funeral, or a marriage order, when we are compelled to work until it is done. I could not refuse work which will support my establishment the remaining time of the year : I must do it when it is offered to me ; I cannot get it at other times. If the ladies could order their court dresses, and their dresses for the Queen's balls, and their toilets for the Spring, during our leisure time, we should make it a very profitable business indeed ; but that cannot be done, inasmuch as the mode is not named for the season, nor are the fabrics ready. The Queen gives very short notices very often. Ladies come to me as late as four o'clock in the afternoon, and say, 'I want a head-dress ; I am going by the four o'clock train to Windsor to-morrow,' and I am obliged to get it ready. Then I have a great many things to get done for the mail train on the next night, perhaps for a wedding in the north of England, or for a funeral in the west : we dare not refuse these orders, because, if we did, the ladies would go to another house and get served, and we should lose their custom for ever."

This is a statement of the mistress's side of the case, made by a competent and confident witness, who was evidently free from any pressure or fear of philanthropic or other patrons. On the other hand, those who plead the cause of the workwomen state that the pressure of the " season's " work is generally too much for the young people in the fashionable houses. They believe that the system could not be kept up but for the constant succession of fresh workers who come from the country to supply the places of those who break down under the exertion. They assert (without stating on what evidence, if any) that not one in a hundred passes through this ordeal with unimpaired health. "In the first place" (say the Ladies' Sanitary Association, before quoted), "the most moderate amount of sedentary labour would be unhealthy if relieved by no exercise whatever. The apprentices seldom cross the threshold, except on Sundays. The rooms in which they work are nearly always badly ventilated; the rooms in which they sleep are worse. Add to this a yearly strain of four months' duration, when all the bodily powers are daily and systematically overtasked, when sixteen hours' daily labour are demanded from these victims of fashion, sitting all these hours in close rooms, or, still worse, standing over some delicate material which must not be injured by a touch, no wonder that they frequently faint at their task; indeed, this is so common that little or no notice is taken of it. Constant headache and pains in the back, loss of sight and loss of appetite, ending in complete prostration and consumption, are the results. We have the evidence of dressmakers who are married or gone into business, to prove that permanent injury is done to the health even of the strongest. Among the former we have numerous instances of distressing weakness from functional derangement, clearly traceable to the work, entailing great debility upon the sufferers, and without doubt upon their children."

The evils resulting from bad ventilation in crowded work-rooms, and from overcrowding in sleeping-rooms, can hardly be overrated, and any agitation or even interference that will lessen these evils, will be thoroughly welcome. Most of the great millinery houses are either in old-fashioned back streets where the rooms are small and dark —as in many parts of May Fair—or in a fashionable thoroughfare, like Regent Street, where rents are enormously high. Of course the best rooms are reserved for show and reception rooms, and no one who has seen the space which a single court dress in all its virgin glory will occupy, can wonder that the largest apartments are secured to display such products of the milliner's art. The dining-room is often a cheerless apartment on the basement; the work-rooms, the low-roofed second and third floors, with extensions, and the sleeping-rooms, the garrets at the top of the house, and a few stray side rooms and lumber closets. Arrangements of this kind, in some measure inevitable, are undoubtedly bad; but we have no evidence to show that there is any anxiety to get into houses where the accommodation is far superior. There are many firms —chiefly amongst the large draper-milliners and dress-makers—where the sanitary regulations are almost perfect, but the managers have no more the pick of the market than other less thoughtful employers, and have to pay precisely the same wages. These employers are undoubtedly acting right in the course they pursue, but it would be more satis-factory to see a more unmistakable demand for good ven-tilation and sleeping accommodation coming direct from the girls, than from philanthropic committees acting as their mouthpiece.

With regard to the vexed question of food, we may safely conclude that the meals provided in the chief houses are wholesome and substantial. It is so easy to get up frivolous complaints about stale bread, salt butter, boiled mutton, roast mutton, tough beef, salt beef, thin milk, stale eggs, or any eatables, that little attention need be paid to such schoolgirl grumblings. Allowances may be made for occasional ill-health and over-fatigue when a fretful impatience of food of any kind may be natural; but, as a rule, such complaints may be regarded as the commonplace criticisms which are met with at all houses where meals are supplied by contract. From the dining-table of a first-class boarding-house, to the eating-hall of a workhouse, such half-fanciful complaints are constantly made, and it is therefore not surprising to find them in millinery establishments.

The great evil, then, that we have to contend with now, is overwork during the "season," or five months in the year, at about twenty court milliners', who employ about five or six hundred needlewomen. "The co-operation of ladies," again says the Ladies' Sanitary Association, "is a necessary element in the social reform to be achieved. They may ascertain with little difficulty the character of the house they employ, and whether its workpeople are treated with consideration. They may refrain from unreasonable demands as to the execution of their orders. They can pay their bills, a duty which has a still more important bearing on the question. Employers with large capital may not care about early payment—indeed, ladies have sometimes to complain that their bills are not sent in, and they do well to complain, for the interest lost by late payments must be made up by large profits, so that they pay for delay, and suffer from the temptation to carelessness and extravagance induced by the habit of keeping a running account. To the smaller capitalist the system of long credit often leads to ruin. One employer stated to us that he had above five thousand pounds due to him, and was thereby brought to the verge of bankruptcy; and this is neither a rare nor an extreme instance. Besides this, the long-credit system keeps the business in the hands of a few capitalists. If ladies paid their bills quarterly, a greater number of work-women would be able to become principals in the business, and this would lead to a fairer division of the profits by making it easier for the employer to increase the number of workers."

The spreading of the business during the height of the "season," and, indeed, all the year round, would materially relieve those who are overworked without receiving the usual benefit of working overtime. "It has been proved," continues the same address, "that no overwork is really profitable—that the worker, when freshness and vigour are maintained by sufficient rest, does more and better work than when exhausted and harassed by fatigue. By secur-ing sufficient out-door assistance in the early part of the season, so as to avoid beginning the late-hour system, the skilled inmates would be kept up to their highest pitch of energy and efficiency, and the result, would, we believe, be found equally if not more profitable in the long run. A wholesome atmosphere would also powerfully conduce to the same end."

We are glad to see that this address, which is more sensible than most philanthropic documents, concludes by advising the workwomen to combine as much as possible to protect their own interests. The good done by the "Association for the Aid and Benefit of Dressmakers and Milliners," is an encouragement to those who feel inclined to act on this suggestion. Anything that will infuse more self-reliance into this class cannot fail to do good. Well-meaning as that paternal system may be which professes to guard the conduct of the in-door workers with a watch-ful eye, it is questionable whether the young women would not make better members of society if they were taught to protect themselves, and to feel that they are responsible for their own actions. A great deal of bad, maudlin sentimentality is uttered about temptations which it is assumed cannot be resisted; but these young women, like all young women, ought to understand that the duty really rests upon them of being their own guardians.

The millinery and dressmaking business, like too many female employments, suffers much from a want of earnestness in those who enter it as apprentices. It is only taken up as a make-shift, a pastime, a temporary occupation, and not as a handicraft which must be practised till death. There are few old milliners and dressmakers, and few married ones, and yet the young people fulfil their destiny and marry like other ladies. It is this matrimonial prospect—this release from the work-room, so certain to come —that creates a difficulty. It is almost impossible to obtain a sound organization for a trade which is supported chiefly by young and marriageable girls, who enter it merely to leave it.

The profits of general needlework would be much greater than they are, if there was less of what we may call amateur work in private families; and they would be greater still, if stitching was not universally held to be so very domestic and feminine.

A middle-class family circle, consisting chiefly of ladies, would doubtless be considered remarkably ill-regulated if the needle and the accompanying work-box were almost unknown within its precincts. If none of the ladies were able to trim a common bonnet, or make a common dress; if they were clumsy hands at hemming a pocket-handkerchief, or at darning a stocking; if they were wholly incapable of making a shirt, and even somewhat careless about stitching on shirt-buttons, it is not difficult to conceive the remarks that would be levelled at them by acquaintances. They would be spoken of as idle, lounging, unfeminine persons—as readers of worthless novels—as would-be fine ladies. And yet if these girls, with their mother at their head, were to quietly practise some handicraft that kept them from needlework or ornamental education ; if instead of the eternal spinning of crochet anti-macassars, or the practising of show-pieces on the piano, they were to thoroughly master some mechanical art requiring taste and delicacy of touch, they would be doing all the practical good in their power towards making a better market for the needlewomen. It might seem strange at first that the tutor ushered in came to teach the ladies watch-making, engraving on metal, artistic wood-cutting, inlaying woodwork, or one of a dozen other similar handicrafts ; but this strangeness would wear off after a few visits. The handicraft would grow in interest day by day, as most mechanical employments do, and would soon be considered less tedious than needlework, or the struggle with sonatas.

If all families of ladies who are dependent upon uncertain or slender incomes earned by husbands, fathers, sons, and brothers, were thus resolutely to turn their backs upon the needle, and to provide themselves with a more marketable accomplishment, they would be far better prepared for those reverses which unfortunately fall to the lot of so many of them. By keeping out of a market already glutted with female labour, they would benefit those poor work-women already in the market, and, at the same time, benefit themselves. They could hardly prepare themselves for any occupation that is not more productive than needle-work, that is not more " genteel," or held in better estimation. Few employments at present sought after by women

—especially young women—are, unfortunately, free from a taint of suspicion, the taint being all the stronger if the average rate of wages is very low. It is uncharitably assumed that poverty and vice must necessarily go together, and as needlewomen are, in the main, the lowest paid of nearly all human hand-workers, temptation is supposed to dog them in every conceivable shape, and to find them with little principle and power of resistance. To avoid entering a labour-market from which at present little profit and less honour is to be derived, can surely require very little strength of mind and judgment on the part of those who have to choose an occupation.

SWEEPS.

It has always been the fashion to regard the fireside as the altar of home—the seat of all the domestic virtues. Round that hallowed spot are supposed to be nourished all those tender feelings and sentiments which soften the harder features of humanity. There it is that the true father, the true mother, the true sister, and the true brother are grown; and there it is that society looks for its brightest ornaments. No patriot or philanthropist, worthy of the name, ever sprung from any other soil, or was really moulded by any other influence.

As the fireside has done so much for the world at large, it seems a pity that it cannot do something for itself, and prevent the perpetuation of a cruel wrong which oppresses the weak and helpless. This wrong is so entirely a fireside wrong, and is so easily destroyed by fireside guardians, that it is difficult to believe in its existence. Public feeling, nearly a quarter of a century ago, condemned the climbing-boy system, and the result was an Act of Parliament,* to render the use of children in cleaning chimneys

* The act now in operation was passed in 1840; it is entitled "An Act for the Regulation of Chimney Sweepers and Chimneys" (3 and 4 Vict. cap. 85). By this act it is provided, that any person who, after the 1st of July, 1842, shall compel or knowingly allow any child or young person under the age of twenty-one years to enter a

illegal, and to compel the use of a machine invented as a substitute. No particular machinery in the shape of inspectors was provided to see that this act was not evaded, it being generally felt that each householder would willingly be his own inspector.

Much reliance was also placed upon informations laid by a few of the sweeps who used the machines against a few others who secretly clung to the old bad system. A few benevolent individuals—chiefly Quakers—formed themselves into associations to save children, under the provisions of the act, from this bitter slavery; but beyond this there was no organized attempt to see that the mastersweeps did their duty.

More than twenty years have elapsed since the passing of this act, and now there is too much reason to believe that the evil, never wholly destroyed, is gaining new life. The Birmingham Association for the Suppression of Climbing-boys—one of the associations we have just alluded to— is compelled to report that within the last few years seventy poor boys have been rescued from this wretched life in the Potteries alone. Mr. Francis Wedgwood, of Etruria, Stoke-upon-Trent, the treasurer of the North Staffordshire Association for Suppressing the Use of Climbing-boys, is compelled, at the close of 1862, to write as follows :—" No chimney need be climbed, and yet there

chimney or flue for the purpose of sweeping or coring the same, or for extinguishing fire therein, shall be liable to a penalty varying from £5 to £10, and in default of payment to imprisonment, with or without hard labour, for any time not exceeding two months. It is also provided, that no child under sixteen years of age shall be apprenticed to a chimney-sweeper, and regulations are made for the proper construction of chimneys to prevent accidents from fire, and to facilitate the use of the sweeping machine.

is no very general strong feeling against the use of climbing-boys. Lords, squires, magistrates, and mayors have their chimneys so swept without shame, and, of course, are very unwilling to convict sweeps for doing the same for others. One justice, if I remember rightly, required the age of a little boy produced in court to be proved by certificate of baptism. Of course such a requirement made a conviction impossible."

Another report, from Leicester, alluding to the state of things existing in 1856 and the subsequent years, says:— "The whole number of children and young persons illegally employed in this town and county was found to be upwards of one hundred." These children were liberated by the efforts of a few individuals acting together; but as soon as the boys were let loose in Leicestershire, they were bought up and carried off to other counties, still to be kept in their cruel and illegal occupation.

This painful subject has recently engaged the attention of the commissioners appointed in the early part of 1862 to inquire into the number and condition of children under thirteen years of age, and young persons under eighteen years of age, employed in trades and manufactures not already regulated by law. In the course of their inquiry much evidence was tendered to them respecting the inefficiency and violation of the " Chimney-Sweepers' Act," and the cruelty consequently often inflicted upon a large number of unfortunate and helpless boys. From the evidence gathered in England, Ireland, and Scotland, it appears that several thousand children, varying in age from five years to fourteen years, and including many girls, are still condemned to this fireside life of slavery. The evil is greater throughout the country and in the second-class country towns than it is in London and the chief cities, but everywhere it shows unhealthy signs of revival. As this state of things could not exist without great apathy or connivance on the part of householders and fathers of families, it is charitable to suppose that they are ignorant of the cruelty which always did and must form a part of the climbing-boy system. What that system now is can best be shown by a narrative embodying the chief features of a sweep's life and calling, compounded from the evidence just laid before Parliament by the commissioners.

My name is George Stevens, and I am now a master-sweep, but I began life fifty years ago as a climbing-boy. I went to sweep at less than five years of age. I remember my first chimney very well, for I was told that there was a pork pie at the top. The masters used to carry a broad belt with a buckle round their waist to thrash the boys with. My master had three little girls who used to climb, and sleep in their sooty skins and clothes like the rest of us, and when they grew up young women they went about doing sweep journey-work, dressed in male dress.

I was so cruelly treated that I ran away. I went to Congleton, and Newcastle, and Chester, doubling back and so to Mold, and then I thought I was safe, but my master was pursuing a day behind me all the time. I had just hired myself to a man there, and was thinking that he looked kind, and his wife was giving me some tea, when I heard my old master's voice, and the tea choked me. I couldn't eat another morsel, though I was very hungry. He took me off at five o'clock in the morning. There was a league then between all the masters, and the sweep at Mold could not hold me against the other. We walked the whole way to Manchester without resting; he waited until we got to the forest, and then he nearly killed me.

Many people will say that this was under the old system, and that things are changed for the better now ; but I can assure them that this is a great mistake. I have given a good deal of attention to this business, and I am sure that in the country, and in many large towns, the boys are as badly off as ever. Mr. Herries, of Leicester, has got twenty-three cases of boys who have been killed in chimneys by being stifled, since 1840. I have known many cases of cruelty. A few years ago a boy died up a court in Manchester. He was apprenticed to a master-sweep in Haslingden. His food was bread which beggars sold to his master. On a Sunday, when his master's family had good dinners, he was still kept to the same hard fare. He had frequent and long journeys into the country, and was forced to leave his heavy and badly-fitting clogs at home. He was constantly exposed, barefooted, to rain and cold ; he often lodged in outhouses upon straw, and had no chance of drying his wet clothes. He was very young, and his health failed, and then, being of no more use to his master, he was sent back to Manchester, with marks of most cruel neglect and ill-treatment upon him. He had a large abscess on his back, and one of his ears was nearly torn off. He lingered a few weeks in extreme suffering, and then died. His death was painful, but I have known worse cases. There was one about seven or eight years ago at Nottingham. A little boy was smothered in a chimney there. The doctor who opened his body said *they had pulled the child's heart and liver all out of place in dragging him down.* That doctor can now be referred to, if necessary, to prove the truth of this.

Unfortunately there is no difficulty in getting boys for the climbing work, and as they are allowed to go about with the masters under the name of assistants, to carry the machine and bags, the law is easily broken. The thousands of climbing-boys are much worse off now, as the masters who keep them are only the least respectable ones. You can buy boys by the dozen. Parents themselves go hawking their children about. A woman was urging me the other day to take her boy, but I would not. Many want to get rid of their children and make a little money by it as well. The women sometimes are more hardened than the men. Only lately a woman who had sold her child to a sweep, followed me, and threatened to pull my hair for speaking against the use of climbing-boys. A man very recently said to me, "You shall have my two lads for nothing," instead of asking for the usual 10s. or £1. I have often had children as young as six years old offered to me in the same way. Sometimes as much as £5 has been paid for a boy, but very seldom. In Liverpool, where there are lots of bad women, you can get any quantity you want. I knew of a boy working at Burslem who was bought from Stockport; he was only six years old. No children can be got in the Potteries. There are no lots of bad women there as there are in the big towns; and besides, the Potteries give too much work for children for parents to want to get rid of their boys to sweeps. I know, however, of three cases at Tunstall, where two women, not married, sold their boys to a sweep there.

Nottingham is, perhaps, the most famous place for climbing-boys, on account of the chimneys being so narrow. A Nottingham boy, for this reason, is worth more to sell. A boy from this place was once stolen from me. As he was in the street a man seized him from behind in his arms, carried him off straight to a low lodging-house, and stupefied him with drugged tea. After the tea, the child fell into a deep sleep and lost all appetite. An inspector and I traced him to Hull. The boy was so glad to find that "master" had come. The man had said that if they had got him to France, they should have had £10 for him. There was another boy found with him. The stealer was a sweep at Hull; letters were found on him giving orders for more boys, and these letters were read before the magistrates. The prosecution was afterwards dropped, as the magistrate said the man must be transported for kidnapping, if it were pressed. He paid £20, and promised not to do it again. About the same time three climbing-boys were missed from Nottingham, and traced by their masters to a cellar where they were hidden. The eldest was not more than ten years of age, and they were going to be sent to Hull, and from there to France.

I have heard of many cases of the same kind in Derby, Leicester, and other towns. I hear from sweeps that come from other parts that this is still the regular thing to this day. I have myself had several letters from distant places asking me to send boys, or to say where some could be got. I had such a letter last summer, offering to pay me well and give me a sovereign. The way it is done is this—to find some poor boy and tell him that you know of a nice place where there is plenty of food and clothes, deluding him all the while, until you send him off by the train. This is more done now, because boys may not be got from the union as they formerly were. Besides this, boys are "trafficked" about from one master to another, 10s. or so being given for the "lent" of them. Whether they ever get back or not depends often on whether they have parents who care to look after them. In some cases they are not heard of for years, and sometimes never again. I remember well two nice little boys (brothers), aged nine and eleven, when I was an apprentice, being sold one Sunday morning for 30s. the two. A brute of a journeyman used to knock them about very much before. They were bought by another journeyman sweep, and put into a country waggon and sent off. They were never heard of again. The poor widow of a mother used to come backwards and forwards to our place to make inquiries, but she could never hear any tidings of them.

No one knows what the boys have to go through to be trained but those who have been climbing-boys, like myself. In learning a child you can't be soft with him; you must use violence. I have kept a lad four hours up a chimney when he was so sore he could scarcely move, but I wouldn't let him come down until he had finished. I shudder now when I think of it. It has often made my heart ache to hear them wail, even when I was what you may call a party to it. I have seen boys go to bed with their knees and elbows scabbed and raw, and the inside of their thighs all skinned. I have seen five or six boys sleeping in dirty straw, banked up with stones, in a dark cellar, covered with soot-bags, which stuck in their wounds. The bags were the same they had used in the day—wet or dry. One could read, and they all subscribed for a candle for him to amuse them with a book when they were in bed. I have seen the steam from their bodies so thick as to obscure the light, so that the boy couldn't read. Dozens of such children die of consumption. They get up to their work in all weathers, and often at two and three in the morning. They are filthy in their habits, and often wear one shirt right through until it is done with. I, myself, have been for fifteen months without being washed, except by the rain, until I was almost eaten away by vermin. Formerly the sweeps, as they said themselves, had three washes a year —viz., at Whitsuntide, Goose Fair (October), and Christmas. I once knew a sweep who had never been washed, and another who had never been sober. The custom of "sleeping black," as it is called, is still very common, and you may often hear the men and boys "dusting" themselves in the morning.

Most masters prefer to take their climbing-boys very young, as they learn more readily. Six years is considered a nice trainable age. I have known two at least of my neighbours' children begin at the age of five. I once saw a child only four years and a half old in the market-place in his sooty clothes, with his scraper in his hand. Some people said, " Look at that little fellow ; he is not four." One man, however, standing by, said, " He's four and a half; his father told me his birthday, and said that he began when he was four, and that he would make a nice little climber."

I have had boys as young as this, but I never liked them. They were too weak, and I was afraid they might go off. It is no light thing having a life lost in your service. They go off just as quietly as you might fall asleep in your chair by the fire after you had had two or three glasses of strong drink. A son of mine, as well as myself, was very nearly gone so once, and I was a long time before I came round.

If, as often happens, a boy is gloomy, or sleepy, or anywise "linty," and you have other jobs on at the same time, though I should be as kind as I could, yet, as I said before, you must ill treat him somehow. Sometimes you will strike him with the hand, sometimes with the brush. It is remembering the cruelty which I have suffered which makes me so strong against boys being still employed. I have the marks of it on my body now, and I believe the biggest part of the sweeps in the town have. I have a deep scar on the bottom of the calf of my leg which was made by my master with an ash-plant—a young ash-tree that is supple and will not break. The limb was cut to the bone, which had to be scraped to heal the wound. I was six years old at the time. I have marks of nailed boots in other parts of my body. It was a common thing with sweeps to speak of "breaking-in" a boy; if he was hard, like a ground-road or a stone, they gave it up. It is necessary to harden the children's flesh when they begin the work. This is done by rubbing it, chiefly on the elbows and knees, with the strongest brine, such as you may get from a pork-shop, before a fire. You must stand over them with a stick while the rubbing is going on.

At first they will come back from their work with their arms and knees streaming with blood, and the knees looking as if the caps had been pulled off. Then they must be rubbed with brine again, and perhaps go off at once to another chimney. In some boys I have heard that the flesh does not harden for years. I once found a boy in the market-place, about eight years of age, who had run away from some place of correction, and who offered himself to me. Part of his knee-caps had got torn off, the gristle all showed white, and the guiders (tendons) all round were like white string, or an imitation of white cotton; his back was covered with sores all the way up. To harden his knees, a salt lotion, simmered with hot cinders, was put on them; and to make him hold them straight under this, he had a brush-tail tied up and down his back, and something else like it in front, and he was made to walk in this way twenty, forty, or fifty times up and down the room. He counted each time, once up and once down, "one." It was like killing him, and I had to stand by and see it all. However, he was the clumsiest boy I ever saw, and had no activity.

Some use the water from a smithy in which iron is hardened, others salt and water; but I think that is no good at all, but makes it worse. Besides all this, there is what the boys suffer from the employment itself; they must go barefoot even on the coldest winter mornings, or the soot would shake from their trousers into their boots, and gall and fester their feet. I have often carried boys myself on my back, out of pity to them at such times. Then, in some, the climbing scrapes the flesh very much; and from "sleeping black" and breathing the soot all night, they get the sooty wart or cancer. The parts which this disease gets hold of are generally eaten away; the sooty warts are sometimes, however, cut out.

Boys suffer much from blisters got in climbing up hot flues, and also in other ways. Sometimes a loose bit of mortar falls and catches them in the waistband of their trousers, and, as there is always very little room to spare, it easily fixes them. The more they twist to get free, the tighter they stick. A piece no bigger than an egg will sometimes do this. Boys get stuck in other ways, especially if they are clumsy at the work. I knew a boy who went up a chimney at nine one morning, and was fixed there till ten the next morning, by which time a bricklayer had opened the chimney from above, and dug him out. A boy was found dead in a flue in this way, at the west-end of London, about two years ago, and his master was only fined heavily. Another man, in Eastcheap, was fined last summer for using a boy. Few informations, however, have been laid in London of late years, although the use of boys is undoubtedly on the increase.

The common price in the London trade for the use of a climbing-boy is half-a-crown for the job, and the nine hundred ill-constructed flues of the Houses of Parliament

have all been lately " cored " by five boys, in direct opposition to the law. An idea of the importance of chimney-
sweeping in large towns may be formed from the fact, that
the Bank of England allows its contractor £400 a year for
this work.

The common hour for beginning work in London is
about four o'clock in the morning, and work goes on at
any hour up to nine o'clock at night. The usual hours
that the boys work in the small country towns are eight
or nine—it is only morning's work; but in the larger
towns they work for twelve or sixteen hours daily. The
younger they are the more they labour, as the masters can
get through more work with the smallest boys. Some
masters work short hours, and give their boys a chance of
going to school, but not always with the consent of their
employers—the householders. A lady in Nottingham who
wished to have her chimneys swept in the evening, and
could not get the work done by her sweeper for this reason,
exclaimed, "A chimney-sweep, indeed, wanting education!
what next?"

When the boys get too big to climb, which in town
chimneys is about fifteen or sixteen, and in the large
country chimneys a few years older, they are unfitted for
other employments, and often do nothing, or worse. They
fall into the ranks as criminals, and no prison is ever without
one at least of this unfortunate, ill-treated class. Scarcely
one in a hundred of them can write, and not six in a hundred of them can read. When they get older they seldom
improve. They have not been accustomed to education
when young, and they don't think of it.

The Chimney-Sweepers' Act, as I have said before, is
not thought much of, and is broken through every day. In
Yorkshire, where there is no association to see the act

enforced, the climbing system is very bad.　In all Sheffield, when Mr. Roberts and Mr. Montgomery were alive, there was not one boy, and now there are twenty-two, varying from five to ten years of age; there are also several in the villages about.　Bury was free for four years, now there is one.　There are fourteen at Chester.　In Nottingham there are twenty; and in all the towns northward to New-castle-on-Tyne (Halifax excepted), there are from two to ten boys employed.　It is the same all over South Staf-fordshire, also at Coventry, Ashby, Leamington, Bridge-north, Wolverhampton, Birkenhead, etc.　I could give the names of fifty other towns where climbing is going on.　As I have said before, it is not abandoned in London and its suburbs, very young boys being employed.　In the county of Kent there are many, especially in Maidstone and Graves-end; also at Greenwich and Woolwich.　At Birmingham, where, during several years, "The Association for the Sup-pression of the Use of Climbing-boys" has been taking active measures to enforce the Act of Parliament, and where nearly five hundred pounds have been thus expended in the last five years, twenty-five boys are employed.　Some are very young, and one poor child, not more than seven or eight years old, can scarcely walk along the streets from sores and bruises received in climbing.　I am told his master is going to have pads made like those of horses for his knees. A child was dragged out of bed at two o'clock in the morn-ing to sweep the chimneys at a certain noble lord's mansion in that county, and at another noble baron's house, climb-ing-boys are always used.　At Wakefield there is a man who has three or four climbing-boys, at Blackburn another, at Preston another, at Rochdale another.　At Stockport, the other day, I saw a child of about eight with a sweep who had just come out of gaol; and I know of another sweep who keeps children, who has been committed more than thirty times, for every kind of offence. At Ashton, last December, a sweep was fined for sending a boy, aged seven, up a chimney on fire, by which the poor child was dreadfully burnt; and at Whitchurch there is a boy with a wound on his head an inch and a half long, which his master gave him with a poker. Those masters who have never climbed are by far the most barbarous.

All this cruelty is not only illegal but unnecessary. Though machines will do the work well, and are not dear, there is a great antipathy to them amongst the old masters. It is mere laziness that causes this. The machine requires working about to make it do the sweeping properly: it is much easier to stand below, gossiping with the housemaid, and send a boy up the chimney. Journeymen who go about with the boys, working, as is frequently the case, for masters who were never apprenticed—travelling tinkers, and such like, who know nothing of the trade—speak against the machine to save themselves the trouble of using it. They generally work with closed doors, so that no one may see what is done. Want of capital has something to do with it at times though not always. A common machine with iron fittings costs twenty-five shillings; a good one with brass fittings, which are much lighter, can be had for about two pounds; and the best, with all extras complete, for three pounds. With yearly repairs and all, I have not laid out more than equal to two good new machines in twenty years, and parts of my first are still in use. Careless workmen, of course, may wear out a machine much sooner, perhaps in about four years.

There may be chimneys which cannot be swept by a machine, but I have never seen one. If there is any slope at all it can be done by means of traps. If people only thought of what the boys suffer they would not have the heart to mind the small expense of traps. Instead of this, the use of boys is much encouraged by householders who will not have their chimneys swept by the machine. I have myself lost a good deal of custom which I should otherwise have, and some which I formerly had, at large houses and public establishments, because I will not use boys. That reason was, of course, not given, but I was sent away after I refused. I have been sent away even from magistrates' houses, and, in some cases, even by ladies who have professed to pity the boys.

In many public buildings now being built or recently built, the Act of Parliament relating to the form of chimneys is disregarded alike by architects, builders, and landlords. Some of the " model " lodging-houses are the worst. All the old chimneys that I have known for more than forty years could be altered to suit the machine; but in Piccadilly and the large houses at the West End of London, where they are generally the worst, the objection to altering them is the strongest. It is these people who make the law, and they are the first to break it. They don't go so far as to positively say they will have a boy, but they say, "I won't have my house pulled about," and leave the rest to take care of itself.

It would be a very good thing to make the law positive, and say, " boys shall *not* be allowed." There should be a penalty on the landlord if his chimneys are so built that the machine cannot be used in them, and a penalty on the tenant for having a boy. A tenant going into a house for a short time, say for a year or two, doesn't like to go to the expense of alterations; but if landlords were made liable they would look into the state of the chimneys when they buy a house. They never think of this now. Of course, at present, they cannot be called to account for chimneys which they didn't build themselves, and I am afraid they are too strong a party in Parliament ever to allow themselves to be called to account for anything.

This is no imaginary narrative compiled to create a sensation. Every statement in it has been collected in the form of evidence, and will doubtless be used to stimulate further legislation on the subject. Further reliable evidence has also been gathered to prove that all fears of the increased risk of fire from what we must now call the proposed abolition of climbing-boys are entirely without foundation.

This is no case in which a large army of government inspectors will be wanted if the public—if fathers and mothers of families—will do their duty. That they have not done their duty hitherto is painfully apparent throughout the course of this inquiry. "We should not do justice," say the Children's Employment Commissioners, "to a large number of master sweeps, were we not to state that many of their number, both in a large and small way of business, have highly distinguished themselves by their disinterested and humane efforts to suppress this cruel system—frequently to their own pecuniary loss. In our opinion, it is the public, more than the sweeps, who are responsible for the revival and extension of these great evils —physical, moral, and religious—which it was the benevolent object of the legislature to suppress." Surely the guardians of the homes of England—those homes that are always referred to with so much national pride—will do something to remove this great reproach from their doors. They will hardly allow themselves to be outdone in humanity by common chimney-sweeps. The full power of destroying this infant slavery is ready in their hands, if they will only rouse themselves and use it. Surely they will not lie snoring in their beds when those hoarse plaintive cries are heard in the late night or early morning at their doors, leaving the duty of watching to their yawning cooks and housemaids.*

* The Legislature has amended the Chimney Sweepers' Act of the year 1840, by an act of the present Session, and it will take effect on the 1st November. From that date a chimney sweeper must not use in his occupation a child under ten years of age, nor is he on entering a house to sweep a chimney to take with him a person in his employ under sixteen years of age. For acting in contravention to each section he is liable to a fine of £10. In order to check an infringement of either statute, and to prevent children from descending or ascending any chimney, the Justices are empowered to imprison the offenders—that is the master sweeps—for a period of six months with or without hard labour. Furthermore, instead of £5 penalties they may be increased to £10. "In any prosecution of a chimney sweeper for any offence against the Principal Act or against this Act, where the age of any young person or child comes in question, the proof of the age of such young person or child shall be on the defendant."

WONDERFUL POLICEMEN.

A POPULAR delusion has a wonderful grip on life. You may jump upon it, you may kick it, you may stab it in the back, or squeeze it by the throat, and still it will not die. It may kill itself, to all appearance, by its own clumsiness, and still it will not die. Like harlequin in the pantomime, it may seem to bury itself in the earth, but only to crop up again in another place.

The detective system is a pre-eminently vigorous popular delusion—a vulgar error that nothing seems to injure. Its reputation is based upon little that is more substantial than an idle feeling of wonder—a gaping curiosity that is excited by the merest trifles. Dress is at the bottom of most popular delusions, and it is at the bottom of this. The scum of a village, after enlisting in the army, no sooner appear in their red garments, than they find themselves objects of hero-worship. Their hats are handled with reverence, their coat-tails are admiringly examined, and they fall into numerous legacies of tobacco and beer. A few months before they would have been hurried to the stocks or the cage: but now they can command the best room in the pot-house. They have done nothing, as yet, but put on a few red coats and military trappings; but this is sufficient to raise them above the village. Their wages and position may be lower than that of the labourer toiling in the fields—their active utility may be far lower—but they have got the magic garments.

In the appreciation of the police force, this coat-worship takes an exactly opposite direction. The army would be looked upon as nothing without their uniforms; the police are looked upon as nothing with them. Wherever half a dozen people are gathered together there is a policeman in the midst, but it is the mob which bring the officer, and not the officer the mob. No town, or neighbourhood, or village ever showed any admiration for the plain blue suit with white binding, and the shiny hat; no drill-meetings of any divisions, from A to Z, were ever attended by an eager public; no triumphs of the wooden truncheon have ever been immortalized on canvas by illustrious battle-painters. Even at the doors of sixpenny photographers—doors that you cannot pass without being stopped by touters—you may see a hundred muddy-looking soldiers figuring in various positions, but never a single muddy-looking policeman. His pay may be good, his labour may be useful and necessary, but his uniform is not popular, because it is not provocative of wonder.

The moment, however, the policeman returns to "plain clothes," without ceasing to be a policeman, he is amply repaid by the public for their former neglect. No celebrated low-comedian walking along the Strand—no literary "lion" at an evening party—no pugilistic champion after a fight for the belt—can produce more excitement than a well-known police officer in "plain clothes." Something very serious must be in the wind when the "indefatigable" and "intelligent" Sergeant Burleigh is seen in a common "every-day frock-coat," and a pair of "sixteen-shilling" trousers. When the round red face of "Meadows the detective" is recognized under a wide-awake hat, over a theatrical-looking smock-frock, and between a pair of false red whiskers, the little knot who recognize him have no doubt that some gigantic robbery will be immediately exposed, or some "mysterious murderer" unearthed from his den. They never reflect that as "Meadows" is known to them, he may be and is known to hundreds more, and especially to those regular criminals whom he is supposed to be working to destroy. He winks—he nods—he puts on many ostentatious disguises—he rejoices in the name of a "detective;" he is often patted on the back by magistrates; he sometimes does a little private business as a spy; and he rather nourishes the growth of crime, by stopping the appointment of a real *preventive* police. He may be familiar with all the small thieves of the metropolis, as many rat-catchers and sewer-searchers are familiar with all the small rats; and in neither case are the vermin checked or destroyed before they develop into far more serious nuisances. " Detective Meadow's " plan—the plan of every policeman in plain or eccentric clothes, is to watch and tend the criminal fruit until it is rotten with ripeness, and then to shake it gently into the lap of justice. He never nips it in the bud. A trial for petty thieving brings as little reputation to the " detective " as it does to the Old Bailey barrister. So, petty thieves are merely marked, and then are left to grow. Sometimes they not only grow, but escape the net that is laid for them, and these are the "detective's" failures, which we seldom hear of. We always hear of the successes, and thus the popular belief in "intelligent officers " is kept up.

When we come to exceptional crimes—to those outbursts of individual iniquity which are even greater disturbers of society than the steady vices of the dangerous classes—we then find the hollowness of the " detective " system. In the first place, it never moves without the promise of a heavy reward, and its notion of its own value is based upon its reputation. In the next place, it seldom does more than constitute itself a centre to which any information may flow; and what is brought to it voluntarily it takes credit for discovering. Its silence is often the silence of those who have really nothing to say, and its paraded " investigations " mere devices to gain time, in the hope that something may turn up.

A little reflection ought to convince the most sensible believers in the detective system that a policeman in plain clothes is not so vastly superior to a policeman in uniform. To make a " detective," such as half the " intelligent officers " are supposed to be, you require a most remarkable combination of qualities. You must have a power of observation such as is given to few, and a logical faculty such as seldom exists in conjunction with this power of observation. You must have the qualities of patience, endurance, and self-possession, no slender degree of imitative talent, and a perception of all the finest shades of evidence. Edgar Poe had many requisites for a good detective; and if the genius Ricardo, the political economist, were boiled down with that of Charles Dickens, we might possibly get the particular combination that we want. It must not be forgotten that the business of a detective, even when it is set in motion for the pure benefit of society, has generally too much of the spy about it to suit the feelings of a gentleman. Those who are best adapted for skilled detectives are prevented from doing the work by high scruples and high taste.

The policeman in plain clothes—the regular and only " detectives "—may do their work as well as their ability will allow them; but it is absurd to suppose that they can

see much farther into millstones than half of their neighbours. Their inflated reputation has been swollen more by
the stupidity of criminals than by their own sagacity. A
forging clerk, or a fraudulent banker, never appears to
have any inventive genius, and while one is sure to go to
Liverpool to embark for America, the other is as certain to
go to Paris. The " detective " has only to hasten to one
of these places, and secure his prisoner, when the public
will exclaim—"What a very intelligent officer !" The
officer may be intelligent, as far as his intelligence goes,
but this is never very far. He will be able to unravel
coarse complications on a level with his own powers; but
when any superior mental agency has been at work, he is
thrown entirely off the scent. The Waterloo Bridge
tragedy—still an unsolved mystery—is a proof of this;
and no detective system ought to hold up its head as long
as *that* murderer remains undiscovered. It is a lasting
disgrace to any body of men, who have nothing else but
" detecting " to do, that they have never got to the bottom
of this notorious crime and many others. If the delusion
about the sagacity of policemen in plain clothes is not to
be dispelled, let us at least not so employ " detectives " as
to defeat the ends of justice.

"CASH PAYMENTS."

THOMAS CARLYLE has declared cash payments to be the sole *nexus* between man and man, and, for once, he appears to have hit upon a truth. Disciples of that school of Political Economy in which John Ruskin is a distinguished preacher, would have us prefer sixpences to shillings, and conduct our business upon sentimental principles. Those who cultivate the " roots of honour " in obedience to such teachers, will find them sprouting, before long, in a Bankruptcy Law Court. The true " roots of honour" are cash payments. If Mr. Ruskin, senior, had acted throughout his long business life as Mr. Ruskin, junior, preaches, the doctrine of sentimental trade would not have been sent forth from such a comfortable pulpit. There is nothing like hard work for a bare living to brush the cobwebs out of a man's brain.

Cash payments are the sole *nexus* between man and man, and have been from the remotest antiquity. In the shield of Achilles, as described by Homer, a tribunal is represented, before which appear the plaintiff and defendant, contesting as to the amount of " blood-fine" to be paid by the accused. In the Northern and Teutonic laws of Europe the varieties of " blood-fines," ranging from homicide to the squeezing of a free maiden's arm a little too tightly, are set forth in the most precise terms. The

Salic law is full of such enactments; the English law is not free from them. We now draw the line at murder. Mr. Greenacre is not allowed to compound with the family of the slain; but violent assaults of different kinds may be indulged in at various prices. You can have a splendid article in this way, from most magistrates, for about five pounds, and an inferior quality of assault at two guineas. The old laws of "the barbarians" assigned a cash payment to the wronged in proportion to the injury inflicted. If one man struck another on the head, so as to draw blood and cause it to flow to the earth, the assailant had to pay to the assailed six hundred pence. If the blow was so severe as to crack the skull, the price was nine hundred pence. Modern civilization has acted on the principle of these laws of the "barbarians," and Lord Campbell's Act restores the old system of "blood-fine," by compelling the wrong-doer to bestow upon the sufferer, or his heirs, such pecuniary compensation as a jury may determine.

While the modern law, however, has provided a scale of penalties, on the one hand, to be inflicted upon assailants and clumsy people, it has provided, on the other, a loophole for escape in the Insolvent Debtors Court. A jury may impose a "blood-fine," and a commissioner may decree that the insolvent is unable to pay it. While the wrong-doer is marked black in one department of the law, he is washed white in another. At this point it is that the system of assurance steps in, and secures that cash-payment to mankind without which life would be an empty name. Divines may speak against money as "filthy lucre," and currency-doctors may quarrel over it as "circulating medium," but it appears to be a very popular salve for broken heads, and most other afflictions of humanity. The dart of death is often tipped with gold, and hardly has the coffin disappeared through one door, when the bank-notes of the " life-office" come in at another.

A curious catalogue is now before us—the list of the different claims paid during the last year for non-fatal accidents by the " Accidental Death Insurance Company." There are more than a thousand individual claims, which vary very much in amount, the payments being regulated by the number of days or weeks the insurer was wholly disabled by the accident, and by the sum for which he was insured. When a man proceeds to insure his life he assesses the vital spark as highly as he can, and pays an annual premium bearing a certain proportion to this assessment. Accident insurances are managed on the same principle, and while one man considers his time worth ten shillings a week, another thinks he is worth ten pounds. The result is, that, according to the company's way of putting the accounts before the public, " contused heads " are quoted at as many different prices as ducks or chickens in Leadenhall Market.

The list is interesting, because it shows the marvellous inequality of the human race. One man's little finger is worth more than another man's whole body ; and one man's big toe is worth the heads of three other fellow-creatures. A fractured collar-bone at Welwyn fetched twice as much as several ribs in London ; and an ankle was injured at Preston for three pounds sterling, when it cost nine pounds to injure another at Ely. A fall, from orange-peel, at Belfast, was eleven pounds seventeen shillings and twopence ; and a fall of iron at Oaken Gates, only one pound and eleven shillings. The breaking of a bottle at Northampton was two pounds seventeen shillings and a penny (the penny probably being paid for the bottle) ; and the breaking of a shaft at Rotherfield, two pounds nineteen shillings and twopence. "J. C.," of Bridgewater, charges forty pounds for crossing a ditch; "T. C.," of Broughton, charges three pounds for jumping a ditch; and "J. S.," of Taunton, charges twenty-seven pounds for stepping over a ditch. The fall of a bottle at Huntingdon is one pound ten shillings; the bursting of a bottle at Colchester is one pound ten shillings and sixpence. "G. G.," of Milford, charges two pounds two shillings and tenpence for embarking on ship; and "W. N. B.," of Shaldon, charges one pound ten shillings for being washed overboard. Falls, cuts, and sprains appear to be the most common "visitations." Broken heads are plentiful; and we are surprised at not finding in this curious price-current the charge for a few broken hearts. These last delicacies are assessed at a money value in cases of "breach of promise," and why not in the list of an Accident Insurance Company? A few of the bruises enumerated, we fancy, must have arisen from fights, for nothing is more easy than to call a black-eye a "contusion." If such an "accident" were charged to the company at three pounds ten shillings, a skilful black-eye artist* would paint over the "contusion" for the odd money, leaving a clear gain of three pounds on the transaction.

The cheapest accident appears to be "a fall of rock" at Bethesda, and for this the company only have to pay twelve shillings and tenpence.

A list like this, where different parts of the human body are quoted, like carcases at a meat-salesman's, is

---

* "BLACK-EYES! AND ACCIDENTS!—Mr. Skrymisher eradicates blackness without pain or injury in half an hour."—See Advertisements, Public Press.

more calculated to teach humility than a hundred tracts
and sermons. It shows us how easily we are reduced to
cash-payments, and cash-payments in the most contemp-
tible quantities. A terrible fuss was made about Shylock's
pound of flesh, when here are dozens of cut legs, hands,
and arms, from one pound one and upwards.

LONGEVITY.

A CASE reported in the newspapers a short time since, under the heading of "Death in a gipsy's tent," shows the strong tendency that exists, even amongst educated people, to accept statements wholly unsupported by evidence. The death which caused a coroner's inquest, and this report, was that of an old gipsy woman, called Barbara Lee, who had once held the rank of a Gipsy Queen. The chief witnesses at the inquest stated that Barbara Lee, at the time of her death, was ninety years of age ; and the coroner, Mr. John Humphreys, without calling for any proof of this assertion, appears to have accepted and enlarged it. He drew inferences from the statement about the superior healthiness of a gipsy's tent compared with the overcrowded dwellings at the East-end of London, without looking to see if his conclusions were based upon any sound premises. He said, "The case is one of an unusual character, and I should not have troubled the jury if the deceased had not died in such a strange and sudden manner. There is, however, no doubt that the habit of living in such open-air places is beneficial, and has in this instance prolonged the life of the deceased, who has almost reached one hundred years."

Who can wonder after this that cases of remarkable longevity have only to be reported to be believed in ? The

late Sir George Cornewall Lewis—a man accustomed to
collect facts and sift evidence—devoted a good deal of
attention to this subject, and came to the conclusion that
nearly all reported cases of longevity were either wilful or
innocent impositions. We all know what little regard the
gipsy tribe pay to the law which enjoins registration of
birth, death, and burial ; we all know how rare it is for a
gipsy child to be taken to a church to be christened, and
have its name and age entered on the parochial records ;
and yet in the face of this knowledge, an important public
officer can be found who believes an old gipsy to be nearly
a centenarian, because another gipsy said she was ninety
years of age.

Cases of longevity, far more extraordinary than Barbara Lee's case, are constantly being reported in the public
journals—sometimes with a suspicious vagueness as to
names and dates, and nearly always without any of those
particulars so essential to establish the truth of such statements. A paragraph of this kind went the round of the
papers only the other day. It ran as follows :—" There
are at present residing in the same mansion in Cardigan-
shire, three sisters, whose united ages fall but seventeen
years short of three centuries. The sisters have reached
the respective ages of ninety-two, ninety-four, and ninety-
seven years, and are one and all in the enjoyment of good
health and unimpaired faculties. Even the eldest of the
three is able at present to dispense with the use of spectacles in reading—a circumstance almost unprecedented at
such ripe age."

It seems to be taken for granted that because a paragraph in a newspaper corner makes a certain statement,
that statement must necessarily be true. The appetite for
the wonderful is always so ravenous, that it will devour

almost anything, without the slightest examination. We are constantly being fed upon remarkable cases—many of them being probably dished up from an old book of lies, called "Wilson's Wonderful Characters." We have remarkable cases of fatness, remarkable cases of leanness, remarkable cases of abstinence, remarkable cases of gluttony, remarkable cases of size and strength, and remarkable cases of smallness and weakness. We appear to be surrounded by wonderful characters, and to live in a world of wonders. There is hardly a village that cannot boast of its Methusaleh, who has long passed the allotted age of man. We have heard of old men and women who enjoy sound health and the "possession of all their faculties," at one hundred, one hundred and five, one hundred and ten, and even one hundred and twenty, and this without going back to "old" Parr and Jenkins, whose claims will hardly bear an hour's patient examination. As to people more or less hearty, at ages varying from ninety to a century, they appear to be almost as plentiful as blackberries.

One favourite form which statements of this kind take must be familiar to most newspaper readers. It is what we may call the wholesale-longevity form. A family, consisting of a grandfather, a father, a mother, a son, a daughter, and sometimes a grandchild, is described, whose united ages amount to something very extraordinary. Young and old are mostly lumped together, and we are left to apportion the years individually, according to our taste and fancy, but the sum total is generally large enough to give the youngest member of the family threescore and ten. Sometimes the scene of this wonder is laid in England, and sometimes in France or Germany. We have seen the wonder increased by fixing the scene at some notoriously unhealthy spot, and representing the aged group as engaged in some rather unhealthy employment.

We are far from saying that there are no living proofs of extreme age—(and we are as much interested as the most credulous of our fellow-creatures in lengthening our mortal span)—but we are afraid that the few real cases are largely adulterated with a good many sham ones. Longevity is sometimes a very paying thing in a village, a country town, or even a compact London neighbourhood. It will often keep its reputed possessor without the trouble of getting into an almshouse, or the disgrace of going to the workhouse. Longevity under such circumstances produces a large amount of gaping curiosity and sincere patronage, followed by gifts of food, money, and clothing. Even when money is not required, longevity will always give its possessor importance. As life is so dear to all of us, except the few " blighted beings" whose digestions are out of order, it is natural to take an interest in long livers. Though conversation with Methusalehs of this kind rarely gives us much insight into the past, we often seek it, and tolerate its barrenness.

When a town or district has once pledged itself to a belief in one of these wonders, it would be very difficult to alter its faith, or even to get it to investigate the grounds of its belief. If any energetic fiction-crusher were to be successful in a task of this character, the result would hardly be worth his labour. Where, however, we look for and are entitled to demand strict evidence for every stated case of longevity, is in those statistics of life and death compiled by the Registrar-General. We have accused a worthy coroner of accepting loose statements as facts, but we are not sure that the accusation will not reach higher functionaries. Every now and then we read in the Registrar-

General's interesting reports of the death of some man or woman at ages over a hundred. Are these cases taken upon mere hearsay, or is the record of birth always strictly demanded? If such official statements only echo the gossip of village alehouses, their value will be obviously lessened for philosophical purposes.

FOOD.

OUR lively neighbours, as it was once the fashion to call the French nation, are somewhat obstinate when they get hold of an idea. It is not ridicule—it is not opposition— it is not even apathy which will induce them to give it up. They may sometimes modify it, but they never desert it. They are logical, loyal, and full of honour.

Some few years ago, when their breed of bullocks was not quite as perfect as it is at present, some one started the notion that horses ought to be promoted to the dinner table. Unlike the fish in Holland, however, described by Andrew Marvel, they were to come, not as a guest, but as a meat. Instead of dining *à la carte*, the Parisians were to dine à la carte and horse. M. Geoffroy St. Hilaire, if our memory serves us rightly, was the chief apostle of the new idea, and he worked hard to overcome the general prejudice. Lectures were given, pamphlets were published, and articles appeared in many newspapers in aid of the new faith; and the hippophagi, as they were called, were honoured with much opposition. They contended that it was far better to eat good horse than bad bullock, and far better to eat horse openly than to be compelled to eat it unknowingly. The mysteries of the restaurants were mercilessly exposed, and it was shown that horses and cooks were very well acquainted with each other. The

horses had substance, the cooks science—science even more
wonderful than that given to Mr. Dickens' pieman. The
seasoning "did it," and Paris was fed upon horse-flesh
without knowing it.

In spite of their telling facts and their powerful style
of reasoning, however, the hippophagi failed to carry their
point, or to increase their followers. Converts to a new
dish are not, perhaps, to be made in this way, and there is
doubtless no converter like sharp necessity. The early
history of the turtle or the oyster as an article of food may
be involved in some degree of mystery, but there can be
little doubt that cannibalism was long preferred to such
very unsightly food. There are certain Robinson Crusoe
conditions in which a Parisian would knowingly eat a
horse, but he would not eat it at the bidding of a "school."
The "school," not to be beaten, have merely shifted their
ground, and Paris is now nourished with horse-fed poultry.
Those who know how largely poultry enters into the
system of French cookery will know how largely horses
are thus eaten through the medium of another animal;
and the following facts, taken from the "Society of Arts
Journal," will show that we are not drawing upon our
imagination :—

"It has been observed that poultry does not thrive
best on a pure grain diet, but that, on the contrary, a
mixture of animal matter has great advantages. Acting
upon this hint, or rather starting from it, and proceeding
to the extremity of the animal food theory, a person commenced some years since at Belleville, an outskirt of Paris,
the production of poultry out of horse-flesh. There are
at present several of these hippophagous farms, which
supply a considerable portion of the fowls consumed in the
capital of France. The system answers well, provided the

creatures are not kept too long on an exclusively animal diet, in which case they become diseased and totally blind. Some time since an enterprising individual introduced great improvements into this system of raising poultry. This new establishment occupies nearly thirty acres of land, and is capable of accommodating about 100,000 poulets at a time. The poulets are divided into parties, according to their age, and each party has its yard and dormitory, both of which are kept with the utmost possible regard for the health and comfort of the boarders. The food consists almost entirely of horse-flesh, supplied from a slaughter-house adjoining the farm, and belonging to the same proprietor."

This mode of feeding, we are told, is kept as secret as possible, as the old prejudice against horse-flesh still prevails; and the hippophagi are, therefore, not much benefited by this application of their principles. They have succeeded in inserting the thin edge of a wedge, but the wedge is very small, and the end is very brittle. The market value of a dead horse—that great economical fact upon which the hippophagi based so much solid argument —is thus stated in the journal we have just quoted:—

" Skin, weighing from 50 lb. to 75 lb., 13 francs to 18 francs; long hair, from one-fifth of a penny to one halfpenny per lb.; flesh from 35 francs to 45 francs; blood about 2.50 to 3.50; intestines, 1.60 to 1.80; tendons, 1.20; grease, from 4 francs to 30 francs; hoofs and bones, about 2.50; and shoes and nails, about 24 centimes to 50 centimes. Total, from 60 francs to 120 francs (£2 8s. to £4 16s.). The number of horses slaughtered averages about 20 a day, and the affair is so well organized that the sales pay all expenses, leaving the flesh as clear profit. This last product is boiled in enormous coppers, chopped up, as if for sausages, and conveyed to the farm, after being seasoned with a small quantity of salt and pepper, which prevents putrefaction, and also contributes to the health of the poultry."

It is not only in the form of poulets that the Parisians eat horse, but the delicate omelette is now largely flavoured with that noble animal. We are told that the production of eggs is more profitable than the sale of chickens, as under a meat diet the hens lay all the year round, and never exhibit an inclination to sit.

"During last winter," says the Journal, "this establishment sent 40,000 dozens of eggs per week to market, at about 6d. per dozen. The hens yield on an average about 12s. per head per annum, and they lay for four years, at the end of which time they are fattened for three weeks with bruised grain and sent to market alive. The steam-hatching apparatus of the establishment is on a grand scale, furnishing employment for fifty or sixty women. The spare cocks are sent to market, and these amounted last autumn to more than 1000 dozens in three months."

There is no sound reason why the hippophagi—the faithful few who are left of that advanced school—should not turn their attention to England. In Paris every part of the horse now appears to be satisfactorily accounted for; the blood of the animals is carefully saved, and fetches a good price; the hides go to the tanners, the heads and hoofs to the Prussian blue makers, the marrow to the perfumers, the large bones to the button-makers, the refuse is converted into manure—a most important product—and the flesh, as we have seen, is given to the poultry. In London we can account for many of these parts of the noble animal in an equally satisfactory manner, but the flesh sometimes disappears a little too mysteriously. We can occasionally trace it to the copper of the cats'-meat boiler, but even then we miss the heart and tongue, which are not used in manufactures. Very little doubt exists in the minds of those who have studied the subject that these parts of the horse are eaten by human beings—perhaps in the form of "Westphalian delicacies."

There is much good work to be done in the removal of old prejudices about eating and drinking, the only question being how best to do it. Our Acclimatization Society has done some service in this way, though not precisely in the direction pointed out by the hippophagi. We have had many international exhibitions, large and small, but they have hardly introduced a new wine on the table, and have left the art of cookery exactly as they found it. There are many dishes mentioned by Mr. Simmonds and other writers upon food which may or may not be as nauseous as Smollett's Spartan broth, but which the inquiring mind would like to know more about than it does at present. The baked donkeys of Tartary; the stewed camel's flesh of Barbary; the fried giraffe of the Hottentots; the baked boa-constrictor of Southern Guinea; and the boiled anaconda of Ceylon, are all dishes calculated to excite our lively curiosity. We should like to know what nourishment and gratification the Havana natives get out of sharks, the Central Africans out of alligators, and certain South Americans out of beetles. There seems to be something like Heliogabalian luxury in feeding, as in Africa, upon butterflies, and something bold and defiant in feeding, as in North America, upon pole-cats. The grasshopper soup of California has a delicate look in print, and the curried ants' eggs of Siam sound far more like luxuries than the baked monkeys of Borneo. Fox-pies, grilled lion and tiger, smoked porcupines, baked elephants' paws, salted hippopotami, hyena steaks, boiled sloth, baked rhinoceros, and seaweed and rattle-snake soup, are all popular dishes in various places—far removed, of course, from London and Paris. The difficulty there has been found in openly introducing the horse on European dinner-tables is no encouragement, however, to culinary reformers, and it will be ages, perhaps, before we are relieved from the monotony of pork, beef, and mutton.

CABMEN.

THERE is only one trading interest in London which is always pulling against the collar, and that is the cab interest. Its masters represent a large amount of capital, its men constitute a large body of labour, and yet the first are mostly looked upon as extortionate usurers, the second as noisy vagabonds and ruffians. No other trading interest works with so little satisfaction to itself, or so little satisfaction to the public. It always seems to be either quarrelling at street corners, driving sulkily over the stones, or paying fines for alleged misconduct to frowning magistrates. It seems to take no pride in its business, but to conduct it as if it were a penal task, like oakum-picking or stone-breaking. It gives us vehicles that are generally dirty, and never comfortable, and horses that are sometimes spectral and always ricketty. We employ it with reluctance, we pay it with dread, and we turn our backs upon it with a feeling of relief; while it serves us with suspicion, is glad when it is able to refuse our offers, and is seldom satisfied with our custom.

As the relations between seller and buyer are generally cheerful, and business is a pleasure in nineteen cases out of twenty, it is as well to inquire why the cab trade is in this singular and unhealthy condition. Neither cab proprietors nor cab drivers are a peculiar race; they behave like other men when they dabble in other trades, and therefore we have not got to look far for the cause of their disease. It lies in the fact that they are over-organized, that they are meddled with by a paternal government, that the price of what they sell is regulated by an inelastic Act of Parliament which recognizes no change of weather, no difference in roads, no variation in the cost of keeping horses. The decree has gone forth that sixpence per mile is the proper charge for driving two persons in an ordinary cab, and the driver who accepts his position is treated as a government machine. He has no power to make a bargain except against himself; he has no power to charge more for struggling across London Bridge, or toiling up Pentonville Hill, than for bounding across Belgrave Square; he is hemmed in by a hundred rules and regulations which are poor substitutes for free action, and he is hourly irritated by seeing omnibus competitors working under a most accommodating sliding scale of charges. Sometimes he must feel like a child, sometimes like a fool, especially if he is so unfortunate as to be of a reflecting disposition. In an age of free trade, when every commercial restriction is being swept away like cobwebs, he stands high and dry as a melancholy monument of protection. Taken with his sulky look, his battered cab, and his wrinkled horse, he forms a pretty picture of the triumphs of Government interference.

If anything were wanted to make this State regulation of a particular branch of trade ridiculous, it would be the recent provisions issued by the proper authorities for the improvement of the cab service. No new cab driver is to be provided with a badge unless he can prove that he can read and write with fluency and propriety. Just as the public are calling out for more vehicles, a rule is published which is likely to check the supply. The quality of the drivers is to be improved, or in other words the quantity is to be carefully limited; while the unchangeable sixpence is still to rule the road, and the usual rise in price under such circumstances is not to be officially permitted. As the feelings of the drivers may naturally be outraged by this tightening of the reins, the precaution is taken to get none but well-educated cabmen. The influence of a little schooling is expected to curb their temper, or at least to cause their oaths to be of a refined and agreeable nature. Nothing is said about vaccination, the use of the globes, or a knowledge of music, but they are evidently expected to drive their horses only to the genteelest of melodies. The connection between reading and writing and the management of horses in crowded streets it is not easy to see; nor is it quite plain why arithmetic is to be left out of this new competitive examination. The cabman's work requires him to be constantly calculating, and a government which undertakes to improve the breed of cabmen should surely not omit to develop their arithmetical faculties.

The evident break-down of all this official coddling of a particular trade is nothing more than might have been reasonably expected. A wish to try free-trade in cabs is now very generally expressed, because it is felt that any change can hardly make matters worse, while it will probably make them much better. There is no proof that cleaner vehicles and stronger horses cannot be supplied at less than sixpence a mile, under a system which will give fair play to wholesome vigorous competition. At present the cab interest is withered by confinement in official fetters, and it is a standing reproach to our good sense and our business habits. Free-trade in cabs may be good for owners and drivers, may have been demanded by some few advanced

men at the recent public meetings of cabmen; but the consumer is the person whose interest we are chiefly bound to
consult, and he can hardly be injured by liberty to make
his own cab bargains. Practically, he does this at present
in many instances, in defiance of the Act of Parliament
and this is another reason for removing these absurd and
injurious restrictions. The sins of cabmen—those peculiar
to their trade—are nearly all produced by official coddling.
The cabman kicks over the traces more frequently than any
other labourer, because the traces are galling, and because
he is intensely human. He has long learnt to lose faith
in the regulating power of the Act which regulates his
fares, and to trust to the generosity of his employers for
an increase of his fees. This stimulates his imagination
to an unhealthy extent, and like all persons who speculate
upon receiving an unknown quantity, he often over-values
his prospects. When the payment comes, liberal though it
may be, it often falls far below his sanguine estimate, and
hence that black unamiable look (to say nothing of rude
remarks) which is so familiar to cab-hirers. A fixed payment at the outset, even though the amount promised be
smaller than the sum paid under the circumstances just
named, always makes a much happier and civil driver, and
consequently a much happier rider.

Many of the vices charged against cabmen, according
to the Hackney Carriage Act, become virtues when looked
at in a broader moral light. One charge frequently repeated
of late is, that cab drivers object to take two people when
they are hailed by four; but what is this but studying the
greatest happiness of the greatest number? Two people
are incommoded that four may be accommodated; and how
has the cabman done anything by which society is a loser?
He has looked after his own interest while studying the

interest of the public, and has unconsciously obeyed a great economic law in preference to one of the most rotten Acts of Parliament.

Cabmen have doubtless many faults which are common to all labourers of the same grade, but there is no need to increase and aggravate these by over-legislation. We have tried the protective government regulation system for our London cabs, and that has notoriously failed; we may now try the opposite system in the name of justice and sound policy. If the cabman is not improved by this much-required change, it will then be time to condemn him as an incorrigible offender. At present he claims the indulgence of the court, because there are many excuses for his shortcomings. Free-trade in cabs, under a few sensible regulations, would doubtless weed out the blackest of the black sheep, and turn those who are left into labourers worthy of their hire.

CABS.

THE pleasure of being brought face to face with a thoroughly bad article is seldom appreciated as it ought to be. There is a mediocrity which is neither loved by gods nor men; but first-rate badness is infinitely superior to this. Perfection is a very good and enjoyable thing in its way, but excellent imperfection is sometimes better and more enjoyable. The man is to be envied who sits down in a dingy, comfortless tavern—a tavern that may possibly be working under the inspection of sheriff's officers—who orders the worst chop in all England; who is served by the worst waiter in all England, or probably in the world; and who feels that nothing can equal the badness of the whole luncheon. Every shortcoming is a source of satisfaction and amusement. The absence of the commonest condiments produces a thrill of delight; the commonest questions become pleasant probes which spy out the nakedness of the land; the paper, a month old, is read with a strange unearthly interest; and when the bill, always extravagant, is paid, the payer almost wishes it could be more extravagant.

The same satisfaction is felt in sitting down with one of the worst books ever written, or in gazing at one of the worst pictures ever painted. A feeling of pity steals over the reader or the spectator for those unhappy fellow-creatures who have no opportunity of enjoying so much excellent badness. The treasures of the richest libraries, of the noblest galleries, sink into insignificance by the side of these two thoroughly bad productions. The book is bought up, and becomes rarer than a certain notorious essay by John Wilkes, or a folio edition of Shakespeare. The picture is carried off by some rich and happy capitalist to be gloated over in secret, or to become a joy for ever to a particular family.

The worst servants, the worst landlords, the worst architects, the worst vestry, the worst member of parliament, and a hundred other bad things may all be invaluable agents in promoting the pleasures of life. It all depends upon the temper in which they are looked at. If those who are largely dependent upon such agents can school themselves into caring very little for their services, and can watch them philosophically, as the movements of insects are watched in a microscope, then their bad qualities, brought out in work and action, become more amusing than a play; and irritation is changed into quiet applause. Any attempt to improve such agents, after they are regarded in this mood, is almost resented as an impertinence. The reformers are sometimes looked upon as dangerous innovators, anxious to meddle with matters which they cannot understand, and shake the foundations of society. Things once abused as nuisances soon mellow into institutions in a conservative country, and any attempt to supplant them only meets with coldness and suspicion.

There is one supremely bad thing—worse even than bad lodgings or bad boots—whose existence is threatened at the present moment: we allude to the London cab. After a stormy reign of nearly a quarter of a century, this dear old stuffy institution is threatened with extinction. There can be no question about its badness—a badness that we are inclined to father upon our legislation; there can be no question about the fleas which it has nourished, about the discomfort which it has caused to riders, about the disgraceful figure which it has cut in the eyes of foreign and provincial visitors. Its warmest friends will hardly contend that in its four-wheeled shape it has given the public a seat upon which any man, woman, or child could sit at ease, or a window which would keep out wind and rain, and ventilate the creaking, jolting box at the same time. No one can say that in its "Hansom" shape it has furnished a vehicle which could be entered without danger, or sweeping the mud off the wheels, or whose bending, clattering window could be ordered down in rough weather without the fear of a broken nose. No one can say that it was ever built to carry the two persons of average size named in its licence, or that it has not been as destructive to hats as theatres or churches. These are defects which are candidly admitted on all sides without any desire to grumble, and yet the institution or nuisance (call it by what name we will) is not taunted about its threatened destruction. Two Joint-Stock Companies are in the field, rich in all the machinery of combined enterprise and the promises of amiable prospectuses, who sound the death-knell of the London cab when they announce a supply of superior hack conveyances. These companies are started for the professed purpose of giving us better horses and vehicles for the same money, and yet we scarcely welcome them. We are not averse to improvements in cabs, we have no objection to use a brougham at sixpence a mile instead of an egg-chest upon wheels; but the promoters of these companies will pardon us if we are suspicious for a reason. We cannot forget the promises which ushered in the Gene-

ral Omnibus Company about seven years ago, and the very
scanty performance which has followed upon those promises. The French system of "correspondence" has not
been imported, the improved vehicles have been very few
and far between, several wholesome attempts at competition have been "nursed" off the road, and the few advanced Exhibition omnibuses introduced from Manchester
have been bought up with rather suspicious avidity. The
Cab Companies may keep better faith with the public than
the great Omnibus Company has done, and, in spite of the
existing absurd legal restrictions on cabs, may be able to
make good service run on all fours with good dividends.
The proof of the pudding, however, to use a homely phrase,
will be in the eating. The buying up of the present ricketty
stock, and the gloss of a few coats of paint and varnish,
will hardly be considered a reform by the cab-hiring public. The new Cab Companies must do more than this
which is nearly all that the Omnibus Company did, if they
wish to obtain an enlarged support for their venture. The
faults of our four-wheeled and Hansom cabs lie deeper than
the travel-stains on their battered sides; they are radical
errors of construction. The Cab Companies must give us
more room and better springs for our money, to say
nothing about less exhausted horses.' They must place
London, which is jocularly called the first city in the world,
upon a level with our provincial towns in public vehicles.
Manchester, Liverpool, and even distant Aberdeen, have
better cabs than the Metropolis, and it remains to be seen
whether the new Cab Companies will relieve us from this
subordinate position. Where we ought to lead we can only
follow, but, by all means, let us follow as quickly as possible. Our population is large enough, our distances are
long enough, and our tastes are luxurious enough, to pay

any one who will accede to our wishes. We shall part with the old London cab, if the separation is ordained, with tender regret, and an admiration fostered by its exceeding badness; but we shall welcome its successor with hope and enthusiasm. One thing alone will check this enthusiasm —the probable mediocrity of the new vehicles. We are sick of half measures in carriage reform. If the new cabs are not to be new, if they are not to be either supremely bad or supremely good, they had better be strangled in their birth.

These things may appear small to grumble about, but life is made up of small things, and he who endeavours to make such trifles pleasant, promotes the greatest happiness of the greatest number. The cab question in London is not so small, when we consider that about seven thousand of these regulated vehicles are let actively loose upon the Metropolis. If the number were smaller, however, it would still involve a great principle. We have tried Government protection, as applied to hackney carriages, and this is all it can give us. It is now time, so it seems, to let this branch of human industry loose, and see what cab-owners and cab-drivers can do for us, with the liberty of fixing their own prices. Manchester, as before remarked, is able to produce a far better vehicle at about equal fares; and finds no dreadful anarchy in a system where every coach proprietor makes his own charge, the simple machinery of appeal being the Town Hall and its authorities. We have been taught many lessons in free trade by Manchester, before now, and it appears that it is necessary for it to teach us another.

NO THOROUGHFARE.

THE partial abolition of all toll-gates within five miles of London ought to draw attention to a defect in our means of internal communication which requires a speedy remedy. The railway undertakings which have been carried out almost remorselessly within the last five or six years, the Bills for new sub-ways and iron highways that are now before Parliament, remove any delicacy which we might ever have felt about speaking out on this subject. We not only want to see every toll-gate swept away which now stands within five miles of London, or even in a far broader area, but we should like to welcome a bold, well-considered measure that would do away with every private barrier. Whether the obstruction be a floriated iron-gate in charge of a liveried porter, which attempts to filter the traffic to and from a particular square; whether it is a row of unsightly posts, like uneven teeth, which dam out a few costermongers' barrows in a back street of the suburbs; whether it is a forlorn "halfpenny hatch" which rots in pernicious idleness in the middle of some withered highway, or a swinging-gate which is a popular plaything for the children of a crowded neighbourhood—no matter what shape it takes, or to whom it belongs, we wish to see it rooted out as speedily as possible. We have no more ill-will against the Duke of Bedford or the

Marquis of Westminster in this matter, than we have against some unknown Mr. Jones or Jenkins who may be the holder of a London cloister. We know the value of peace and quietness as fully as the hero of a certain well-known farce; we know how charming and snug it is to live in a settlement, which is as much like the cathedral square of a remote city as bolts and bars can make it, although pitched in the very heart of the metropolis. We are not blind to the selfish advantages which may thus be enjoyed by a select few, to the manifest inconvenience of the vulgar many. We have long felt, however, that a city is not made for one man, or one body of men, but for everybody whose lot may be cast in it. In much of our recent legislation this truth has been half recognized, but only in that petty way which shows either ignorance or timidity. No one has been bold enough to propose the removal of these numerous barriers, on the ground that the owners were maintaining them in defiance of all good citizenship and public morals. Attempts have been made, from time to time, to get rid of one or two of these obstructive gates, but nothing like a general movement with fixed principles has been organized. We have a recollection of something like a parochial riot about the barrier at the end of Devonshire Place, but the local Rebeccas were defeated by the strong arm of possession. Other points have been attacked in these London barricades, but by troops who had neither leaders, force, nor sustaining power.

It will not be necessary, in order to prove that we are not fighting with shadows, to give a detailed list of London streets which are kept under lock and key by their private owners. Every Vestry—every district Board of Works within the metropolitan limits can furnish a long catalogue of these obstructions. A locked-up meadow, or a private road, may be tolerated at the side of a country highway, or even in a country village, but certainly not in the midst of three millions of busy people. It wants no quotations from great authorities, the acknowledged sources of political wisdom, to prove that the rights of property will not morally sustain such an occupancy. If we object to the stand-and-deliver system of collecting public tolls, how much more strongly must we object to a power which shuts a public door in our face, and will only open it in accordance with its own peculiar fancies? The uncertainty as to the hours when these barriers may be open or may be closed, is a fruitful source of annoyance to Londoners and their visitors. If the owners closed them altogether, they could hardly injure the public more than they do by admitting a few vehicles and pedestrians at very uncertain specified periods.

This baronial mode of dealing with large tracts of metropolitan ground that ought, by their position, to be thoroughfares, may seem very grand and feudal to many people, who affect to worship the barbarous and the mediæval. We respect the rights of property fully as much as these adorers of the past, but we see a right of property which they are probably blind to. This right is the ancient right of way—the power to command the use at all seasons and at all hours of anything like a road or pathway from one part of the City to another. Nothing in the shape of landed proprietorship, private convenience, or the desire to preserve unnatural solitudes within a gunshot of Temple Bar, ought to stand in the way of this greater right and convenience. When bills like the one which empowered the formation of the Underground Railway were brought before the House of Commons for its sanction, every personal and private objection was overruled for the sake of the general public. When the railway was being constructed, during a painful and never-to-be-forgotten period of three years, its legalized nuisances were tolerated for the sake of the public benefit. When several lunatics and a score of bankrupts were made, and a vast amount of house property was undermined and depreciated, all these injuries were tolerated for the sake of the public benefit. In the face of this and similar undertakings, where nothing has been allowed to interfere with a work which is thought to be for the public good, we should like to know why any hesitation should be shown in dealing with our London barriers. Powers, of course, must be got from Parliament, and the vigorous opposition of many landowners and property-champions will probably have to be encountered; but if compensation were freely and liberally offered, much of this opposition would either be withdrawn, or deprived of its strength by the force of public opinion. This question, like the abolition of tolls question, must not be looked at in a penny-wise manner. As a general metropolitan tax will be the only equitable financial substitute for tolls to pay for the maintenance of the public highways, so a similar tax ought to furnish the funds for this purchase of thoroughfares. This task is an important part of that greater work which is necessary for the improvement of London, and if undertaken in an earnest spirit it will not be merely tilting at windmills.

A WEST-END THOROUGHFARE.

WE have thousands of streets, and courts, and alleys, scattered throughout London, that make us doubt our humanity and civilization, and even the existence of our boasted "local governments." We have close, square blocks of human dwellings, built at the back of busy thoroughfares, and approached by narrow passages like the mouths of ovens, whose roots lie soaking in stagnant cess-pools, and whose walls go up to the little patch of heaven like the sides of a deep well. We have mockeries of English homes where children crouch upon rotten vege-table matter, and where every kind of contagious disease is nourished as in a hot-bed. We have not to search for these blots in any particular corner of the metropolis. They may be found in Shoreditch, in Bethnal-Green, and in Lambeth; but they flourish just as rankly in Maryle-bone and courtly Westminster. If Soho, St. James's, and St. Martin's can boast of no physical superiority over poorer and distant parishes, they have nothing to be proud of in their moral condition. A more frowsy, utterly shame-less, festering neighbourhood than that which is rotting round Leicester Square, can hardly be found in any part of the world. The coarse sensual dens of Holland and the half-fabled receptacles of Parisian immorality are refined gold compared to these gilded hives of vice and pollution.

A popular notion prevails that this quarter represents France in London; but no fouler injustice was ever done to the French nation. If Leicester Square, the Haymarket, and Piccadilly were in Paris instead of London, the good-will of their wretched debaucheries would not ¦be worth a half-penny.

We will take the Haymarket, and all that it includes. We know we are treading on the skirts of a very delicate subject; but there are times and seasons when all mock-modesty must be thrown aside, and we must look our "social evils" full in the face. No good public purpose can ever be served by a studied silence upon these offensive themes. Many rampant, full-blooded national nuisances are encouraged in their encroachments, because they see that their enemies fear to speak about them. If all the moral lepers of our modern Babylon could be collected in one quarter, walled and fenced in, ticketed in plain, unmistakable characters, there would be much wisdom, perhaps, in giving them an exchange, or market-place, where every London fool or gaping rustic could go to be fleeced. If our really dangerous classes were so attractive that, though dammed up within certain limits, they still gathered a certain per centage of victims, it may be a question whether the State would have any further right to interfere. Government is a fine thing, a useful thing, and a costly thing; but it is not its duty to extinguish all candles that fairly attract moths, nor to protect all moths that *will* fly into the candles.

The Haymarket, however, with it gaudy dens and brazen-faced loungers, is not one of these recognized licensed markets for vice. Though the really dangerous classes have taken forcible possession of nearly the whole of the west side, and are now beginning to occupy the east, there are many respectable business residents still remaining, who have to live daily and hourly in the midst of these nuisances. They look from their windows upon a long and growing line of "cafés," whose doors are nearly always crowded with evil-eyed old women, representing the capital of prostitution, or low, bearded, ruffianly-looking men, who are its champions, and its guardians. All through the morning the flaring shutters of these dens are generally closed, but towards the afternoon their owners begin to prepare for work, and dull, fishy-eyed servants sweep out the fragments of the last night's orgie. As evening approaches the usual revel begins, to die out a little between the hours of nine P.M. and eleven P.M., when the different casinos and singing-rooms in the neighbourhood are in full swing, and to revive again with fresh vigour a few minutes after midnight. Then bright-eyed, hollow-cheeked, painted women sweep along in their borrowed silk; crowds of idle, thoughtless men pour out from the different oyster-rooms; others look in as they pass from the opera or the clubs; countrymen visiting London, who wish to see what they are told is "life," rush up in cabs from theatres and concert-rooms. Old men, who are not aware that manners have changed since the days when morals were very loose and cravats were very stiff; young clerks who have an ambition to be men of the world, and who, in all probability, are trembling on the verge of embezzlement; half the celebrities of crime in the metropolis—everything, in fact, that is false, rotten, and bad in London, may be met with in this public thoroughfare during the small hours of the morning. The lights in the different "cafés" are turned on to the full; most of them are doing a roaring trade; they have no spirit or wine licences, and are consequently free of the police, whilst any fiery stimulants their customers want can be easily obtained from neighbouring taverns. The new act compelling public-houses to close between the hours of one and three in the morning scarcely touches them. The gaudy cotton velvet couches are crowded with noisy occupants; and a stray nobleman or two of not over pure tastes may occasionally give an aristocratic flavour to the orgies. A quarrel will often ensue between certain Guelphs and Ghibellines of the lost class. Bonnets will be torn, windows smashed, marble tables overturned, and the whole motley crowd—half drunk and wholly excited—will flow out from the different dens into the highway. The air will then perchance be rent with cries of " Murder ;" and oaths and imprecations, foul allusions, shrieks, the noise of heavy bodies falling against closed shutters, will rise up to the sleeping chambers of those few respectable residents who are compelled by the interests of business to live and bring up their families in this infested neighbourhood.

When things get to the worst they are supposed to mend, and the Haymarket, with all that it includes, ought to be dealt with promptly and vigorously. It answers no useful purpose—not even in the economy of vice. The harpies who live in it and around it feed as much upon the " unfortunates," who are used as decoys, as they do upon the fools who are caught in the net. When the ordinary blandishments of vice are found to be powerless, and men of supposed respectable position are known to be present, a " row " is often arranged, during which some article of small value—such as a wreath or a bracelet—is palmed on to one of the unsuspecting visitors, and a charge of robbery is at once made in the hope that fear will produce a liberal offer to hush the matter up. Prostitution and café-keeping doubtless pay very well on the average, but there are times when "little plants" like this are found to be much more productive. We hear of the cases that are brought before the Marlborough Street police court, but how many are nightly settled without any magisterial aid ?

The persons primarily responsible for the present leprous state of the Haymarket are the police, the local authorities, and the owners of house property there. The police are easily and systematically bribed; the most reliable officers put over this district become corrupted in a week; and, after a loud and united complaint on the part of the respectable inhabitants, there is a fitful exercise of authority—nothing more. Local inspectors of nuisances make occasional reports when something more gross than ordinary is brought under their notice, but three-fourths of the Haymarket eyesores are not in their "department," and the best report is useless unless it is soon followed by action. Those owners of local house property who feed upon and encourage vice are the leading offenders, and it remains to be seen whether they can continue much longer to evade and defy the law. They sell their shops and houses in the dearest market, lease them, let them, and sub-let them to the very scum of the earth, and doubtless draw such a rental in short and substantial payments as secures them against every chance of prosecution or loss. Their tenants require neither music licence, wine licence, nor spirit licence, and, so far, they can snap their fingers at the whole bench of magistrates. They may be upheld in their pernicious course by the knowledge that the Crown owns houses in this thoroughfare, and is actually the proprietor of one of its vilest dens. The immediate communications with vice and fraud in such a case are made through ordinary Crown tenants, who hold the property on the usual terms ; but the State is the first landlord, and, as such, receives a certain portion of the tainted money drawn from sharpers and prostitutes.

NUISANCES.

Am I to become the sport of my nerves? Am I to be a slave to my senses of sight, smell, and hearing? Or am I to stand up against the encroaching power of these four secondary parts of my mental and physical organization, and to say boldly, I will acknowledge no government but that of my head and my heart? Am I to try everything by the eternal standard of self—the everlasting me—and to ignore all that is done by my fellow-creatures, unless it happens to harmonize with my own petty tastes, and feelings? Who am I, what am I, that I should set myself up as the judge of what is correct and agreeable—the putter-down and mover-on of what is improper, or repugnant to my standard of taste? What is my standard of taste? Is it something infallible—something that may be trusted under every change of circumstances, every variation of temperature, every condition of bodily feeling, or is it not rather the slave of all these things, a compound of physical weakness and mental prejudice? What right have I, a poor, weak, erring, insignificant atom upon the great earth, to sit in judgment upon anything, and call it a positive nuisance? A floor-cloth manufactory—is that a nuisance? Not absolutely or altogether so. The smell of the paint acts differently upon different constitutions; and although I cannot say that it excites in me any very agreeable sensation, I know that an open gas-pipe does, and I have a right, therefore, to assume that all men are not disgusted with a floor-cloth manufactory. Anyway, there are the work-people and their families—and no mean number of these things are to be settled by majorities— who would be sorry to hear that the nuisance which provides them with bread was put down according to act of parliament.

The fat man, with the broad, opaque back, who always sits before me in a theatre, and interferes with my personal comfort in a public conveyance, becomes at times such an intolerable nuisance, that if I were to give way to the savage impulses of my nature, I should smite him down with the first destructive instrument at hand. A little reflection, a little communion with my better humanity, convinces me, however, that he is a far greater nuisance to himself than he is to those around him, and that I am not altogether guiltless of various little acts of an annoying character by which I irritate him, and deprive myself of the pure right of complaint. At the theatre, my sharp, attenuated knees painfully penetrate his yielding back; and in the omnibus, the hard, keen angles of my pocket-book, or my snuff-box, find a resting-place in the soft substance of his incompressible sides. As I see him weltering in perspiring agony in the boiling caldron of a crowded, unventilated stage-pit—in the close, musty depths of a public vehicle—or waddling as the butt and football of every hurrying passenger on the Queen's highway—my antagonism is disarmed, and I pass him tenderly, as I should one who was blind.

Slow people in the streets are nuisances, especially the two young ladies and their dowager-mamma, who will walk three abreast with a snail-like movement almost

imperceptible to the naked eye. If I gave way to my
feelings as I hasten to attain a given point by a certain
time, I should unceremoniously break the self-complacent
line of the fair promenaders, and scatter them on each side
to the gutter and the wall; but a glance backward at the
indignant faces of the persons whom I have rudely passed,
convinces me that my haste is a greater nuisance to society
at large, than the calm tardiness of the three ladies who
form an elegant barrier across the footway.

The street-vendor of hardware, who stands at my area-
railings with a couple of tea-trays under his arm, which it
is a gross, unpardonable insult to my taste to suppose that,
under any circumstances, I shall buy, appears a thorough
nuisance to my one-sided vision, when he will not move
on, under repeated hostile signs, which I make to him from
behind the blind of my dining-room window. But if I
have the heart, or take the trouble to look at the other
side of this nuisance—the side that is not immediately
presented to my sight—I shall see, in all probability, an
anxious, struggling, itinerant trader, with a small capital,
moving from house to house, in search of a humble living
for the family dependent upon him. As he passes up one
hard, unsympathizing street, and down another, meeting
with nothing but closed doors, and the eternal hasty shake
of the frowning head, it may be that, in his melancholy
reflections, society appears to be a greater nuisance to him
than he ever appears to be to society. If I changed
places with him this instant, should I conduct myself with
more propriety of demeanour? should I carefully draw the
line at that nice point where praiseworthy perseverance
ends, and troublesome impertinence begins, with the ever-
increasing cry for bread, bread, bread, ringing unceasingly
in my ears?

Let any man whose nervous system is cultivated to the highest pitch of sensitiveness, try to see in the noisy huckster of the streets a fellow-labourer, whose lot has fallen upon more stony ground, and he will hear from that moment a plaintive music in the most uncouth sounds that ever issued from the lips of street-trader or street-minstrel. There will be an end to those fretful starts of impatience when the sharp, short, quick beats of the Indian tom-tom burst upon the ear, and he will learn to look with pity upon the poor copper-coloured performer who chants his wild lay in calico and a March wind. Rude and unmusical the performance may be, but not more so than Professor Gamma's illustrations of Greek harmony, to which the learned flock in crowds, and in the crabbed, four-note combinations of which they affect to discover a simple melody that is not altogether unpleasing to the ear. I have had my horror of the oriental nuisance long ago, but it fled before a day-dream picture of myself in Singapore—the temperature lowered to freezing-point, the European population rooted out, and I singing, to an unsympathizing populace, for my daily food and my nightly bed, one of the wild songs of my native land.

The organ nuisance, I must say, never annoyed me, because I am not a learned and indefatigable man, like my neighbour, Dr. M'Verbose, who is preparing his great work upon the currency for a not over-expectant public. He is continually calling in the assistance of the Vandal policeman to stop the *Casta Diva* abruptly in the middle, because the subtle theories of a man who is about to open up upon paper unbounded supplies of paper-wealth to pacify the insatiable hunger of the directors of a delusive commerce, cannot be properly worked out while an Italian scena is being performed upon a barrel-organ under the

window, with a fluto-harmonicon accompaniment. A
nuisance, no doubt, to Dr. M'Verbose is that poor, pinched,
dirty-faced, slouched-hatted, idiotic, smiling, nodding, me-
chanically-musical emigrant from the sweet south; but a
far greater nuisance to a large circle is the learned doctor
—even before his great work is published—without having
the excuse of the Italian, that he is fighting for a living.
The nuisance of the organ-player begins and ends in himself, but the nuisance of Dr. M'Verbose and his theories
will become multiplied in the persons of a hundred
active disciples. As for me, I am content to stop for a
time the working of the mental mill, and look out into the
falling snow, to dream—as I listen to the melodies of the
Italian composer—of a land where the people live in contented idleness under the sun, where the street-minstrel is
welcomed by young and old, and not moved on by every
uncongenial hermit who dwells in the social isolation of
eight rooms and a kitchen.

In nothing are men so inconsistent as in their horror
of nuisances, the most sensitive being usually the greatest
offenders. The hardened snuff-taker, who sneezes with
the roar of a wild beast in the middle of a solemn service,
will leap off his chair at the sound of a postman's knock;
and the man whose nerves are irritated by the ringing of
church-bells, will play complacently upon the bagpipes in
the bosom of his family.

AN UNNEIGHBOURLY ACT.

THOSE who live in society should either learn to tolerate society, or should retire to those deep solitudes and awful cells where the evils and advantages of living in crowds are unknown. Every man who comes out of the wilderness to dwell in London, and to form part of any given street, crescent, or square, should leave his castle, and all notions pertaining to castles behind him, and should amiably and tranquilly accept the new conditions of citizenship under which he lives and moves. Books, pictures, architecture, gas, water, and police—all the appliances of civilization are brought within his reach at the smallest possible cost, and in return he is expected to give up much of that individuality, that rugged independence in which the country resident may fairly indulge. The moment he takes up his abode in the town he becomes a neighbour, with all a neighbour's rights and duties. He is part of a great and delicate machine which is easily thrown out of gear. To use a common expression, he must " give and take ;" he must bow to the wishes of majorities ; he must do unto others as he would be done by, and he must study the greatest happiness of the greatest number. If he fails in these duties, he will be a bad neighbour, and a bad member of society.

One way of encouraging the growth of bad neighbours

and bad members of society is to make bad laws; and Mr.
Bass's Metropolitan Street Music Bill will be a law of this
kind if it is not rendered inoperative by the superior morality of the public. It will not only give power to individuals
which they may use against the wishes and pleasure of the
mass, but it will nourish a belief that the exercise of such
power is a praiseworthy act performed under the highest
sanction. It will stigmatize a harmless commodity much in
demand as a "nuisance," and the men who sell this commodity as "rogues and vagabonds." Mr. Gladstone may
well say that the bill "treads on dangerous ground," for no
measure could well be framed which would more pamper
private rights at the expense of public duties.

Mr. Bass's bill, which is very short, enacts that any
householder, personally, or by his servant, or by a police-
constable, may require any street musician or singer to
depart from the neighbourhood of the house; and a penalty
of forty shillings or three days' imprisonment, as the magistrate may think fit, is imposed on every one who, after
being so required to depart, sounds or plays upon any musical instrument or sings in any thoroughfare near any such
house. It is to be lawful for a police-constable to take the
offender into custody without a warrant. The bill extends
only to the metropolitan police district.

A measure of this character would hardly have been
tolerated if the so-called "nuisance" which it sought to
remedy had not been grossly exaggerated. To justify such
an interference with the open sale and purchase of music
and amusement, it was necessary to describe the music as
discordant, the amusement as low, and as rather forced
upon than sought by the public, and the annoyance to
minorities of one or two persons in particular streets or
districts as something which no man could bear, and yet

pursue his avocation. No attempt has been made to show that the measure has been actually demanded even by these minorities of one or two, here and there, if we except Mr. Babbage, and we must, therefore, assume that it has been benevolently supplied without an order. It may seem ungenerous to look a gift horse in the mouth, but there are many horses which are not worth their salt. This piece of spontaneous benevolent legislation is a horse of this character, got by well-meaning fogyism out of blind misrepresentation. Caricatures, superfine articles in a few journals, and one or two pamphlets have sustained those who ask for this exceptional Act of Parliament—this licence to put down the harmless pleasures of the many for the sake of gratifying a fretful few. Highly-coloured pictures have been drawn of ugly, grinning brigands, armed with knives to defend their hurdy-gurdies, and who, like the "wandering minstrel" of the play, are well acquainted with the value of peace and quietness, and never "move on under a shilling." This is the fancy sketch, but what is the reality? Generally a weak-faced smiling Italian—too indolent to be greedy, with a well-tuned organ, correct because mechanical, discoursing the best music of the day, and educating the ear of hundreds for a few halfpence. Such a visitor in poor and middle-class neighbourhoods is welcomed eagerly by young and old. Little children, the most sensitive and truest judges of humanity, crowd round him, and pay him for his pleasant labour with the coins given them by friends or parents. This is the organ-fiend that Parliament is solemnly asked to exorcise, of whom the following anecdote was told the other day by a respectable contemporary :—

"For years past one of the much-abused 'organ-grinders' has been a regular Tuesday-morning visitor in the streets of Pentonville; and his instrument, so far from being voted a nuisance, has made him welcome, not only to juveniles, but to parents and others, who have an ear, if not for music, for childhood's joyous play. Yesterday he appeared as usual, and, to those who had been accustomed to reward his efforts, he sent in a neatly-written English circular, returning thanks for the patronage afforded in the past, and intimating that the state of his health required his return to his warmer native land. He desired, therefore, to bid his friends a grateful farewell. There is little doubt that this was a genuine outburst of feeling; and we can only wish that the poor man might bear with him some better fruit of an English sojourn than the pence of his patrons."

More appeals like this might be made to the better feeling of good citizens, if the question was to be settled by feeling, and more evidence of the same kind might be produced, if the bill had been based upon evidence. Evidence and feeling, however, have been set aside, and prejudice has been the chief law-maker. Organ-playing is to be "put down," and we all know what putting down leads to. It sets class against class, and produces a bitter, uncharitable spirit, a desire for revenge, very injurious to social morality. If street-music, good, indifferent, and bad, is to be sweepingly called a "nuisance," and to be "regulated" off the face of the earth, how many more "nuisances" are there which might be so treated, but which are tolerated for the sake of our neighbours? Take the smoking-nuisance, the pipe and cigar question, for example. This has been leniently dealt with, without special acts of parliament, in the true spirit of good citizenship, because the majority are supposed to be smokers; but suppose a "factious minority," who may be really annoyed by smokers in most places and at all seasons, were to get some courageous member to plead their cause, and to ask for some such enactment as the following:—" The existing law is found to be insufficient for the protection of house-holders from annoyance by smokers, and, therefore, be it enacted that any householder, personally, or by his servant, or by a police-constable, may require any smoker, or even chewer of tobacco, to depart from the neighbourhood of the house ; and a penalty of forty shillings, or three days' imprisonment, as the magistrate may think fit, is imposed on every one who, after being so required to depart, smokes or lights any pipe or cigar, or chews tobacco in any thoroughfare near any such house. It is to be lawful for a police-constable to take the offender into custody without a warrant, and the bill (for the present) is only to extend to the metropolitan police district."

A bill like this would only be directed against an intensely selfish pleasure which is often productive of great annoyance to many worthy and responsible people ; while Mr. Bass's bill is meant practically to destroy a recreation which is open and liberal, and which has a refining influ-ence in places where such influences are most needed.

THE TRAVELLING ENGLISH.

No people travel so much abroad as the English, especially in the hot months of the year; no people are so little skilled in speaking any language but their own; and no people run so much after scenery, parks, palaces, and picture-galleries. The Rhine during August and September is as much an English "silent highway" as the Thames between London and Gravesend, and Paris receives every week in the short tourist season from twenty to a hundred thousand English visitors. When the thermometer in that delightful city stands at a hundred degrees in the shade, and all the chief theatres are closed, and dogs, under a penalty payable by their owners, of many francs of fine, are compelled to drag on a miserable existence with their mouths fastened in tin canisters or wire baskets, and when every Parisian who can scrape together a few napoleons is away at some sandy watering-place or leafy spa, then a few favoured districts of Paris are flooded with British tourists. Americans, commercial travellers, and French provincials are there to keep them company, but the pleasure-seeking English are the people who take visible possession of nearly all the chief shows, bazaars, and boulevards. Like the ordinary French in London, however, they seldom move beyond a certain circle. It is true, they have no quarter as thoroughly English as Leicester Square with its tributaries is French, but they move in a beaten track marked out for them by guide-books, and see little of the real city and less of the real people. There are streets in Paris—in spite of the "improvements"—in which an Englishman is never seen, and where he would be stared at like a white man at Timbuctoo. There are men and women in Paris whose ways of life are as unknown to the British tourist as the habits of the Fans or Aztecs. The tomb of Napoleon, the galleries of the Louvre, the waters of Versailles, the churches, the Champs Elysées, a dancing garden like Mabille, perhaps a theatre or two, and certainly a circus, some half dozen hotels, and about as many cafés, form the ordinary travelling Englishman's Paris. At the hotels he meets none but his compatriots; and though he sits upon French furniture, and skates upon a waxed floor, he is waited upon by Germans or Swiss, who speak a kind of talkee-talkee English; he is fed with legs of mutton and "trimmings," cooked in the supposed British manner, and he drinks windy British bottled beer in preference to the wine of the country. When he moves from place to place it is generally in a solitary phaeton, with his nationality wrapped round him like a cloak, or in a first-class railway carriage, where he finds no one but his countrymen.

This "Rule Britannia" style of travelling is not calculated to remove many illusions and dispel many prejudices, but still it is better than no travelling at all. Few, even amongst the most bigoted Englishmen, now believe that all classes of Frenchmen are fed upon thin soup and sour wine, and that they eat frogs when they require more solid nourishment. Something more than a suspicion has now got hold of the British mind that frogs are as much a luxury in France as turtles are in England. The belief fostered by caricaturists at the beginning of the century, that Frenchmen are a nation of scraggy dancing-masters, has faded away, with many other vulgar errors, after fifty years of observation. A large number of such mistaken notions, however, still prevail, and these will probably never be got rid of until travellers travel a little more philosophically. The worst preparation for a foreign journey is to start with an assumption that you are about to visit some very curious people, whose manners are strange, quaint, and peculiar, and unlike anything else in the world. The British tourist, no matter where he may be going to, will do well to cherish a conviction that mankind are pretty much alike in all countries. The differences which exist are differences of condition, not of nature. A careful study of these differences of condition may save the British tourist from jumping to many hasty, sweeping, and unjust conclusions. For example, we hear far too much in this country about the "dirty foreigner." We are too apt to crow about our superior cleanliness, because our bed-rooms are not furnished with milk-jugs and sugar-basins instead of good-sized washing apparatus. This is taken as evidence that the foreigner has no taste for a clean skin, not only by our new school of fanatics who look upon the tub as the one thing needful, but by people who make very little use of cans and footbaths. Why one "foreigner" should be unlike another foreigner—for the English, strange as it may seem, are foreigners in relation to the French—is never explained, and the statement stands only as a broad assertion, sustained by and sustaining a diseased national pride. It is never remembered that Paris—we will still keep to France—has an atmosphere of so much higher purity than London, by reason of its wood fires, that the difference is as great as that between the atmospheres of London and the Potteries. It is never remembered that the water supply of the Paris houses is very defective, and that this is counterbalanced, in some measure, by the conveniences for bathing in the Seine. In no city are the baths so numerous and cheap; and it is just possible that a people who probably bathe more than the English, and who are not made so dirty with soot and coal smoke, may after all be quite as cleanly as our fanatics of the tub.

Many such prejudices as this exist, which it is good to try and dispel; and the French, on their side, have much to learn in this matter. In their dealings with the British tourist, there is what we may call the great beefsteak delusion. The popular notion in France, and even in Belgium, Holland, and other parts of the Continent, is that the travelling Englishman is always pining after beefsteaks at every hour of the day. The travelling Englishman has certainly too little toleration of national variations in cookery; but he is not such a worshipper of the beefsteak as the French imagine. He has no faith in being able to get the article in a state of British excellence; and here, as in many other things, he shows his ignorance of the country. There are places in Paris, not frequented much by the English, where this dish may be got in higher perfection than at many of our dingy taverns, and simply, we presume, because it is much eaten by the natives. The Frenchman, after all, is your great beefsteak eater—devouring it, with many adjuncts, at eleven o'clock in the day, long after the British tourist has breakfasted on eggs and bacon.

No international delusions ought to stand long in these days of free and cheap communication, if travellers would only study streets and people as well as palaces

and picture-galleries.   Perhaps, when the British tourist
has wandered for another quarter of a century he will
discover that Frenchmen are not mercurial, but somewhat
sad and earnest; that Dutchmen and Germans are rather
light, gay, and riotous; and that Italians are not always
breaking into tarantellas and flourishing stilettoes.

ON THE PARISH.

A CERTAIN story tells us how two gentlemen attended to hear a charity sermon, and while one was visibly affected by the preacher's eloquence, the other was totally unmoved.

"Beautiful discourse," said the impressionable listener; "so simple, and yet so full of spirit."

"Very likely," replied the listless member of the congregation, almost yawning. "I belong to another parish."

History has not handed down the name of the last speaker, nor has it told us anything about his position and occupation; but whatever he may have been, he was a parochial genius. Those few words contain the philosophy of a thousand vestries—the rule of action which guides, or ought to guide, their officers. That mysterious line or boundary, which is "beaten" every year; which disappears behind factories; dives under houses and gardens; comes up again in thoroughfares; embraces churches, skittle-grounds, and theatres; the tracing of which few of us ever considered a necessary part of our geographical knowledge; is the railing of a pen which encloses us as securely as sheep are secured in the market-place. To know it not, is to argue yourself unknown—a parish beneath the notice of rate-collectors on the one hand, beyond the sympathies of "relieving officers" on the other. This mysterious line is the great regulator of vestry taxation, of workhouse charity, and of those laws which preside over " settlement and removal." In some cases, it softly encloses a happy family of housekeepers, who have much to give, and no paupers worth speaking of, to maintain ; in others, it binds tightly round a hard-working district, where the empty mouths are almost too numerous for those whose duty it is to fill them. This is one result of the changes and varieties in house-property, the system of rating, and a want of an equalization of poor's-rates.

We are all familiar enough with the strange and the remote ; learned, to a fault, in distant boundaries of foreign states, the limits of disputed principalities, the quarrels of ministers at Vienna, or St. Petersburg. But how many of us ever looked into our Vestry Hall in the next street, or can tell the name of the man who "represents" us in that building ? We shrink from the heavy demands that are made upon our purses by our local assemblies ; we are surrounded, perhaps, by small nuisances, and sometimes suppose that the turnpike-man, the crossing-sweeper, the policeman, or the fire-engine-keeper, is the proper officer to remove them ; we pay for vast underground tunnels, new roads, new lamps, and a hundred other things that may have no existence, as far as we know, except upon paper ; and we seldom ask for information, because we laugh at a beadle, and dispise an overseer. The beadle grows, however, and so does the overseer. New districts spring up, and fall into their hands ; while old districts expand until they become as large as all London a century ago. The money these despised officers command and deal with, would have astonished our imperial chancellors of the exchequer in our great-grandfathers' days. The "local expenditure" of the United Kingdom, in the present year, for county, town, and parochial purposes, will be eighteen millions sterling; or within five millions sterling of the *whole expenditure, government and local,* of the thirty-two states of America, for the same period, with a greater population!*

If figures like these are not sufficient to arouse us from our sleep of parochial indifference, a number of parish newspapers are now printed and published, to teach us something about our local affairs. The oldest of these may have been born about eighteen hundred and fifty-three— the youngest, only the day before yesterday; and one or more may have " gone away, leaving no address;" but, at present, to the number of about five-and-twenty, there they are. The abolition of the stamp and advertisement duty has brought them into life, and the abolition of the paper duty will possibly swell their numbers and increase their size.

To those who remember what a leading French newspaper was, and what a leading American newspaper is, a *halfpenny* journal, like the "Clerkenwell News," which appears four times a week, or the "Islington Times," or the "Islington Gazette," must appear a wonder of trading enterprise. In the first of these journals, nearly two thousand advertisements in a single impression have appeared—a proof of the business activity of the district. The others show signs of vigorous health, and their general literary contents present little that can be cavilled at.

The work they set out to perform, and do perform, with

*	Population (1860).	Whole Expenditure.
United Kingdom . . .	30,000,000 . .	£94,000,000
United States . . .	31,000,000 . .	22,884,000

more or less judgment, taste, and skill, is essentially parochial. Nothing occurring within that boundary can be
too small and insignificant to interest their readers ; as
nothing occurring outside it can be large enough to
interest them. The " City Press," the largest of the district penny papers, is a model in this respect. If we
search its columns week after week, we shall find nothing
that is not strictly within the shadow of St. Paul's. It is
so conducted that hundreds outside the limits of the City
welcome it as the most complete record of City life ; and a
century hence its " files " will, perhaps, be found amongst
the most valuable materials for history in the British
Museum.

The " City Press " is a faithful representative of that
large gathering of small parishes, districts, and liberties,
included under the general title of the City of London.
The turbulent parishes of Marylebone and St. Pancras, including the smaller and distinct parish of Paddington, are
looked after by the " Marylebone Mercury," the " St.
Pancras Reporter," the " St. Pancras News," the " St. Pancras and Holborn Times," and " Marylebone and Finsbury
Advertiser," the " Holborn Journal," and the " Paddington
News." The important parish of St. George's, Hanover
Square, with the smaller parish of St. Martin's-in-the-
Fields, and Westminster generally, may consider themselves watched by the " West-End Examiner " and the
" West Central News." Chelsea, Kensington, Bayswater,
and their intermediate districts, are attended to by the
" Chelsea Chronicle," the " West Middlesex Advertiser,"
the " West London Observer," and the " Bayswater
Chronicle." Clerkenwell and Islington are happy in pos-
sessing the " Clerkenwell News," before alluded to, and
the " Clerkenwell Journal," with the " Islington Times "

and the "Islington Gazette," while the distant district of
Hackney, with all that it includes, is represented by the
"North-East London News." The Hendon, Hampstead,
Highgate, Colney-Hatch, and Hornsey clans of the London highlands are regulated in print by the "North
Middlesex Weekly Express," a full-grown quadruple-leaved
pennyworth, nearly as large as the "Times." In the low-
lands, the great parish of St. Leonard, Shoreditch, boasts
of the "Shoreditch Observer" and the "Shoreditch Advertiser;" while the greater parish of Lambeth, and the
wide-spreading district known popularly as "over the
water," is provided with the "South London Journal," the
"South London News," the "South London Chronicle,"
the "Clapham Gazette," and the "South-Western District
Times."

Of course, in organs giving full reports of every
meeting in the parish, and every discussion in the vestry,
there must, of necessity, be much that is "personal." Such
journals have no right to alter the utterances of parochial
speakers, to make a vulgar vestryman genteel, and a
ridiculous vestryman dignified. What their readers demand
from them are exact, word-for-word reports, and the public
good is best forwarded when these demands are complied
with. The vulgar and ridiculous vestrymen, and the small
jobbing contractors, are more likely to bridle their tongues
and curb their rapacity, when they know that every word
they utter, and everything they do, will be brought before
their constituents.

A reader of average discernment and industry may
take up the advertisement sheet of a paper like the
"Clerkenwell News," and, by reading its contents, may obtain
a fair idea of what life is in that district. A leading
article may instruct or amuse him, a letter from a cor-

respondent may tell him something about a local grievance; but a short pithy advertisement will give him facts, and give them to him in as few words as possible. There is seldom any of that stuff which is known as " English composition" in an ordinary trade advertisement; it is astonishing what a check is exercised upon exuberances of style when money has to be paid instead of received for what is written and printed.

Such a reader, on looking over the local papers of " The Well" (as it is familiarly called in the neighbourhood), will always find a thousand sacks of sawdust waiting his pleasure. Whatever may be the high and rising price of meat, of bread, of coals, coke, wood, and potatoes, it is some comfort to know that a quantity of material " fit for burning purposes" can always be had gratis for the trouble of fetching.

The same reader will also discover, what he may not have been aware of before, that he can have black eyes— the result of " accidents"—" eradicated in half an hour, without pain or injury." He will also see that credit is freely offered to him by strangers, and that he never need be without " bedding, furniture, boots, hats, and clothes," as long as he can prove himself to be " respectable." Cash loans he can have in all directions, from twelve shillings to two hundred pounds, " without delay," or " with no office fees," either at taverns, public offices, or private houses. If he wants to go into almost any conceivable business, it is ready to his hand; if he wants any conceivable kind of lodging, from a drawing-room to a back-kitchen, it is open to receive him. If he has a fancy for bargains, he can purchase pawnbrokers' tickets for almost any article; and if he can work at almost any mechanical trade, he is offered employment. If he wants a servant, a number of boys, lads, girls, young women, and "persons," press themselves upon his notice. If he wants a child's caul, a diving-bell, a mangle, or a printing-press, all are offered to him upon the most reasonable terms. If he is not a graceful dancer, the defect can soon be remedied, for a dozen professors stand forward eager to teach. If he wants recreation, he has a choice of many "music-halls," from the humble room over a tavern bar where the visitor is expected to contribute to the harmony of the evening, to the more ambitious building with the Corinthian portico, where the renowned Sam, Bill, Tom, Harry, and Dick Everybody are to be heard every evening at stated hours. If he lives in the neighbourhood, and is desirous of destroying bugs, a friend in need steps forward to "banish them for ever." "A lady, after trying, without success, numberless so-called remedies has at length discovered a speedy and never-failing method of utterly destroying these insects," and she kindly offers to communicate it for twelve postage-stamps, "to defray expenses." If he is in search of "happiness"—and who is not?—he hears that "wandering husbands can be reclaimed, recreant lovers brought to their mistresses' feet, and happiness imparted to all—high, low, rich, and poor—by an invaluable remedy known to the advertiser. The everlasting twelve postage-stamps are still required, and without them the secret can never be discovered. Occasionally, he is addressed in a style of rude familiarity, and reproached for his scanty patronage in some such terms as the following:—" * * * returns his thanks to those who *did* support him in his unfortunate shop — their name was not legion — and having completed his schedule, has four oil-paintings, good subjects, after Morland, Constable, Cooper, etc., and one hundred and sixty books, all standard works, to dispose of for nine pounds, so as to make his passage through Portugal Street as easily as possible. The goods can be seen at his venerable father's, the working furrier." . . . .

If the same patient and discerning reader were to wade through all the local newspapers of London in search of amusement, he would mostly find it in other parish organs than his own. We can always laugh at the follies of our neighbours. The following true report (I have altered the names) of a meeting at a " Board of Guardians" appears to me to put the authorities in a rather ridiculous position, because they are some one else's authorities, and not mine.

" Mr. Thornintheside got up, and said he had been informed that one of the guardians had taken two lunatics to the asylum; surely, they must have been remarkably quiet !

" Mr. Willinghorse admitted that *he* was the guardian alluded to. He had fetched one lunatic from Camberwell, and had taken another to the asylum from the ·House. Another guardian had promised to accompany him, but as he did not do so, he (Mr. W.) had taken a friend with him.

" Mr. Thornintheside would like to know what refreshments were charged for.

" Mr. Willinghorse had charged refreshments for himself only.

" Mr. Thornintheside would like to see the bill.

"Messrs. Brutus and Cassius quite differed with Mr. Thornintheside, and thought that, instead of censuring Mr. Willinghorse, a vote of thanks ought to be passed to him for doing the work of the overseers while they were engaged.

" Mr. Cromwell said Mr. Willinghorse went to look after his own freehold land at Camberwell.

"Mr. Brutus was surprised that Mr. Cromwell should impute any motive to a guardian who had kindly done that which very few people would like to do, for accompanying a lunatic could not be a very pleasant thing.

"After a few observations, the resolution that a vote of thanks be passed was put, and carried by 4 to 2.

"BOILED TEA!

"Mr. Thornintheside called attention to the fact, that he had been informed the inmates were in the habit of having boiled tea. He should think it might be easily arranged so that tea could be made in messes for six or seven persons.

"Several guardians spoke to the incorrectness of the assertion. The tea was fit for any one to drink, and Mr. Thornintheside ought to give his author of such an erroneous assertion."

If all this discussion had taken place in my own or my imaginary reader's parish, I have no doubt we should have both regarded Mr. Thornintheside as a very vigorous reformer.

In another case, the same reader will doubtless smile at the importance given to an annual parochial operation, called "beating the bounds." It has its descriptive account, in the style of "our own correspondent," accompanied by a list of the persons composing the procession :—

Two Police Constables.
Lamplighters with Ladders.
Parish Engineer.   Fire-Escape Conductor.
Beadle in Livery.   Beadle in Livery.
Headborough and Constables.
The Master of the St. Solomon's Boys' School.

THE SCHOOLBOYS.
(Two and two.)
Boys from the Workhouse.
DISTRICT INSPECTOR OF POLICE.
Constable of the Vestry.
THE CHIEF SURVEYOR.
THE ASSISTANT SURVEYOR.
THE INSPECTORS OF NUISANCES.
The Vestry-Clerk.
THE CLERGY.
(Two and two.)
THE SENIOR CHURCHWARDEN.
THE JUNIOR CHURCHWARDEN.
THE OVERSEERS.
(Two and two.)
Members of the Vestry.
(Two and two.)
Members of the Board of Guardians.
(Two and two.)
THE ST. SOLOMON'S RIFLE CORPS.
(In file: two deep.)
PARISHIONERS IN PROCESSION.
(Two and two.)
Police Constables.

These things may appear very small, but life is made up of small things. We are not all destined to shake the world, and those who are so distinguished are not always shaking it. There is a popular idea that every vestryman is an oratorical greengrocer, or a discontented tailor, with mean views, a loud voice, and an abusive tongue. Some vestrymen may be of this order, like some members of parliament; but, underlying this sort of scum—scum always floats to the top—there is often a solid substratum of sound sense and discretion. The faculty of ready utterance is generally possessed by small minds which have little in them to check volubility. It is the mere parochial orator who brings ridicule upon the good old system of local self-government; while those men who do credit to it, and who are the working bees amongst the buzzing drones of the parochial hive, are seldom heard. It is they who do the work: the others talk about doing it, but really obstruct it, and are, happily, the minority. The revenues of the larger London parishes amount to sums which many a full-blown Continental State looks upon with envy. Yet, on the whole, these are collected and dispensed with reasonable accuracy and judgment. The majorities in vestries must, therefore, consist of men of unsullied principles and active business accomplishments, who work hard and talk little; otherwise, parochial affairs could not be so well carried on as they are. It must always be remembered that the short-comings of local administrative bodies depend, not upon the noisy ungrammatical speech-makers, but upon those who elect them. Parish government is representative government, and the ratepayers pull the strings. They, above all others, should support the local paper; for the local paper adds to their ability not only to pull the strings well, but to keep the springs of their parochial puppets in good working order.

PHASES OF THE FUNDS.

THE Stock Exchange is regarded by many persons as the pulse of the country. Its register of prices, especially that portion which records the fluctuations in the public funds, is watched as eagerly as a physician's face when he comes out of a sick-chamber. When it cheerfully announces "par," a technical money-market phrase for one hundred, as far as Consols are concerned, the quarter of a million of steady investors who really *hold* the national funds, consider Britannia to be in a very robust and thriving condition. When it shakes its head and announces ninety, the pulse is considered to record a weak and sinking condition; when it can give no better account than seventy, sixty, or even fifty, Britannia seems to have exchanged her spear and shield for a crutch or a coffin.

If the Stock Exchange be really the pulse of the country, what a number of times, even during the last half-century, poor old England has been gasping in the arms of death! There was the year 1802, when Consols, or Consolidated Three per Cent. Annuities, stood as low as seventy-nine, and fell to sixty-six and a quarter, in consequence of the menacing attitude of Bonaparte. As Consols form nearly one-half of the National Debt of eight hundred millions (speaking in round numbers)—the rest being made up of South Sea Debt, Bank of England Debt, eight or nine different kinds of annuities at different rates, Irish Debt, India Bonds, and Exchequer Bills—they are the most easily affected by all those circumstances and events which directly or indirectly affect the price of Stocks. Whatever tends to shake or to increase the public confidence in the stability of government, tends, at the same time, to lower or increase the price of Stocks. They are also affected by the state of the revenue, and, more than all, by the facility of obtaining supplies of disposable capital, and the interest which may be realized upon loans to responsible persons. A low rate of discount at the Bank of England means a high price for Consols ; and a high rate of discount means a low price for these securities. From 1730 till the Rebellion in 1745, the Three per Cents were never under eighty-nine, and were once, in June, 1737, as high as one hundred and seven. During the Rebellion they sank to seventy-six; but, in 1749, rose again to one hundred. In the interval between the Peace of Paris, in 1763, and the breaking out of the American War, they averaged, says Mr. McCulloch, from eighty to ninety; but towards the close of the war they sank to fifty-four. In 1792 they were at one time as high as ninety-six; but this state of rude health was of short duration. In 1797, the prospects of the country, owing to the successes of the French, the mutiny in the fleet, and other adverse circumstances, were by no means favourable; and in consequence, the price of the Three per Cents, with all their " elegant simplicity," as the Rev. Sydney Smith phrases it, sunk to forty-seven and three-eighths. This was on the 20th of September, after the receipt of the intelligence that the attempt to negotiate with the French Republic had failed. In August of the next year, the month famous for the battle of the Nile, and the presence of the French army in Egypt, they fell to forty-seven and a quarter, or the lowest price they have ever touched.

To come to times more within the memory of some few living people; there was the fall of these very sensitive securities in 1803, on the breaking out of hostilities with France, when they went down rapidly from seventy-three to fifty and a quarter. Those were glorious days for the "*bears*," or all the jobbers who speculated for a fall. The stagnant days of peace provide no such splendid opportunities for money making on the bear side of the Stock Exchange, and no wonder many of the members are often heard singing, as they look abroad for an invasion bogie :—

"Stir up the wars again, the trade it will be flourishing,
 This grand conversation is under the rose."

In 1814 there was another drop from seventy-two and a quarter to sixty-two; and in 1815 a similar drop from sixty-five three-quarters, to fifty-three seven-eighths. This was at the close of the war period, and it was during this time that one of the greatest Stock Exchange frauds on record was organized and carried out. We give the substance of the narrative as we find it recorded in Mr. Francis's History of the Bank of England.

On the 21st of February, 1814, the Bank of England and its neighbourhood wore an appearance of great excitement. The military operations of Bonaparte, by which he checked the great allied powers, had depressed the funds. Deep anxiety for the result was felt throughout England. On that day, however, although it was what is termed a "private day," the clerks in all the stock offices of the establishment were busily employed in preparing transfers, which, contrary to the custom on such a day, poured in from the members of the Stock Exchange. Reports and rumours spread rapidly. Many of the transfers remained unfinished, as a plot, intending to deceive all London, was discovered in time to prevent their execution.

On the 21st of February, 1814, about one o'clock in the morning, a violent knocking was heard at the door of the Ship Inn, at Dover. On the door being opened, the visitor announced himself as Lieutenant-Colonel Du Bourg, aide-de-camp of Lord Cathcart. His dress supported the assertion. His military-looking clothes appeared wet with the sea-spray, and he stated that he had been brought over by a French vessel, the seamen of which were afraid of landing at Dover, and had placed him in a boat about two miles from the shore. His news was important. Bonaparte had been slain in battle, and the allied armies were in Paris. A great victory had been gained, and peace was certain. He immediately ordered a post-chaise and four horses to be prepared, inquired the residence of Admiral Foley, and, with the appearance of great haste and excitement, wrote the following letter :—

"To the Right Hon. T. Foley, Port Admiral, Deal.

"Sir,—I have the honour to acquaint you that L'Aigle, from Calais, Pierre Duquin, master, has this moment landed me near Dover, to proceed to the capital with dispatches of the happiest nature. I have pledged my honour that no harm shall come to the crew of L'Aigle. Even with a flag of truce they immediately stood out for sea. Should they be taken, I entreat you immediately to liberate them. My anxiety will not allow me to say more for your gratification than that the allies obtained a final victory; that Bonaparte was overtaken by a party of Sachen's Cossacks, who immediately slayed him, and divided his body between them. General Platoff saved Paris from being reduced to ashes. The allied sovereigns are there, and the white cockade is universal. An immediate peace is certain. In the utmost haste, I entreat your consideration, etc. Signed,

"M. Du Bourg, Lieutenant-Colonel, and

"Aide-de-Camp to Lord Cathcart."

A special messenger was despatched to Deal; and the letter reached the admiral between three and four o'clock. The morning proved foggy; the telegraph (the old hill telegraph) could not work, and Admiral Foley was thus saved from an involuntary deception. Immediately after the letter was forwarded, Du Bourg entered the post-chaise, and with every appearance of haste, departed for London. Wherever he changed horses, the news was spread, and the postboys were rewarded with napoleons. On his arrival at Bexley Heath, the intelligence was acquired that the telegraph could not have acted; on which he told them not to drive so fast. He then added that the war was over; that Bonaparte was cut into a thousand pieces; and that the Cossacks fought for a share of his body. At the Marsh Gate, Lambeth, he entered a hackney-coach, after informing the postboys that they might spread the news as they returned. In the mean time, the information had reached the Stock Exchange; and by a little after ten in the morning, the market was filled with rumours of general officers, dispatches for government, victories, and post-chaises and four. Expresses from the various places where Du Bourg had changed horses, poured into the principal speculators. The funds rose on the news. Application was then made to the Lord Mayor for confirmation of the important tidings, but, as his lordship had received no intelligence, the funds declined again.

On the morning of the same day, about an hour before daylight, two men dressed like foreigners landed in a six-

oared galley, called on one Mr. Sandon at Northfleet, and
handed him a letter purporting to be written by a person
whom he had formerly known, begging him to take the
bearers to London, as they had great public news to communicate. The request was complied with. Between
twelve and one o'clock in the afternoon of that day, three
persons, two of whom were dressed as French officers, proceeded in a post-chaise and four, the horses of which were
bedecked with laurel, over the then narrow and crowded
thoroughfare of London Bridge. While the carriage proceeded with an almost ostentatious slowness, small billets
were scattered among the anxious crowd, announcing that
Bonaparte was dead, and that the allies were in Paris. The
occupants of the carriage drove in this manner through
Cheapside, down Ludgate Hill, over Blackfriars Bridge,
and rapidly to the Marsh Gate, where they got out, took
off their military hats, put on round hats, and speedily dis-
appeared. The news again spread far and wide; and the
Stock Exchange was once more full of exaggerated reports.
The funds rose. How could they resist such accumulated
evidence ? The aide-de-camp of Lord Cathcart at Dover ;
two foreigners at Northfleet with despatches; private
expresses from various places; all tended to convince the
members that there must be some foundation for the
reports, Application was made to the ministry, but they
knew nothing. Large bargains were made. The excitement at the Stock Exchange is described by those who
witnessed it: "To this scene of joy," says one, "and of
greedy expectation of gain, succeeded, in a few hours,
feelings of disappointment, shame at having been gulled,
the clenching of fists, the grinding of teeth, the tearing of
hair. Some showed their consciousness of ruin, and all
desired revenge."

A committee was appointed by the Stock Exchange, and many circumstances proving a conspiracy were discovered. On the Saturday preceding the Monday on which the deception was attempted, Consols and Omnium (the aggregate articles of any particular loan) to the extent of eight hundred and twenty-six thousand pounds were purchased for various individuals, many of whom were seriously implicated. The late Earl of Dundonald, then Lord Cochrane, was dragged in as one of the accused conspirators, tried on the 21st of June, 1814, with some others, at the Court of Queen's Bench, and sentenced to twelve months' imprisonment. His lordship and another were fined one thousand pounds each, and were also condemned to stand for one hour in the pillory, but this part of the sentence was remitted. His lordship remained for several years under the cloud of this misfortune, steadily affirming his innocence, and stating that he was more sinned against than sinning. Many influential friends believed him, and it was reserved for her present Majesty to restore him to his honours. His spirited autobiography, recently published, contains his own version of this Stock Exchange story.

This great stockjobbing fraud could only have met with the limited success that attended it, in a time of great warlike excitement, and defective means of communication from place to place. Even if we were not more honest nor scrupulous now than our grandfathers, railways and electric telegraphs compel us to change the plan of our frauds.

After the war fever had subsided with the peace of 1815, the fluctuations in Consols reached the next most marked point in 1819, with the resumption of cash payments by the Bank of England. These securities then dropped from seventy-nine to sixty-four seven-eighths, mainly because Sir Robert Peel's (then plain Mr. Peel) celebrated Currency Bill was passed in that year, declaring the bank note once more to be a convertible security, payable in gold upon demand. There ought to have been nothing very terrible in this—the mere payment by the country and a large trading corporation of a just debt; but the fundholders seem to have thought otherwise, and hence a fall in their confidence in England's stability, of more than fourteen per cent.

The next marked fall in Consols, and of course in all other Stock Exchange securities, occurred in 1825, the year of bank failures and bubble companies, when they went down from ninety-four and a half to seventy-five. "The glut of money," says Mr. Morier Evans, in his excellent History of Commercial Crises, "and the consequent low rate of interest that had prevailed during the greater part of the year 1824, and at the beginning of 1825, had induced private bankers to advance money on securities not readily realized, and hence, when the merchants applied to them for assistance, they were unable to afford it, and several commercial failures occurred as the commencement of a state of distress which soon reached the bankers themselves." A monetary panic soon comes to a head, and is always fruitful in curious anecdotes, most of them without any foundation in fact. One is told on this occasion about Lombard Street, which is worth relating. A poor woman having met with a slight accident, seated herself, to recover strength, at the door of one of the banks. A crowd immediately collected, and a report soon ran through the City that the house was unsafe. In less than an hour there was a fierce panic-stricken "run" upon this bank, and with difficulty it was able to meet the sudden demand upon it. One thousand eight hundred and twenty-five saw the downfal of some seventy-nine banks in town and country, with fifty-eight branches, whose liabilities amounted to fourteen millions sterling. The loss to their customers on the liquidation of these concerns, was about three millions and a half ; and the loss in the next year (1826) by twenty-five similar failures was about a million and a half.

From 1825 to 1830 Consols appear to have had a stormy time of it, and on the rejection of the Reform Bill, in the latter year, they went down from ninety-four and a quarter to seventy-seven and a half. In these calmer days, the rejection of a Reform Bill is seldom marked by any sinking variation in the funds more alarming than one-eighth, thereby showing that the fundholders value the rejection of such measures at exactly half-a-crown.

In 1847, the famous year of the railway crisis, Consols again went down from ninety-four to seventy-eight seven-eighths. The railway projects that had been stigmatized as " bubbles" in 1825, had all grown into substantial realities, with hundreds of companions who called out loudly for unlimited capital. There was at the same time a rage for joint-stock speculation in every conceivable branch of trade, though not for so many schemes in the fish and dairy line as there were in 1825. The potato disease, and the consequent Irish famine in the autumn of 1846, and the French revolution of 1848, also tended to make the timid fundholder nervous, so that Consols were not called "firm" for several years.

In 1851, notwithstanding the *coup d'état* in Paris in the December of that year, these sensitive securities showed a strong upward tendency, and maintained it until December, 1852, when they reached one hundred and one and three quarters—their highest price during the present century. In 1853, the Turkish complication and the Russian war came upon the field, and the timid fundholder, after asking one hundred and one, was willing to sell at ninety, and in 1854 at eighty-five.

During all this time, and throughout all these fluctuations in Consols, the timid fundholder never had to complain that his dividends were either lessened, or not punctually paid. On the 5th of January or the 5th of July every year, when he applied for his three per cent. per annum, it was always ready for him, less the income-tax. When his security stood "in the market" at one hundred and one, he got no more; when it fell to fifty, he got no less. He was not conscious of being treated with more or less respect by the dividend clerks at the Bank of England according as he presented a Consol paper at one price or the other. They knew nothing, officially, of the fluctuations out of doors, and when he wanted to learn more upon this interesting head, he had to visit the Stock Exchange.

The market for the purchase and sale of public securities has never stood very high in general estimation. It has always been looked upon as a mixture of Tattersall's and the betting nuisance in Bride Lane. A stockbroker has often been confounded with a stockjobber; a stockjobber with a "stag," or outside hanger-on of Capel Court. Every now and then the neighbourhood of the Bank of England is paraded by men with huge boards on their backs advertising another "exposure of Stock Exchange iniquities," and the booksellers in that quarter are always well supplied with pamphlets detailing various financial grievances, or putting forward various financial theories. It is some comfort to the Stock Exchange to know that it is not abused in print half so much as the Bank Charter is, and never will be, while two men out of every three are gamblers, and want capital to be as cheap when it is scarce as when it is plentiful.

The Stock Exchange is a large square building in the City of London, lying at the back of the Sun Fire Office, near the Bank of England. At present it is supported by about eleven hundred members, who each pay ten pounds per annum, besides finding securities for between eight hundred and nine hundred pounds. There are also fifty authorized clerks allowed to transact business within "the house," as it is called, upon an annual payment of five pounds, and some three hundred unauthorized clerks, who are admitted to the same privileges for a smaller annual subscription. This body is governed by a stringent set of rules, carried out by a committee of thirty members, possessing great power.

The building is regarded as a mysterious temple by the general public, simply because only the authorized members are privileged to enter it. A visitor, if he can find the entrance up a court in Throgmorton Street, may go as far as the door, and watch the excited crowd of brokers, speculators, and jobbers, through a glass partition, but this is all. If he ventures inside the building he will stand a fair chance of being hustled, and of having his clothes torn and his hat battered in, amidst howling cries of "fourteen hundred new fives."

On the wall at the left side of the building is the "black-board," a register of the names of defaulting members who have failed under disgraceful circumstances, and have not given up their estates to be divided amongst their creditors by the committee of the house. As the law does not recognize stockjobbing transactions, such creditors have no more hold over their debtors than one betting man has over another. The debts are merely debts of honour;

but, as such, are generally very scrupulously paid. The black-board does not seem to be very full of names; and some explain the fact by saying that it is not used with strict impartiality. During 1850, particularly, individuals, whose conduct merited the penalty of this public exposure, are said to have escaped the ordeal by influence with the committee.

In the further right-hand corner of this building is the Consol market, a place where nearly all transactions take place in the public funds. Immediately under the glass screen at the entrance, on each side of long tables, like school tables, is the "rubbish market," as it is contemptuously called, a spot where nearly all the transactions take place in "miscellaneous" shares. Twenty years ago, railway scrip, or subscription paper, was classed under this head; but now it can command a market to itself; and its capital of four hundred millions sterling makes it as important as Consols. The other stocks dealt in, represent foreign railways, banks, mines, waterworks, gas and coke companies, bridges, docks, canals, and insurance companies.

The mode of transacting business in the Stock Exchange has often been explained; but in consequence of the numerous technicalities and intricacies surrounding it, it must always be learned from professional experience rather than from books. The small capitalist, wishing to invest his money in the funds, or any other Stock Exchange security, goes to a recognized broker with an introduction, and gives him an order to buy. The broker goes upon the Exchange, where he seeks a stockjobber—one of the class of members who remain stationary inside the stock market always ready to buy or sell to any amount. Much of this buying and selling, by dexterous manœuvring,

becomes little more than a "time-bargain" in practice, or
a bet that certain stock will be at a certain price by a
certain day; but it is necessary for the furtherance of business on the Stock Exchange, that every seller should be
able to find a buyer without delay, and every buyer a
seller. The jobbers reserve a margin for themselves of
one-eighth per cent. between the buying and the selling
price, the lowest price quoted being the selling price, and
the highest the buying price. This eighth per cent. added
to the broker's commission of an equal amount, makes a
difference of five shillings per cent. against the outside
capitalist who wishes to invest his money in the funds.

Certain dates have been fixed by the committee of the
Stock Exchange as settling days, for the purpose of balanc-
ing time-bargain and stock-buying accounts. These dates
occur once a month, as far as Consols are concerned, and
at intervals of a fortnight as far as concerns shares and
foreign stocks. On these days all bargains have to be
adjusted and closed, and many fearful settlings are recorded
in Stock Exchange annals. We need not go back to the
beginning of the present century for examples of Stock
Exchange panics, as we have the history of one recorded
by Mr. Morier Evans, which occurred only the other day,
about the middle of 1859. The whole Stock Exchange,
according to the account given, appears then to have been
on the verge of bankruptcy, the causes being injudicious
speculation for a rise, or a "Bull" account, and the fall
occasioned by the "Italian difficulty," and the rumoured
alliance between Russia and France. Many members of
the house owe their ruin to the movements of the Emperor Napoleon in that year—an Emperor who is at least
no unworthy successor of his uncle, in the effect he is able
to produce upon the Stock Exchange. Twenty or thirty

failures occurred in a day, and the link of connection between the different stock markets was so close that the suspension or embarrassment of one member frequently jeopardized the position of seven or eight. The panic continued all through April, and the fall in Consols was often as much as one and a half per cent. At least a hundred members of the Stock Exchange broke down on this occasion—a number not equalled since 1825—and many men of large fortune lost all their previous accumulations. All this havoc was produced by a wide and general depreciation of foreign securities, and a fall in Consols from about ninety-five to eighty-eight, a price which they touched a few weeks ago.

To read an account of this late panic by a sympathetic observer, any one would suppose that Bartholomew Lane, Old Broad Street, and Throgmorton Street, were haunted by withered, anxious capitalists and speculators, who twitch their thin fingers, slouch along with heads lowered and peer from under broad hats with thin faces, like the conventional type of the miser. The members of the Stock Exchange and their outside parasites are not of this order; but are stout and cheerful-looking middle-aged "bucks," in huge double-breasted waistcoats; or full-whiskered young "swells," in turned down paper collars, and unexceptional trousers. They talk about business, in easy lounging attitudes that would not disgrace the steps of the most aristocratic club in Pall Mall, and seem to show no vulgar money-grubbing anxiety in their faces about the course of the market. Outside the house they act and look like gentlemen, but inside the house they reverse the old school-boy order of things, and are riotous, disorderly, and much given to practical joking. Towards two o'clock on a "ticket," or settling day, before the fatal rattle is heard, they crowd and leap and hustle and shout, until the stentorian porter, whose duty it is to call the names of the members inquired for at the door, is almost unable to make his shrill ringing voice heard. They have a fancy for " bonneting " each other; for chalking caricatures on coats; and for throwing ink on shirt fronts. Some of the members have a rough talent for comic etching, and this is often exercised at the expense of other members whose appearance presents any tempting peculiarity.

No man's origin is safe from their prying curiosity, and if it present any materials for a ballad or a squib, such a production is at once manufactured. Names are a great source of joking of this kind, exactly as they are in schools, and the thirty members who sit upon the committee are favourite targets for the comic satirical muse. The peculiar titles of the mine stocks furnish easy themes for budding rhymesters, and a young scion of the house is happy when he can put together and hum something like the following :—

> Fare thee well, my Wheal Mary Anne,*
> And fare thee well for a while ;
> For your prices are steady,
> And your calls are all ready,
> Then fare thee well for a while,
> Mary Anne!
> Then fare thee well for a while.

Sometimes their talents are exercised in the cause of commercial morality—when their fingers have been burnt by touching damaged trading shares; and they put forward some such song as the following, supposed to be sung by bank shareholders at general meetings :—

* The name of a Cornish mine.

[TUNE—JOLLY YOUNG WATERMAN.

Did you ever hear tell of our stupid old auditors,
    Who into bank ledgers pretended to pry,
And made such a show of accountants' dexterity,
    Winning each heart and deceiving each eye ;
They looked so neat, and they wrote so steadily,
We all of us voted them in so readily,
And they eyed all our clerks with so searching an air—
Oh! these auditors ne'er were in want of a chair.

But all this deportment deceived only shareholders,
    Our clerks were too knowing in figures and books,
And Watts, Robson, Pullinger, Redpath, and Durden,
    Have shown us the folly of trusting to looks.
They took out our money—as much as they wanted
    (God bless them for not taking more than they did!)
And then by a system they called " double entry,"
    Oh! they balanced accounts, and our losses they hid.

In the mean time our drowsy self-satisfied auditors,
    Who into bank ledgers pretended to pry—
Who'd made such a dazzling show of dexterity,
    While pass-books were tampered with under their eye—
Still looked as neat, and still wrote as steadily,
And signed their dear names to the " balance " as readily,
And eyed all the clerks with a confident air—
Oh ! these auditors *must* be kicked out of the chair !

It must not, however, be supposed that all the members of the Stock Exchange are practical jokers, comic song writers, caricaturists, and happy-go-lucky speculators. Many of them are far-seeing earnest men of business, with a vast range of knowledge and an European reputation. Among past members we have the founders of the Rothschild and Goldsmid families, the anecdotes about whom—mostly fabricated—would fill half a dozen volumes. The old business man is often highly romantic, even during business hours, and the wonders he will relate about the elder Rothschild and the days of "pigeon expresses," ought to make a story-teller's mouth water.

A greater man, however, than any of the most eminent loan-mongers, about whom we hear so much, was David Ricardo, the stockbroker and political economist. He had one of the keenest and clearest intellects for grasping abstract subjects ever known, and besides winning a prominent position as a writer upon political economy, he did good service for theory in its everlasting battle with practice. Starting with what is called nothing in popular histories of self-made men, he ended by making an enormous fortune for his family. This has not only secured to his name the respect of a money-making country, in a money-making age, but has proved that those who can think often know how to act, and are not easily distanced in the race of life by mere bustling stupidity.

NAMES.

OUR godfathers and godmothers have certainly much to answer for. They often start us in the world with names which doom us to a life of misery. A want of taste or imagination—a bad ear for music—a weak sense of the ridiculous, and a foolish desire to flatter one or more wealthy relatives, are at the bottom of half our absurd christenings. They sometimes brand us with titles which are stumbling-blocks in our business, which often lead us to change our identity, and which often lead us into the Court of Bankruptcy. An unfortunate gentleman appeared in the "Gazette" the other day as an insolvent debtor, whose name must surely have helped him into failure. His full title was Johannes Fidelius Edwardus Segers, and he was described as a general merchant, of Southwark. A title that would have figured well in a history of some Norman Conquest, or on the roll-call of an ancient abbey, or on a tombstone in St. Paul's Cathedral, was doubtless found very clumsy and unmanageable across bills of exchange, and not at all impressive at the heads of invoices. A man who started in business with such a name as that was heavily weighted for the race, and he would have done well to have imitated the policy of our Polish trades-men. When Kosciusko Poniatowsky opens his little café on the borders of Leicester Square, he transforms himself

at once into Herr Kosk or Signor Poni. By this course he
does all he can to deserve success, and is not quite such a
problem to his creditors and the postmen.

The struggles to get rid of an ill-fitting name are constantly finding work for our judges. The Court of Queen's
Bench is occasionally turned into a Divorce Court, where
unhappy suitors pray to be released from their worst
halves. It was not long ago that a gentleman, pining
under the depressing name of Bugg, came forward and
begged to be changed into Howard. The homely moth
wished to be transformed into the aristocratic butterfly,
and applied to the proper authorities in that case made
and provided. Some people are pardonably discontented
with their surnames, others with their Christian names,
and some with both. The other day an attorney, who had
borne the insufferable burden of five not very harmonious
Christian names for half a lifetime, applied to the Court of
Queen's Bench for liberty to drop two of his titles. When
addressed in full he was called Edmund Jonathan Hornblower Watkins Clarke, and it was doubtful how many of
these titles were Christian names and how many surnames.
He had no objection to Edmund, nor to Hornblower, but
he wished to be relieved at once from Jonathan and Watkins.
He found that the compulsory use of all these names in
legal documents was a great inconvenience and expense,
to say nothing of their want of harmony to a refined ear.
He kept Hornblower, however, because it was a family
name, though it was open to many objections on the score
of taste.

The Court had their little jokes while discussing the
application, and it is surprising how little jokes tell when
they are uttered from the Bench; but Mr. Edmund Jonathan Hornblower Watkins Clarke was not allowed to cut

off half his tail without a scolding. The judges were
evidently not disposed to encourage these applications,
and were inclined to let a man suffer for the folly of his
sponsors.

The weight of absurd surnames is always felt in society,
as a man can often drop his first titles, but never his last.
We can all call to memory a host of surnames which have
to be softened in the mouth for the sake of decency.
Though a man, by the mere accident of birth, may be
afflicted with one of these names, there is no reason why
he should not cast it off as he would the clothes of his
grandfather. The law is made for men, not men for the
law; and it is bound to assist the citizen in making himself and his neighbours comfortable. The question of
identity ought to be set at rest by a system of registration
as cheap and accessible as a transfer share list. There are
a hundred names now in our " Directory" which no man
could follow into a drawing-room; and a thousand which
are never uttered without a laugh or a titter. A host of
titles seem to have been framed for no other purpose than
to afford an easy theme for jokes, and to keep alive a few
puns which have descended from the Deluge. We have
no wish to deprive the world of any wholesome food for
wit, but jokes upon surnames tasted stale even in the days
of Joe Miller. Many names that were once fit for gods
are now hardly wearable for dustmen, and it is foolish for
any man to sit under them for a single moment. A nick-
name has no right to live beyond the life of its owner, and
yet we see it transmitted to the twentieth generation. A
sturdy giant, who thrashed half a village, or who threw a
skittle-ball over a church steeple, was probably called
"Stronginthearm," in a moment of beery hilarity. As
Stronginthearm he lived, as Stronginthearm he was buried,

but the name, unfortunately, was not buried with him. It was transmitted, perhaps through a consumptive race, until it reached a feeble dwarf, who could hardly cross a bridge on a windy day in safety. To call such a mannikin as this by such a title is a cruel mockery, and both reason and humanity demand a change of title.

The influence of names on occupations is another reason for the utmost freedom in exchanging titles. We never hear of "Mr. Twopenny," "Mr. Caudle," or "Mr. Kitchen" as great statesmen or great orators—not, probably, because they are deficient in the impudence and talent necessary to make such distinguished men, but because they are smothered by their names. No amount of energy can pull against many names, which must have been invented to keep their owners in obscurity. No amount of natural genius can pull against many other names which have been owned by men who are the world's idols. A poet had better be born as Master Twopenny than as Master Milton, if he wishes to make his mark; and the greatest painter would hardly succeed in his art if his name happened to be Titian. "Michael Angelo Titmarsh" would do better as a sculptor than "Mr. Chantrey," because he could drop the first two names and work down the absurdity of the last. A bad name is like a tin kettle tied to the tail of a hapless dog, and the law, like a good Samaritan, should relieve the animal cheerfully.

RE-CHRISTENED.

THE great family of the Browns, and Jones's, though they never seem to be aware of it, have very much to be thankful for. The bare simplicity—I will not call it vulgarity—of their names may not place them very high in the social scale, but it lands them on a level far above that allotted to scores of their fellow-creatures. They may be despised by the aristocratic Montmorencies and De Grenvilles, they may be pitied by the more homely Barclays and Harrisons, but they can relieve their overcharged feelings by despising and pitying their inferiors. They may laugh at Cockles (Antibilious, not Horatius), they may affect to be disgusted with Giblets, and they may patronize Pighead or Rawbone. They can ease their wounded vanity in a dozen other ways by tormenting a hundred other unfortunate victims of absurd surnames. I know they can do this, because I am one of these victims.

My name is Rottengoose. I got this name fairly from my paternal grandfather, but where he got it from I have never been curious enough to discover. It is one of those names that an owner is not likely to make much stir about. I have never had the courage to follow it into a drawing-room, nor even to hear it announced by a parlour-maid. I slink about with it like a branded criminal. I shudder when I see it in print, or anything approaching to it; and

am only induced to break silence now to publish a short
and important narrative.

A few months ago, a gentleman appeared as the correspondent of a leading journal, and gave a list of absurd and
repulsive surnames, which he said a friend of his had
extracted from the wills in Doctors' Commons. The names,
I have too good reason to know, were not invented for the
occasion, though I question the story of their discovery.
The melancholy catalogue was, I believe, neither more nor
less than the list of members of a club, started in self-defence
by a few victims of hereditary nicknames. Its founders
were two gentlemen named Honeybum and Mudd, who had
been blackballed six times at six ordinary clubs, entirely on
the score of their titles. This club, which is now broken
up, was known as the Refuge, and it drew into its peaceful
fold all those wanderers about London who had been compelled to pass half their time in dull chambers and tavern
coffee-rooms. The Refuge was not remarkable for architectural embellishment, its charm was found rather in a
certain unobtrusive plainness, which suited the character of
its supporters. It gave each member a certain amount of
society, without the formality and annoyance of introductions; in fact, introductions, though not absolutely forbidden
by the bye-laws of the club, were silently, but strongly discountenanced. No member was held to be properly qualified
to enter the club, unless his name was more or less absurd
and repulsive, but once admitted, he was never addressed
by his title under penalty of a fine. The servants were
selected on the same principle as the members; they were
never allowed to address the members by their names; and
all letters, when brought in on trays, were carried with
their faces downwards. Our community, except in these
last particulars, was very like the House of Commons; we

were each and all known as " honourable members," and
were never "named " on any consideration.

The Refuge, like all clubs, was not free from cliques or
parties, and from individuals who affected to be superior to
their companions. There was the Bungler clique, the Sponge
clique, and the Booby clique, the latter comprising nearly
all the aristocrats of our society. We had several members
who were sulky and solitary in their habits, who neither
joined any of the cliques, nor conversed with their fellow-
members. We had a butt, a glutton, a bore, a professed
wit, a teller of coarse anecdotes, a member who made a
counting-house of the place, transacting all his business
there, and another member who used it as a bed-room,
sleeping there for hours in an easy-chair. We had several
notorious grumblers who found fault with everything, and
our little society was as much like all other clubs as one pea
is like another.

As much happiness as can be found in clubs was found
in the Refuge, and enjoyed for several years without any
sensible interruption. Bit by bit, however, the club was
being silently undermined by the admission of members
who were not properly qualified. Gentlemen bearing,
amongst others, such inoffensive titles as Shave, Cuckoo,
Dolly, Cake, and Shuffle were admitted by the electing
council without consulting the wishes of the majority.
Old members, whose names could not be pronounced without a laugh or a shudder, or without being mumbled for the
sake of propriety, were thus brought into contact with men
more highly favoured by their godfathers and ancestors. I
am far from saying that all these new members made the
club feel that they belonged to a higher level. Some of
them were well-behaved modest gentlemen, and even those
who felt most inclined to assert their position, were outdone

in presumptuous vulgarity by a few of our most offensively-
named members.   Still the introduction of this refined alien
element was calculated to ruin the club by making it too
self-confident.   Our society soon clung less to that obscurity
which had been its best safeguard, and courted publicity
with a blind disregard of consequences.   It began by allowing strangers—no matter what their names might be—to
dine with members ; it ended—I may well say ended—by
giving a grand evening party.

The same recklessness which had entertained the idea of
turning the Refuge into an Assembly Room, also presided
over all the arrangements of this party.   Invitations were
issued to the female relatives and friends of members, doubtless in imitation of a very bad precedent established by the
leading clubs on the day the Princess of Wales arrived in
England.   The regular servants of the club, with names
and habits that were agreeable to the old members, were
placed under a new body of men engaged and regulated by
the "purveyor" who furnished the refreshments.   None of
the conventional ceremonies of assemblies were consequently
dispensed with, and the company, instead of being silently
ushered into the drawing-rooms, were announced by a
gigantic footman with the lungs of a Stentor.   His memory
was very retentive, his feelings were very blunt, and his pro-
nunciation was terribly clear, the result being that not one
name—presentable or unpresentable—was lost upon the
company.

Mr. Asse, Dr. Bub, Mr. Belly, Mr. and Miss Boots, and
Alderman Cripple, were amongst the first arrivals.

They were quickly followed by Messrs. Fat, Ginger,
Drinkmilke, Beaste, Dunce, and Buggey.   Mr. Honeybum,
one of the founders of the club, but who now had little
voice in its management, got in unobserved and unan-

.nounced, like me, at a side door amongst a crowd of waiters. Several other members were clever enough to imitate this trick, amongst whom were Messrs. Screech, Spittle, Cheese, and Kidney.

The announcing footman was not idle, and his voice was heard above the hum of conversation :—

." Mr. and Miss Milksop, and the two Miss Pigges."

" Mr. Vittles; Mr. Kneebone; Mr. Jugs."

" Dr. Poopy; Mr. and Mrs. Gotobed; the Reverend Mr. Shrimps."

" Mr., Mrs., and the two Miss Jellies; Mr. Leaky; Mr. Rumpe; Mr. and Mrs. Taylecoate."

" Dr. Cauliflower and Miss Sprat; Mr. Demon; Mr. Cod; Mr. Funck; Mr. Mug; Mr. and Mrs. Radish."

" What funny people; it's like a play," said the youngest Miss Pigge, loudly; a young lady who ought not to have been brought so early into society.

" Hush," returned Miss Milksop, an elderly unmarried lady, who had charge of this young person and her sister, " let us seek for some refreshment."

The announcements still continued :—

" Mr. Lambshead; Mr. and Mrs. Looby; Mr. Bonfire; Mr. and Miss Sawney; Mr. Butter; Dr. Whiteleggs; the Reverend Mr. Stump; Mr. Licie; Mr. Gullet; Mr. Meatyard; Mr. Smelt."

" 'Pon my word," said Mr. Kneebone, at this point, addressing Dr. Poopy, " they ought to make a gathering like this a little more select. That last batch of names is enough to make a fellow sick."

" My dear sir," returned Dr. Poopy, " the same feeling came over me; but you know there are many people who *must* be invited on these occasions."

I moved away from this group and drew near another,

by which time Messrs. Clodd, Cheek, Bones, Humpe, Prigge, Cockey, Sprawl, Swine, Tick, Fever, Deadhorse and Hardup, with several ladies, had been announced, and had mingled with the crowd.

"My dear fellow, there's Deadhorse just come in," said Mr. Mug to Mr. Buggey; "let me introduce him to you."

"I'm not equal to it to-night," replied Mr. Buggey, affectedly; "I've not been very well lately, and the name calls up unpleasant associations."

The visitors still kept pouring in, announced by the stentorian footman :—

"Mr. and Mrs. Pricktoe; Mr. Spratt; Dr. Mountebank; Mr. Corpse; Mr. and Miss Hussey; Mr. Scragge; Mr. Phisicke; Mr. and Mrs. Muddell; Mr. Flashman; Mr. Gaby; Mr. and Mrs. Swette; Mr. Lazy; Mr. Monkey; Mr. Mule; Mr. and Miss Poker; Mr. Squash; Mr. Pott; Mr. and Mrs. and the two Miss Headaches; Dr. Gready; the Reverend Mr. Sheartlifte; Mr. Idle; Mr. and Miss Maypole; Mr. Skim: Mr. and Mrs. Gull; Mr. Simpleton; Mr. Rascal; Mr. Barehead; Mr. and Mrs. Dam; Mr. Shoe; Mr. and Miss Vile; Mr. Bulley; and Mr. and Miss Shirt."

"I say, Rottengoose, my boy," shouted Mr. Sawney, who fancied himself a bit of a wag, "there's something wrong with the gender of that last name, isn't there?"

"I don't quite comprehend you," I replied, rather nervously, for the way in which he shouted my hated name was very embarrassing.

"Don't you see," he returned loudly, "Mr. and Miss Shirt—Mr. Shirt is all right, but Miss Shirt ought to be Miss Shift; eh, Rottengoose, eh?"

"Ha, ha," I responded, very feebly, "glad to hear from you again."

The shouting of my name attracted the attention of Mr.

Mrs. and the two Miss Jellies, whom I had bashfully avoided, though I often visited them in private. To put me at my ease in their society, they had kindly softened my name to " Writingcase, " or something that sounded very much like it, and by this title they always addressed me.

" We never heard you announced, Mr. Writingcase," exclaimed Mrs. Jelly, in which remark she was echoed by her husband and daughters.

" No," I said, nervously, fearing that Mr. Sawney would rally me upon the way in which my title had been softened ; " I was here—that is in the building—before the doors were opened."

At this moment I saw the dreaded Sawney coming towards me with his mouth wide open. Much against my inclination, I tore myself from the Jelly party, and hurried away with my tormentor. He had invented a wretched conundrum turning upon their names, and though I felt that I could have knocked him down, I was compelled to listen to him.

I will not dwell any longer on the events of that party. The club, as I fully expected, withered gradually after that night ; as the members had been coarsely aroused to a sense of their degradation. A hundred applications in one form or another were made, to the legal authorities, for a change of name within a week of the meeting, and there was a great run upon classical and aristocratic titles. My Christian name being Julius, I selected Cæsar to follow, and this advertisement appeared in the daily journals :—

THIS IS TO GIVE NOTICE, that I, the undersigned JULIUS ROTTENGOOSE CÆSAR, lately called Julius Rottengoose, now and for some time past residing in Pall Mall, and the Marshes near Stratford, Essex, gentleman, have determined to assume and take from the 10th day of November, 1863, and thenceforth and at all times hereafter to

USE the SURNAME of CÆSAR, in addition to the surname of Rottengoose, but as my last and principal surname, and by a Deed Poll under my hand and seal, bearing date the 10th day of November, 1863, and duly enrolled in Her Majesty's High Court of Chancery, I have, in-order to give effect to such determination, and for the purpose of evidencing the same, declared, and I do hereby declare, that I shall at all times hereafter, in all deeds, writings, documents, letters, and other instruments of writing, and in all dealings, transactions, and in all intercourse with other persons, and on all occasions whatsoever, set, subscribe, and use the surname of Cæsar in addition to the said sure name of Rottengoose, and as my last and principal surname, and by the said deed, I have expressly authorized and desired, and I do hereby ex-pressly authorize and desire all and every person and persons whomso-ever to designate, and describe, address and call me at all times and on all occasions whatsoever by such surname of Cæsar accordingly.

Dated this 12th day of November, 1863.

JULIUS ROTTENGOOSE CÆSAR.

Witness, G. A. Scragg, Solicitor,

Bow-legged-lane, Waddling-street, E. C.

I need scarcely add that though I retain the name of Rottengoose for legal reasons, I shall use it even more sparingly than is indicated in the above deed. Whatever windfalls of property—expected and unexpected—may fall to the share of J. Rottengoose C., will be immediately seized and enjoyed by J. R. Cæsar. My change of name is likely to lead to another, before long, when Miss Jelly will pro-bably become Mrs. J. R. Cæsar. We shall probably go abroad for a lengthened period to avoid the detestable Sawney, who is still satisfied with his repulsive title. *

* All the names used in this paper are veritable titles.

END OF VOL. I.

MARRILD, PRINTER, LONDON.

Check Out More Titles From HardPress Classics Series In this collection we are offering thousands of classic and hard to find books. This series spans a vast array of subjects – so you are bound to find something of interest to enjoy reading and learning about.

Subjects:
Architecture
Art
Biography & Autobiography
Body, Mind &Spirit
Children & Young Adult
Dramas
Education
Fiction
History
Language Arts & Disciplines
Law
Literary Collections
Music
Poetry
Psychology
Science
…and many more.

Visit us at www.hardpress.net

CPSIA information can be obtained
at www.ICGtesting.com
Printed in the USA
BVHW070202120819
555624BV00026B/4491/P

9 781318 678341